# The H... of God

by

# Guy Steven Needler

OZARK MOUNTAIN PUBLISHING

PO Box 754, Huntsville, AR 72740
800-935-0045 or 479-738-2348
www.ozarkmt.com

For permission, serialization, condensation, adaptions, or for our catalog of other publications, write to Ozark Mountain Publishing, Inc., P.O. Box 754, Huntsville, AR 72740, ATTN: Permissions Department.

**Library of Congress Cataloging-in-Publication Data**
Needler, Guy, 1961 -
    *The History of God*, by Guy Steven Needler
Dialogues through meditation with the Origin, the Source Entity and other beings in frequencies and dimensions above those of mankind.

1. Origin   2. The Source Entity   3. Dimensions   4. God   5. Metaphysics
I. Needler, Guy, 1961-   II. God   III. Metaphysics   IV. Title

Library of Congress Catalog Card Number: 2011928633

ISBN: 978-1-886940-16-1


Cover Art and Layout: www.noir33.com
Book set in: Times New Roman, Arial
Book Design: Julia Degan


Published by:

OZARK
MOUNTAIN
PUBLISHING
PO Box 754
Huntsville, AR 72740

WWW.OZARKMT.COM
Printed in the United States of America

# Table of Contents

**Part 3: Communication with Aliens**

# Forword

When I initially started to write this book, I fully expected to focus on the technical aspects of the universe and not the personal progression side as well. Indeed, the start is very mechanical in nature, which can be seen from the way I initially prepared myself to talk about content that was based upon the physics of the universe with the entities, the *Origin* and the *Source Entity*. In the early days I needed to literally *count* myself up the energetic levels to reach those with whom I would spend the next couple of years communicating. The process would occur via my computer on Friday afternoons unless I was on holiday or out of the UK. The subject matter that we discussed over the years chopped and changed from week to week and has had to be edited to make it flow. I also seemed to develop a style of contacting the entities only long enough to generate only a thousand words or so, plus or minus 10-20%,which was interesting, to say the least.

Some of the chapters are clearly longer than 1,000 words while others are 2,000+ words. This depended upon the difficulty of the subject being discussed, or, in fact, how broad it was. Sometimes these words took a couple of hours to generate with every word being painful. At other times it flowed like a river, and it was all that I could do to keep it in my memory long enough to type it into my computer. As you can imagine, this, in itself, generated a level of frustration that at times could stem the flow of communication.

Nevertheless, I have gotten to the stage now where it is time to cut and run, to publish and be damned. I am not a fan of books that are as thick as door stops as they tend to bore me. As a result, I have a deep sense of not wanting to bore my readers with 600+ pages when they could get more enjoyment out of the staggered introduction of the information that I received. It also gives me a break and allows me to pass it on to my editor, who while I am writing this text, does not know this is about to come over the wall. In actual fact, the reason for stopping here is this:1) I need a rest; and 2) I want to contact the other Source Entities that have been mentioned in this text with a view to describing their universes and giving the world the opportunity to see the wider reality through their senses and achievements.

I apologize for the changes in style as I progressed, but this is how it came to me. I guess that this in some way adds authenticity to it. Nevertheless, I hope you enjoy the reading the text and the things that I gleaned as a result of being able to communicate with these entities.

So just what does one do when a channeled work is finished? For one thing, I knew that this would not be the last, for I knew that I personally was interested in the universes that were indicated to be controlled by the other 11 Source Entities, each one trying to understand itself and its creativity and feed its own learning back to the Origin.

Next, it was clear that the concepts that were being presented to me would, in a lot of instances, go straight over my head. Indeed this was the most annoying side of what I was doing, for I really like to understand the mechanics of what I am being shown, no matter how rudimentary that understanding may be. I felt that if I could understand the information being presented to me, then those who read these texts will also understand. I guess the fact that my dear wife, Anne, also understands a great deal of what I have channeled in this book is a result of the high level of understanding that the Source Entity and the Origin have of humanity's ability to assimilate information in our low frequency existence. In essence, they know what we can digest and offer concepts to wake us up in a manner that we can understand in our limited capacities.

I was surprised at the duality of the book as it unfolded. First, I would like to remind the reader that this was supposed to be a work that focused upon the history of God and the universe

He/She/It has created. I was not comfortable with the dialogue dipping into the more esoteric aspects of how to live our lives to the best of our ability while being of service to others. Also, there seems to be a strong link between the two subject areas, not because of its spirituality but because of the interconnectedness of living life according to the rules of the universe. Going against the physics of the universe ultimately results in our early demise as physical beings but also irrevocably links us to the lower energies of the physical in a way that is truly difficult to reverse without a significant change in our personal nature. Learning to forgive what others do to us is one of the hardest things to do as is shrugging off the greed that we have acquired from living in a materialistic society; however, these two together are without doubt the route to our own personal evolution and ultimately the evolution of humankind incarnate, the route back to the Source and the Origin.

We have to understand the physics of the universe to understand the esoterics. The two are intertwined as they create the path to correct efficient existence in the other. This helps us go with the flow rather than against it. For this reason, I decided to keep the two types of channeled work under the same cover. The physics and the esoterics. The one provides the living space and how it evolved; the other provides the rules for existence in this space. It would have been logical to create two books and maximize on the sales potential, but that would have been materialistic and would have missed the opportunity for people to have it all in one place, for why would you buy a book when it has only provided one side of the argument and not offered an answer or a way forward?

Approximately two years prior to starting this work, I had written some 180 pages of my "meditational meanderings," some of which I noted later were relevant to this work. These I have also included as I now know that they were, in effect, the start of this dialogue and have their own relevance within the text. As such, they are now fully integrated and help to provide a fuller picture of God's universes and the energetic creatures that exist within them, each of them helping the Origin to understand Its Self and the universe It created through the Source Entities and ourselves. The universes are truly full and vibrant environments, offering myriad opportunities for entities to evolve and, therefore, grow closer to the Source and go home to be part of the whole, but this can't be done without understanding and working with the rules. In reality, this is what this book tries to do—offer us all a way out of the darkness with a light to help us on our way home.

# Part 1

# The Mechanics of the Origins Universe and Where We Fit In

# The Author Awakens

Throughout my life I have been interested in the paranormal; indeed, I had a constant feeling that I was *more substantial* than my current self. In one of my earliest memories on this subject I distinctly remember being told by my mother that I could not see the wind when I clearly saw it whistling up and over the roof of a building. I practiced meditation as a young teenager and felt that I could astral travel and levitate/perform telekinesis, even though I couldn't when I tried. I had previously awakened several times in dreams to find that I was out of my body, levitating at will, outside our house. In my late teens I practiced meditation diligently every night trying to gain control of the faculties I was sure I had. Then one morning I had a waking dream. In this dream four white robed individuals stood before me, each of them smiling. They communicated with me by telepathy and told me that all that I believed in was correct. I could do everything I felt that I could do, but not yet! They told me that it was not the right time and that I needed to learn my Earthly lessons first. From that day forward, my interest in the paranormal waned, and I concentrated on doing the best I could in the physical world. That is, until a friend introduced me to Reiki, which led me to other energy healing arts. I became a student of a direct student of Barbara Brennan. My interest was reawakened!

During the years of being trained in the energy healing arts, I noticed that I could sense and feel energies. Not only this, I could talk to the chakras to find out what was wrong with them and sense other entities. I also noticed that I could go well above the energy levels taught me by my teacher and was, subsequently, reprimanded for not staying grounded. The problem was that it felt *right* to be *up there*.

## The Author Meets the Om

It was during one of my initial healing course meditations with a guest instructor that I first met the Om and was identified by a fellow student as being one of them. Little did I know that during a trip to see a friend who was working in Sweden, I would have the connections I required to communicate with energy beings and manipulate energy, thanks to a group of aliens.

# Chapter 1:
## *Sweden, a Reawakening*

The energy at my friend's house in Sweden was high. It was surrounded by ley line energy which was not connected and was moving around wildly, rather like a high tension wire whipping across the land, grounding out. The stones at the bottom of his garden felt like they were part of a shrine that focused and directed the ley line energies (rather like the stones at Avebury and Kilmartin). I felt energized.

## The Author's Attunement by Aliens to Balance Other World and Earth Energies

One day, during a walk with my wife and my friend, I felt the need to go to a certain rock which was by the river. The river was in a small valley. At the rock I had a desire to sit in the lotus position whilst meditating. During the deepest meditation that I had ever experienced, I sensed a lot of light come into my head and my eyes flicker uncontrollably. A voice in my head told me I was being attuned to the Earth energies and that I should stay calm. I also had the impression that a craft of some sort was hovering in front of me. The impression was validated when I saw the strange movement of the water just after I came out of the meditation.

During the time I was in meditation on the rock, my wife, who is also quite sensitive, was standing on a suspension bridge upstream. She said she perceived a number of UFOs approach the area, which was a portal between universes. The bridge was at the point of a triangle/cone, and the UFOs were coming in towards the point. She further stated that she was told that the aliens wanted to communicate with me to give me "*other world* ways of using energy." To do this, she said they worked directly on me (particularly my brain)—the word *rewiring*

5

came into mind. After a while, she felt the UFOs leaving and the portal closing. My friend, who also practices the healing arts, said that the stone I was on was aligned to a point on the bridge, and that this was where the energy flow was. He said it was as though the energy collected at the point by the bridge was channelled into the hill via the stone in the river.

A year later I was traveling to Sweden again with my friend as a traveling companion as he had moved back to the UK. During the journey I meditated. I logged into the aliens; they were excited that I was coming, and I heard a voice in my head saying, "He is/they are coming." Beforehand, a strange feeling had come over us in the hours around 11:00 A.M. to 12:00 P.M. before the flight. Both my friend and I felt a bit lethargic (stunned) and weren't able to think straight. I now know that this was a result of tapping into the energies that the aliens were using, which at that time were overwhelming. I thought I was coming down with a bug or something. As a result, I mixed up the flight times, and we missed the flight. I wondered if perhaps we were supposed to miss the flight for other reasons. Maybe we missed an accident or something. I never did check to see if there were any traffic accidents. Maybe I would have arrived at the wrong time for the aliens and their plans. Maybe I'll never know. I'm sure there was a reason. We finally caught a flight the next day and arrived without issue.

The next day while we were walking towards the river and bridges where the aliens' portal was located, I had the feeling that they were accessing me, especially my autonomic functions. As we walked along the river side path, I felt energy in my hands and arms increase. My friend said that he felt we were going through waves of energy. When we arrived at the bridge, we both knew that the aliens were coming through the portal. I then received a command in my head and walked back down to the rock I had sat on the previous year. I was told that I should expect nothing strange or anticipate anything special/strange happening because this would block the work that they would be doing—more *fine tuning* and opening of my skills and abilities/functions. As I continued my walk to the rock, I saw images in my mind's eye of aliens working with machinery and computers. They were getting the machine and equipment ready and tuned into me for when I arrived at the allotted place.

Once at the rock, I made myself comfortable, sat in a lotus type position and meditated. I eventually had the impression that the aliens were working on my third eye and were fully opening it so that I could *see properly*. I was told that this would happen slowly over the next five to ten years. They further told me that they had to attune my third eye to the present time line as it was capable of seeing past, present, and future. They said that I would get confused with seeing this more complex level of information. Suddenly I felt they had turned on my hearing and noticed that, for a split second, I could hear my friend's thoughts as he stood by the bridge. Then a series of instructions were transmitted to me. I was being told that I should not hang onto any one function that I would receive and that I was to treat each one as a tool and not as my world task or *my work* or *only ability*. The initial attuning work in 2002 needed some time to stabilize before it could be *turned on*.

## Alien Dimensional Warping Device

I opened my eyes, and as I did, I noticed my vision was a bit wobbly at my left and right hand side as if my vision was out of phase with the normal visible spectrum. I thought I saw a large orange object in front of the trees in front of me. The object had no form. I just managed to see similar objects in other parts of the tree-lined bank. Suddenly I picked out the outline of an object that I can only describe as machine like. It was totally invisible, but for a split second or two, I saw its outline and its 3D depth of perception. The aliens told me that they were using some sort of dimensional warping device that made it blend into the background. However, if you had the ability, you would just be able to see its outline as it mirrored the visual appearance of its surroundings. I also noticed that although there was a bit of wind, the trees in the area of the objects were moving like they were being blown by the downwash of a helicopter's blade. I was then told that I shouldn't try to see these things too hard as I would put too great a strain on the tuning and alignment work they had done.

To help the reader understand what I saw, the outline of the craft is in the illustration below. Its visual appearance was like an upside down triangle with a round top and some protrusions on the bottom that I can only describe as being sensor or antenna-like. The trees and surrounding rocks looked as if they were on a convex plate or lens.

**Figure 1: Illustration of craft outline seen**

The trees within the internal vicinity of the outline of the craft effectively *stood out* from their usual environment.

## A Dimension Within a Dimension

As we sat on the rock before going back to my friend's house, we both felt that the aliens lived here in a complex that was within the hillside and supported by dimensional mechanics.

That is, it is a dimension within a dimension, and that this was a local phenomenon.

My friend said that he thought the rock was a focal loci for energy between two dimensions and that the rocks either side of the bridge were special because they allow the transference of energies (spiritual, cosmic and Earth) to occur and blend together, creating an inter-dimensional portal. He also thought the abilities of these rocks in this configuration on Earth was rare; therefore, this was a special place.

For a day or so after both of these attunements, I felt very wobbly and could hardly string a sentence together, like being mildly drunk. It was a very strange feeling.

## Some Independent Proof

### A Contract with Aliens

A few months later, I showed some pictures of the landscape around the river and rock in Sweden to a medium I was visiting in the *College of Psychic Studies* in London. I had not previously talked to her of aliens and my association with them. She immediately recognized the presence of aliens there and clearly stated that I had a *contract* with them. It was shortly after the visit to the College of Psychic Studies that I started the Barbara Brennan-based energy healing courses where I learned to use some of my abilities and started communication with energy-based entities, two of which are the Source Entity and the Origin.

# Chapter 2:
## *Contacts with Beings on the 14$^{th}$ Through the 27$^{th}$ Levels*

## Building My Link to Spirit and the 20$^{th}$ Level

Over the course of many meditations I often tried to clear my mind to help allow the helpers and other entities from all the other dimensions to connect me or make my link to Spirit. It was during one of these meditations that I noticed their help in action. At the start of this particular meditation, as I allowed myself to be at peace, I noticed a couple of cherub-like entities building what I can only describe as a scaffold of one pole or an antenna like that on a car or transistor radio. It was as if they were putting all the pieces or links together one by one—putting them together until they eventually were high enough to go into the ionosphere and beyond. Each time I let my mind wander and lost focus on the greater reality, it would be as if they would be held in suspended animation. When I pulled myself back into meditation, I would see them start up again with vigor, delighting in the fact that they were able to start building again. As I came back each day, the antenna or link got higher and higher until it was outside our solar system. When I projected myself to the top of it, I could see the rest of my home galaxy below me. When I looked at this construction (2004), I started to see the rest of the other galaxies in my universe coalescing into a single ball of light. When I asked Earth's Source Entity [you'll hear more about this Entity soon] about this, He/She/It was very pleased and was surprised at the speed at which I was able to make progress in my meditations—which subsequently helped my helpers to make my link.

*Note:*
*During the editing of this text for publication (February, 2011), I noticed that the link had progressed beyond the physicality of our universe. The single pole had split off like the branches of a tree, creating a web-like network of connections that ventured through the multiverse of our Source Entity and beyond to the Source Entities' creator, the Origin, and the eleven other Source Entities (again you will read about the Origin and Its creations later), and the environments They created. It was an amazing sight to behold. Momentarily I felt the Origin as It smiled Its approval. GSN.*

# The 20<sup>th</sup> Level

## Traveling Through the Crown Chakra to the 20<sup>th</sup> Level

The extension of my ability resulting from the construction of this scaffold was illustrated during a morning meditation by an old apple tree in our garden, I had grounded myself by taking in Earth hara line energy through my Tan Tien and was opening up all my chakras when I received the impression that I should also open my higher chakras. To do this, I imagined a trap door that opened upwards above my crown chakra, and I would go through it to the next level. Opening and spinning the chakras was a method I was taught as part of my healing training to assist in raising my frequency levels to those of the levels in the aura or chakra I wanted to work with. I counted up, eight, nine, ten, eleven, etc., to the 15<sup>th</sup> level where I had been before and then had the impression that I could go higher. I continued to count up the chakras to level 20. At this point I could go no further and felt that this was the highest level I could go to at the moment.

## A Bypass from the 14th to the 20th Level

Upon arrival, I thought about the level where the Om came from and realized that I had just gone straight past it (the 14th level is where I first encountered the Om). I then had the impression that I could create a link of pipe between the 14th and 20th levels so that the Om could come up to the 20th level. I then received the impression that they had, in fact, come up the pipe to my level. I also had the impression that this was the way wormholes are used in the physical levels. A pipe goes from one level to another and then back to the original level but in a different location which then allows instantaneous travel between distant points in the same reality. The Om answered.

Om:   Om originally came from the 14th but can go up to the 20th and beyond. The only reason that you first encountered us on the 14th was that we needed to go *down* to the 14th to meet you. You only just understood that there was a 14th level and didn't even consider that there was a 20th. The 14th level is the lowest we can descend because going lower is painful and energy-depleting for us. Going any lower requires incarnation into the physical bodies relative to that frequency. The Om made a big sacrifice by coming this far down in the frequencies, and because of that, you are special. Although it was a big sacrifice, it was essential to their work here on Earth.

I felt that other beings, including my guides, were present as well. I asked them why I couldn't see any stars or galaxies at this level (the 20th). They said there weren't any as such at this level and that if I dropped down to the 14th level, I would see them again. This I did momentarily, and I again found myself at the far end of the galaxy (the Om were with me). I returned to the 20th.

13

Om:     You are not ready to and are not able to perceive or
        understand at this level whilst in your earthly body, so
        the area looks black; however, it serves its purpose.
        You can get up to that level and communicate without a
        problem.

I was then told that this was enough for that day, and I zipped
down the levels and back into my body.

## Slipping into Various Dimensions and Universes

Another meditation saw me rising up to the 20th level. I looked
around in my mind's eye to see if anyone was there, only to
find that I was surrounded by entities. Om and others whom I
could not identify were present. They were all pleased and
honored to meet me. (I was starting to be embarrassed by this.)
I also expected to see many stars and galaxies as I do when I
visit the 15th level, but I received the answer that the neutral
color I was seeing in place of the stars and galaxies was
because I was in all levels and all universes/dimensions at the
same time. This surprised me, but it did make sense. I then
made sure that I was grounded. When I focused my attention
on a star system in a particular galaxy, I found that I could go
there at will. Slipping into different dimensions/universes was
like slipping through the layers of a spherical Russian doll. On
my way to another planet, I saw a couple of space ships; one
was like a flying saucer and the other like an orb of light. I
went into the ship that was like an orb and found myself in a
control room of sorts. There I was met by three beings of
humanoid shape with big black eyes who bowed with hands
together as if in prayer when they noticed I was with them.
They also said that they were pleased to see me. I asked them if
they knew why I was on Earth, and they said that I was there to
evolve. I then asked what my job on Earth was, and they said it
was to help the Earth and its inhabitants to evolve. They said
that everything would become apparent when the time was
right, when I had learned my lessons and had a firm

foundation. I then thought about my task in life, and they said I could do two or three world tasks, including my own evolution, all at once because I am multidimensional. This was funny to me because at that time I had been having the feeling that I had been living three or four lives at once!

Later when walking to my car to go to work, I had the impression that we evolve faster by incarnating here on Earth because of the short life span and subsequent accelerated learning opportunities. I then noticed that I felt a bit spaced out and heady. This I supposed was because of the level that I was working with. It was good that I was grounded!

## The Power of Thought

The next day when I opened my chakras in the same way, I was aware that I was literally bursting my way through the trap doors that allowed access to the higher levels. When I got to level 20, I stopped and looked around. Again I was surrounded by beings, but this time I had the impression it was just the Om.

Om: We are both surprised and pleased in the progress you have made in this short period of time. You are progressing faster than anticipated.

*ME:* *Why do you say "we"?*

Om: Because We answer collectively, not singularly.

*ME:* *Why are you surprised?*

Om: Because the 20<sup>th</sup> level is very high, and you have to be very grounded. You are learning fast; you are awakening fast. It will not be long before you are fully aware. But don't try too hard as this will block your progression.

*ME:* *So where am I now?*

Om: You are everywhere, in all places at once.

I looked out at the universe and found that each universe was represented as a separate sphere.

15

ME:  *It must take a long time to travel between the universes?*

Om:  Traveling in a higher frequency is easier because the molecules are further apart and create less friction; therefore, they allow you to travel much faster—as fast as the speed of thought.

This confirmed what I had previously received and understood in meditation.

Om:  We use the power of thought a lot. Thought has three parts: thought, intention and action. Thought is the start of the process and initiates the desire. Intention focuses the thought and gives it inertia. Action is the end product, thought taken form.

ME:  *Why do I need to know this?*

Om:  Because it is a universal process, and it is one that you will need to understand and fully believe in the future.

## The Effect of Alcohol on Evolution

I had been thinking about being able to drink the real ale that I love and how it affects contact with my higher self and other beings, including my ability to rise up to the higher levels. I asked the Om a question on this.

ME:  *What part does alcohol have with me?*

Om:  It clouds the communication between your physical and higher self. It removes your intention and, therefore, your focus.

ME:  *Do I drink too much?*

Om:  You were on the verge of it. We do not understand this need to poison your bodies, but your method of limitation and extending your "dry days" slowly over a period of time is a good way of removing dependence.

*ME:*   *I try to give myself three to four dry days a week now, but I still like a tipple with my friends.*

Om:   Poisoning yourself to be sociable is a very foreign concept to us.

I had to go to work then and came down the frequencies by diving down through the trap doors that represented the higher levels until I got to the 7<sup>th</sup> and my body. The grounding must have worked as I did not feel heady this time.

## The God Collective

Another meditation saw me rising through the levels to the 20<sup>th</sup> level. I was jumping up the levels in a series of uneven numbers: 7, 9, 12, 13, 15, 17 & 20<sup>th</sup>. This I found surprising and wondered for a moment why this was. I was suddenly told that this was because of my intention. I was reminded of the three stages of thought: thought, intention, and action.

*ME:*   *Who am I talking to? One of the Om?*

HSME (Higher Self ME): In a figure of speech, yes, but it is you. You are speaking to your higher self and your higher self is Om.

*ME:*   *I wonder what we are going to talk about today?*

HSME:   We can talk about whatever you like. It depends upon whether you want it to be about mundane or interesting things.

*ME:*   *Should I wait until I am at my computer before I start to talk to you, so that I can remove the forgetting bits and pieces process.*

HSME:   You can if you want, but would you have the time to do it? This works for you and not all of the information you get will be required to be presented in the conversational format.

*ME:*   *Why pick that method?*

HSME:   Because it makes it easier to read and, therefore, accessible to everyone, not just the intellectuals. The conversational method is a very good way of conveying the information you will be receiving to the general public.

I then saw an image of a bacterium, which was round in shape, with billions of small tentacles surrounding its periphery.

HSME: That's right. That is a good image to use to describe what we are. We are all tendrils or sensors of the main entity going out to learn information and bring it back to the whole. Some of us want to return, and some want to remain in the learning/experiencing loop or even help other tendrils in their process of learning/experience. Do note that we still retain our singularity even though we are part of a collective, as our knowledge gained is specific to one Source and that Source can be recognized.

ME: *You just said "we." I thought we are all one. How can God be "we"? Does that mean there are other Gods?*

I was having difficulty seeing how big this was in terms of how the universes/or continuum could create more than one god-like entity. My limited Earth mental capacity was truly limiting my ability to understand this concept.

HSME: If you would take a temporal or dimensional slice of the cake at any one time, you would see Us, we the God collective, as separate entities separated by thin slices of dimensional layers or time. Don't forget that although time is an Earth concept, it will do for this explanation. All you would be doing is seeing parts of Us, We, Me, God (the bigger part of us) through different layers of reality. Separate out all these realities, and you have many Gods/beings. Put them all together, and you get one being, one God that exists in all times, in all spaces, in all dimensions, in all continuums at the same time. Consider the total entity or God as a tall building, the number of floors representing the total number of dimensional realities that I, We, God encompass. Each floor is a reality all of its own with people/civilizations working and living on that one level only. The beings on a particular floor experience Me, We, God only at that one level, that one part of God that covers all of their level of existence, one level of the building. Put all the levels together, and you make a tall building or an entity that covers all of the beings in all of the levels all at the same time. That is what We, You, God is—an entity that is literally everywhere simultaneously. The point is to get as many people in the world questioning their environment and paradigm as possible.

ME:  *I have to go now. I need to get to work, and I am late. I hope I don't forget this stuff.*

HSME:  You won't. I will make sure that you remember. Let's go over it again in brief indicating topic headings.

This we did, and it only took a few seconds to get some topic datum so that I could remember. I then went back down the frequencies, again missing a couple of levels at a time until I arrived at the physical levels.

I walked to my car and thought, "I hope I don't forget."

"You won't," came the reply from a distant place in my mind. My higher self was still in communication with me!

## The Myriad Shapes and Sizes of Galaxies

Another meditation saw me once again soaring up through the levels and landing in the 20<sup>th</sup> level rather like jumping on the edge of a rather comfortable bed. As I sat there, I saw all the other galaxies in the third dimension and was told by an entity that I could change my view at will. I zoomed in on one of the other galaxies rather than the one I was currently close to. I had

19

no idea which galaxy it was; it looked pretty similar to our own Milky Way, but I was told that it wasn't. I was then advised that I could see the galaxies in another dimension, one where the ambient light was actually white rather than the black of interstellar space. In this dimension there were many different shapes and sizes of galaxies: from flat shapes to totally round shapes to shapes that were like a red ball in the middle with two corkscrew-like tendrils of stars trailing off in an upwards and downward fashion, and others looking like they were just pillars of light. I was told that there are as many sizes and shapes of galaxies as there are stars in the galaxy that Earth inhabits.

On this note, I descended down the levels to my 7$^{th}$ level home and went to work.

# The 27$^{th}$ Level

## Meeting the Dragon

The next day I was opening my chakras and realized that I was not totally in my body. I was slightly beside and above myself. I raised my level up to the 20$^{th}$ level, this time going one level at a time. When I reached the 20$^{th}$ level, I felt that I could go further because the 21$^{st}$ level felt easy to penetrate. I pushed harder and established that the next levels up to the 27$^{th}$ level were pretty much the same in response. Moving from one level to another was like pushing my hand through an elastic curtain that suddenly gave way when I pushed past its elastic limit. At this point I realized that I needed to be grounded and quickly sent a line down the levels to the Earth plane and imagined that I had placed an anchor in the ground with the line attached to me. When I completed the grounding work and looked around the 27$^{th}$ level, I noticed that there was another being by my side. The level looked black all around me, and I perceived the being as being black on black and rather dragon-shaped.

D:     What are you doing here? You shouldn't be here.

ME:   *Why not?*

D:     You are not the right vibration level.

ME:   *Why is it so black and dark here? I thought that the 27th level was full of light.*

D:     It's black because that is all you can perceive here.

ME:   *Why are you dragon-shaped?*

D:     I am trying to frighten you away, but it obviously didn't work.

ME:   *I thought everything here was supposed to be good.*

D:     We are mostly, but you shouldn't be here.

ME:   *If I am not the right vibration level, how did I manage to get here?*

D:     You just used brute force and pierced the veils between levels. I sense that you are stronger than you could possibly know.

ME:   *O.K., I must go. I also have things to do on the Earth level (go to work).*

## The Difficulty of Decoupling from Levels Above the 20th Level

As I descended, I got the impression that it was actually difficult to decouple myself from the levels above the 20th. I felt that I was traveling down a tube with graduations printed on the outside and that the journey down was constrained to being in this tube. I think upon reflection that I had found another shortcut or was allowed to use this shortcut to get me out of the 27th level ASAP.

# The 60th Level

## The Necessity of Grounding on the 60th Level

The next day after the trip to the 27th level, I opened all my chakras and decided to go up to the 27th level again just for a look-see. I shot up the levels and hardly saw the numbers in my mind indicating where I was. I noticed that I was missing numbers and that I was leap-frogging levels. When I got to the 20th level, I kept going and noticed that I had accumulated quite alot of momentum and was literally tearing up the levels as I went—so much in fact that I completely missed the 27$^{th}$ level. I had a mere glimpse of the outline of the dragon on the 27$^{th}$ level as I flew past! Surprised, I saw the 30$^{th}$, 40$^{th}$ and 50$^{th}$ levels go past me before I finally managed to focus my attention on stopping. I finally stopped on the 60$^{th}$ level and realized that I should send out a line to the Earth plane to ground me. I quickly did this as I envisioning a hook truly embedded in the ground and a rope leading up to me. I wondered how I could have gotten so far when the dragon on the 27$^{th}$ level had told me that I shouldn't have been there. I looked around, and it felt like I was on the outer edge of what looked like a very big onion with all the layers representing the levels I had just traversed. A voice then spoke to me.

## The Author's Home Base

V:      You got here because you can.

*ME:    How can I get to this level when the dragon entity on the 27$^{th}$ said that I shouldn't be there?*

V:      Because you live here, you come from here, and you traverse all these levels all of the time.

*ME:    Who are you? Are you my higher self?*

V:      In a way I am you, and you are me.

*ME:    So you are not my immediate higher self then.*

V:      No, but we are one in the higher sense.

*ME:    So are you the entity we refer to as God or the Source Entity?*

V:      Yes, you could call Me that.

*ME:    If this is the 60$^{th}$ level, are there any more levels?*

V:      There are many above and below your current position.

*ME:    Why did the dragon entity not know that I could traverse to his level and stay there?*

V:     Because it saw you for what you currently are, an incarnate being in the lowest levels.

ME:    *Oh, I see. Can I come here again?*

The next response came to me as I typed this.

V:     Yes, but remember where you come from and the work you have to do. Don't get distracted. It's easy to get distracted.

ME:    *O.K., I will try not to get distracted. I had best be going now—low level work to do.*

V:     Go in peace.

As I descended the levels, I noticed that I was again dropping down the levels in decades rather than in single-level numbers. As I passed the 27th level, the dragon entity noticed me passing and issued a friendly word of advice.

D:     Be careful. Don't get lost!

ME:    *I will. Thank you.*

I then slowed down as I got to the sub-20 levels and finally stopped as I integrated with my Earthly body. This is one trip I didn't expect.


## An Explanation of the Levels

### Reasons for the Presence of 100 Levels

A morning meditation in August 2003 saw me connected with my hara line. I opened up my chakras and wondered what I was going to receive this time. As my thoughts went to the number of levels and the Source Entity's comment that there were levels above and below the 60th level, I found myself being told that there are 100 levels. I was a bit suspicious of this as it is too round a number. I then heard the voice of the Source Entity in my mind:

SE: Why not a hundred? It suits my purpose.

ME: *It's a bit of a round number, that's all. It would provide suspicion. I am surprised that you can contact me at this level (I was only at the 7$^{th}$, maximum).*

SE: I can talk to you at any level.

My thoughts went to the 27$^{th}$ level and the dragon entity.

SE: That entity no longer has the appearance of a dragon, but he will use it when you need to contact him. It will help you to discern/recognize who it is.

ME: *O.K. Why did you choose 100 levels? Why not 12 or 96?*

SE: I chose 100 because it gives the individual soul something to strive for. I could have had as many levels as there are souls in the multiverse, but 100 sounded like a nice number. It's also a number which is recognized by most of the incarnate beings in the multiverse. Each level gives an increase in possible knowledge, ability, and understanding. A soul can only progress through the levels by the process of experience gained.

## Differences Between Levels

ME: *So what is the difference in the levels?*

SE: They are a distance away from Me. The closer a soul gets to returning to me, the higher up the levels it is able to access or live within. Each level is like the differences in the auric and body levels with the exception that once you have evolved past the need to incarnate in the lowest form (what you are in now) or you no longer need to help out in the physical levels, you move upwards and exist in the higher levels, but you are still subject to the need to evolve to get closer to Me. It's just that the evolution is done on a much finer scale. The difference between the levels that you currently exist in (1 to 7) is quite marked. The difference in the levels above, say in the 50s is much more subtle as you are now focusing your evolutionary attention to specific issues, issues that are really the very fine detail.

## Relationship of Levels and Dimension

*ME:* *How does this relate to the need for dimensions?*

SE: Dimensions allow for many things to be done at the same time. To put it another way, it allows the individual part of Me, You, the soul to evolve faster as you are learning and experiencing many things at the same time. Call it parallel processing.

*ME:* *Fascinating, so we really are multidimensional.*

SE: Of course.

## The Mission of Enlightenment

*ME:* *Is it O.K. for me to put this stuff in a book that I propose to write?*

SE: Yes, of course. It all helps in the mission to enlighten people. I am not saying it will make you famous or make money, but it will fill in some of the gaps that others have left out. It is important for the whole picture to be made available rather than just parts of the picture. Everyone who is helping to accelerate the evolution of humankind on Earth at the moment is one part of the jigsaw; each is just as important as the other. It's just that some will resonate with more people than others, and, as a result, they will become more popular, making the individual writer more money by default. But they all are important; they all add to the whole. Money is NOT the issue here.

25

*ME:*   *O.K., I have to go now. Can I talk to you on this subject again?*

SE:   You can talk to Me at any time. You don't need to rise up to the 20<sup>th</sup> or 60<sup>th</sup> level to contact Me; all you need is the intention.

# Back to the 27<sup>th</sup> Level

## The Dragon Entity on Helping Others Awaken

The following day I connected with the hara energy and opened up my chakras and waited a moment before going up the levels. When I eventually decided to move up the levels, I moved straight to the 20<sup>th</sup>. I thought this was a bit too fast, so I decided to start from the bottom (7<sup>th</sup>) and work my way up level by level. I have to admit I was surprised by how fast I went to the 20<sup>th</sup>. Then I decided to move to the 27<sup>th</sup> level to visit the dragon entity. When I got there, the entity welcomed me and I gave him my love. He then transformed into the light being I had expected to encounter at this level. He had the appearance of a human figure wearing brilliant white robes. His skin and the robes emitted a brilliant white light. Even though he was now transformed, I will still refer to him as the dragon entity for continuity.

D:   The Source Entity is pleased with you.

*ME:*   *Why is that? I haven't done anything special.*

D:   He was pleased that you were able to contact Him. There are not many people who have managed to do that. Although all are able to, very, very few do. This is because most people are tied up with living their lives and doing what they need to do to evolve; they are totally engrossed with living on the Earth plane. People who contact Him/It are starting to or have already awakened to who they really are. When they do this, they naturally want others to experience the same wonders they are experiencing and then dedicate themselves to the greater task of enlightening the rest of humanity. Their ultimate aim then is to raise the vibration levels to a point where everyone is enlightened or awake again. They do this by spreading the word as you are with this book and discussing this subject with others who are open-minded enough to also spread the word.

## The Great Catastrophe

*ME:* *Why would they want to do this?*

D: It is just the same as anyone who has been involved in an accident or a great catastrophe (such as the great forgetting—that was a huge catastrophe!). The survivors naturally help those who are injured with a view to saving their lives because they would want someone to help them if they were in the same situation.

*ME:* *So this is the same for those who either are enlightened or in the process of waking up. They naturally want to help others become the same?*

D: Yes, and this is why the Source Entity is pleased with you. He now has someone else helping Him/It to get the other parts of Himself/Itself back to Himself/Itself faster.

*ME:* *Oh, that's beautiful.*

D: It certainly is.

*ME:* *O.K., I must go now.*

I started to go down the levels one by one, and as I did so, I heard the dragon entity call to me.

D: You can go straight to the level you want, you know. All you need is the intention, but you already know this.

I dropped down to the Earth plane thinking, "He's right. I don't need to go through each level. I can just pick a number."

## The Source Entity Identifies the Dragon Entity as Byron

The next meditation was short but nevertheless interesting. I connected with the hara, opened my chakras, and went directly to the 27$^{th}$ level where the dragon entity being was. Again he was radiating a brilliant white light. I then perceived an iridescent golden light in the shape of a sphere next to him (I will refer to this entity in the masculine as it is easier to have one point of reference). I knew instantly that this was the Source Entity.

SE: I am gold because this is what people expect to see. Also, it differentiates Me from the other entities when we are together, and I represent Myself as a similar size to My creations.

He appeared to be hovering above and to the right of the dragon entity.

SE: His name is Byron, and he will help you with your questions. This is a better name than the dragon entity, is it not?

ME: *Yes. I thought I could contact You personally.*

SE: You can. You are contacting Me through him through yourself. We are all connected, and We are all one, are We not? He will be your guide. When you need to speak to Me directly, you will.

ME: *I have to go now.*

I was late anyway.

SE: You always need to go, but even these little sessions are useful.

28

## Characteristics of the Om Entities

The next meditation I had saw me going straight to the 27th level and seeing Byron immediately in my mind's eye. I was interested in what Byron did in his level, so I asked him.

ME:     *Where do you live in your level?*
B:      On a planet in a solar system in a galaxy in a different universe than you and, of course, in a different dimension.
ME:     *Do you have a physical existence?*
B:      Not in your sense of the word, but things can be considered as physical in the dimension and level that I exist within.
ME:     *What do you do on your planet?*
B:      We do things similar to you. We live to evolve and get closer to the Source Entity. We work on a universal level.
ME:     *Do you incarnate into bodies?*
B:      Not in the way that you do. We exist for as long as we want in the form that is necessary for the environment for as long as we need to do our job.
ME:     *What is your job?*
B:      To evolve and to help the planet evolve and to keep the frequencies high. We all work to keep the frequencies high. Most of what we do is for the whole; we work for the whole to ensure that the whole is able to progress together.
ME:     *How do you do this?*

I was receiving pictures of people working with the Akashic records.

B:      We are collective beings; all of us are linked so all work we do is for the good of the whole.
ME:     *So you are part of a gestalt collective?*

29

B:      We are still individual, but we are one and all. We do not ignore one another or work against each other as your race does for the benefit of the individual. We work for the all; we all want to progress towards the Source Entity at the same time. We get great satisfaction in this goal.

ME:     *Can you create things by pure thought?*

B:      Of course, one only needs the intention.


## The Om's Work with the Akashic Records

ME:     *Do you work with the Akashic records?*

B:      That is some of the work we do, but this is for the greater whole. We look after histories and knowledge.

ME:     *I get the impression that the histories are past, present, and future.*

B:      That is a reasonable assumption for a being that is tied in one dimensional time for most of his consciousness in this incarnation. There is more to it than that because we record the full range of experiences (emotion, pain, joy, love, stress, telepathic communications, etc.) that go with the knowledge. The list of experiences we record is too long to mention here, and again this is only some of the work we do for the greater whole.


## The Author as an Om

ME:     *Do I always have to meet you at the 27$^{th}$ Level?*

B:      To initiate communication, yes, but once you have linked in and your intention is to communicate with me, you can move around to the other levels and still communicate with me.

ME:     *Why is this?*

B:      You are of the Om, and you are able to move around a number of levels. I think you can go up to the 80$^{th}$.

ME:     *Are we the same type of entity?*

B:      We are similar but not the same. The similarity is
        insomuch as we are energy-based beings and not of the
        low density/vibrations and levels needed to become
        incarnate as you currently are.

ME:     *What do the Om do?*

## The Focus of the Om

B:      They do what most highly evolved beings do; they
        work for the good of the whole with the express goal of
        returning to the Source Entity. The Om also help the
        spirits on the Earth plane since this is a pivotal
        experiment. There are many Om working with the
        Earth, and you are one of them.

ME:     *Earth is an experiment?*

B:      Yes.

ME:     *What is the experiment?*

B:      To pave the way for individual free choice rather than
        collective choice. This is required as it allows faster
        evolution of the entities involved. It has been
        interesting to see the progression up and down the
        frequencies.

ME:     *I hope I will be able to remember all of this when I
        finally type it up.*

B:      You will always remember, and I will always be with
        you when you are typing.

ME:     *Thank you.*


I went down the levels to the Earth plane, and as I reached the
Earth level, I heard his voice in my head say:


B:      Be careful on your motorcycle.


It was a nice day, so I was going to work on my old 1977
Triumph Bonneville.

*ME:    I will.*

## Byron on Intention and Mental Constructs

A week later I went straight to the 27th level, and Byron was there waiting for me. I greeted him. I then perceived that we were standing on a balcony with a steel railing and looking out into space with a couple of planets very, very close by.

B:    This is an example of what we can do by using a mental construct.

The next thing I knew we were looking over a gorge or valley that looked like it could be Earth.

*ME:    This is impressive. How do you do this?*
B:    We simply have the intention and follow through.

We were then back in space. Byron had taken me back to the same position with the planets close by.

B:    This is your solar system.
*ME:    How can the planets be so close to each other?*
B:    I have brought you to a point in time in your vibration level where they were close together so that you can have a good view.
*ME:    Do you use space ships to travel in space?*
B:    Not usually. We generally just go wherever we need to go by using our intention. If we need to come into your vibration levels and travel in physical space, we need to construct a mental barrier to protect ourselves.
*ME:    Are these what we call UFO's?*
B:    You have many ways of perceiving them. You see them as golden orbs and even disk-like space ships. You interpret the information in your own ways, depending on what your physical knowledge is and what your mental capacity is for dealing with such information.

The object is to show you that you are only limited by your own imagination—an imagination that is limited by your experience of what you believe can be done here on the Earth plane. You could do quite a lot, but you don't fully and unequivocally believe that you can do certain mental tasks and functions, and so, therefore, you fail.

## Byron on Spherical Time

Today Byron said as I reached the 27$^{th}$ level, "I am going to tell you about time." This I thought would be interesting as I believed I was quite adept in the philosophy of how time worked.

B:      Time is spherical.
ME:   *What? (Out for a golden duck! [See Glossary.]) How do you mean?*
B:      Time is spherical. All the events in time that have ever happened or will ever happen are happening now or are all happening at the same time.
ME:   *Can you explain what you mean?*
B:      Basically your perception of time is linear with three points: a past, present and future. You don't perceive an end point, and you can't remember a starting point. However, you do know where you are currently, or so you think, so you perceive the future as in front of you and the past as behind you.
ME:   *You mean we think of time as in a straight line.*
B:      Yes, but this is not the case. Everything that has already happened and will ever happen is happening all at the same time. Call time a finite series of happenings. If you travel in one direction in the sphere, you will experience the events that are a result of that which has gone before in that direction. But if you change direction . . .

33

ME:    *A whole set of other interactions take place that causes that event to take place?*

B:    That's correct. If you travel from event point A to event point D via event points B and C, you know what other events took place to get to point D. However, if you went from event points A to D via B1 and C1, another set of events could have occurred to change the event point D, or not change it, as the case may be. Actually you can also use the term "holographic" to explain the happening of events since the sphere has an interior and not just a surface.

ME:    *Why is time finite?*

B:    Because the Source decided when our departure would end, and we would all be together with the learning and experiences completed. Hence, the task is finished and the individual concept of events happening is, therefore, no longer necessary and is removed.

## Overlapping/Simultaneous Time and Space

ME:    *How does this relate to space?*

B:    Obviously there is physical space, non-physical space (higher frequency or spiritual), dimensional space, and level space—all happening at the same time. All happening *together* is a better way of putting it. You can travel to wherever at whatever event point instantaneously and experience what is happening at that event point when you get there.

ME:    *How does level space come into it? I thought the levels were relative to the auric bodies.*

B:    They are up to a point, *but when you get past the relationship with the physical worlds and you get closer to Me . . .*

## Levels of Perception

ME:    *Hang on. Who am I talking to now? (I had noticed the voice change). Am I talking to the Source Entity?*

34

SE:    Yes. You see, the closer you get to Me, the more like Me you become as an individual, so you go higher up the levels until your bodies are My body. They are anyway, but it will help your conception to consider them as being separate for a moment or two. Essentially, the higher your perceptions of the levels between us, the closer to Me you get. This distance is called the levels of perception or auric body levels at your position in the game.

ME:    *And all this is happening at the same time.*

SE:    Yes. You can perceive or visit any point in time in any level of perception in any dimension in any spiritual frequency you want. If you had the mental capacity (and at this point in time you haven't), you could experience it all at the same point or from all the different points. I refrain from using the word *time* here, as it is misleading.

My head was spinning as I thanked them both and came down the levels to the Earth plane. This head wasn't big enough.

## The Fallacy of the Time Loop

The next day we talked about time again. I was back with Byron.

B:    Time is not linear as you now know, and because of this, the popular depiction of the time loop doesn't exist.

ME:    *What? I thought that this was a well-proven theory. What about the classic grandson killing the grandfather scenario?*

B:    Yes, provided that you are in linear time, and you assume that the time line change is such that the grandson's existence is terminated, but time isn't linear. When you consider that the time line—really a series of events—is changed and the effect is that the grandson is still born but has a different grandfather, then the need to go back in time to kill the grandfather may not exist, and the time line continues. You could also consider that once the grandfather is killed, the grandson stays alive in that time event because that has not changed his personal time line. The series of events after this event, i.e., that his parents were the same, compensate for the change. Everything that has ever happened or will happen is happening now, so the natural thing for the event stream to do is go from the nearest event to the next event that should have happened because it has already happened.

ME: *Has this something to do with time being spherical or holographic?*

B: Yes, remember that you experience time as a number of events and that each event and all its variations are happening all together. Hence, the individual who traverses the events to affect an individual person in one event switches to another event automatically, one that is similar to but not exactly the same as the one he was just part of.

ME: *So this means that the loop theory fails.*

B: Yes, of course.

ME: *This is taking some time to get my head around, even with my interest in temporal concepts.*

B: It's bound to. You exist in an environment where it is hammered into you that time is linear.

**Figure 2: Spherical Time**

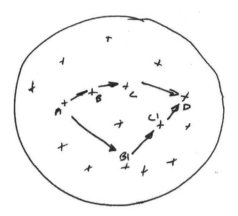

# Chapter 3:
## *Byron and the Source Entity*

## Visits at the 100$^{th}$ Level

## Appearance/Forms of The Source Entity and Byron

In a later meditation I decided to go to the 60$^{th}$ level bypassing all the other levels on the way up. I then decided to go up to the 100$^{th}$ level. When I arrived, I sensed the Source Entity. The Source Entity visually appeared to be like a galaxy or nebula in a space that was all black. I was positioned on the edge of this nebula. I spoke to the Source.

*ME:*   *So this is what you look like.*
SE:    Yes. I have no form, but I have form.

Byron suddenly appeared by the side of me, but his appearance was not that of a humanoid. He also looked like a loose ball of energy.

SE:    This is what Byron really looks like. When he is with Me, he has no need to look as you or any other being that communicates with him would expect him to appear, so he adopts his natural state.
*ME:*   *I thought he lived on the 27$^{th}$ level.*
SE:    He does, but I brought him here to let you see what he really looks like.
*ME:*   *Can only people who access the higher levels, the 60$^{th}$ and above, speak with You?*
SE:    I will speak to anyone on any level if they wish to speak to Me, but generally it is only people who are evolved enough or remember who they are that are able

39

to visit the 60<sup>th</sup> level and above that manage to contact Me the way you have just done. I use the 60<sup>th</sup> level as a buffer.

ME:    *That's interesting. I will chat about this some more tomorrow.*

SE:    I will be here.

## The Source Entity—Time as an Event Stream

The next day I decided to go back to the 100<sup>th</sup> level and talk with the Source Entity again. I went straight there with no need to jump up one level or a series of levels at a time.

SE:    Ah, you're back.

ME:    *It's been exactly a day on Earth. How long has it been for you?*

SE:    No time and all time. It is as if you were never away, or you have been gone two years.

ME:    *Oh, where is Byron? I expected him to be here.*

SE:    He is doing things in his realm.

ME:    *So did You notice me gone?*

SE:    I noticed a lack of attention on your behalf.

ME:    *How do You experience time?*

SE:    All at the same time and one event at a time. It depends on what I want to focus on; it can be fast or slow. You will also experience time this way when you return to the energy state and to the Source/Myself.

My thoughts went to the comments that the late Adrian Divir made in is his book "*X3, Healing Entities and Aliens*" about communicating with aliens. He talked about only a week having passed between communications with a particular individual, but the alien he was communicating with said that a year had gone by in his dimension. The Source Entity picked up on my thoughts.

SE: That is because they are experiencing the event stream (or *time* as you call it) at a different speed. It is also why they appear to travel and change direction very quickly when they are seen in their craft in your dimension. They are going in and out of their event stream and your event stream to aid their travel in your dimension. The result is that they seem to appear and disappear or move and change direction very fast. The aliens haven't contacted you yet, but they will.

As I pondered on this comment, I saw the Source from a distance. It appeared as a vast galaxy of energy in the darkness. I tried to enter its light, and the Source spoke to me.

SE: You can't come in here yet. You are not capable of experiencing the total unconditional love of the Source in your current incarnate form. You will, of course, when you are disincarnate (in between lives) and when you return to Me but not now. It will distract you.

## Contact with Aliens

ME: *O.K., I understand. What about the aliens? Why have they not contacted me yet?*

SE: They have on the subconscious level, but they find it hard as your mind is too busy. You are truly multidimensional in your mental activity, but you need to allow yourself to focus on one thing at a time. This will allow them access to you. The "Violet Flame" meditation you are doing is helping, but you need to be more resolute. Only when you have quietened your mind will they be able to contact you properly. Also, you try too hard when you start things. You are too intense; this acts as a block. You need to let go and go with the flow. Only then will things happen. You are getting there, but do it slowly and don't try to force it.

ME: *Thank you. I will do my best.*

SE:    Don't try your best, just *be*. Sometimes just "being" is the best thing to do. This is at the heart of meditation. You should try it.

## Byron on Just Being

One morning meditation I found myself just being and not trying to contact anyone, such as the Source or Byron.

B:    Just being is sometimes the best thing to do. It slows the mind down.

*ME:*    *Who is that? Is that the Source? Where is Byron?*

B:    This is Byron.

*ME:*    *Oh, hello. How can you contact me on this level? I am still on the Earth plane.*

B:    I can contact you on any level; it is only you that have decided to come up to my level to communicate, and you think this is the only way. This is no longer necessary.

Not convinced, I shot up to the 27th level to see Byron. We walked in a lovely wooded glade filled with flowers.

B:    Just *being* is one of the best things you can do. It allows you to just be yourself without the urgencies of the material world. It allows you to think and rationalize and communicate with yourself properly. It will slow YOUR mind down, allowing you to access the spiritual side of yourself, the real you.

*ME:*    *How is this?*

B:    Your mind races with a list of things to process; it is constantly planning and scheming on things/jobs that you believe are more important. They appear to be so important that they even override your ability to meditate. This is your conscious mind fighting for supremacy, for it knows that it will eventually lose control of your Earthly existence as you become more spiritual. It wants to perpetuate itself. It will even try to disguise itself by being part of your spiritual agenda and making you think that you need to have your abilities *now*. In effect, it will make you try too hard and subsequently block your progression—a perfect way to maintain its existence.

ME: *So just* being *really is good for you?*

B: Yes, provided you don't focus on it as a means to an end and make it *formal*. Just enjoy the moments when they appear and don't think that you need to communicate with me or the Source and write something every day.

## Accessing One's Core Essence/Core Star

I discussed the *just being* principle with my wife one night, and I mentioned the information I received about it being an essential part of getting in contact with our core essence. I also talked about the feeling that I had been getting that the material world was feeling more and more like an illusion. I said that I thought "The Matrix" movie was a very important concept for people to think about in terms of understanding the difference between the realities of the spiritual world compared to the great illusion of the material world. We also discussed the need to access levels individually when we are in contact with our core star. We considered that when we are in contact with our core essence, we will be operating on all levels at the same time and will not, therefore, need to think about *going* to a level to communicate with an entity or being. This also came up in my morning meditation the next day.

SE/B: Just being is a key part of getting in contact with your core essence.

ME: *Who am I speaking to? The Source or Byron?*

SE/B: Both of us and one of us, for we are one and the same. You understand this on a deeper level.

ME: *I am getting the feeling that I no longer need to "go" to a level to communicate with you.*

SE/B: That is correct, for when you are in contact with your core essence, you are truly everywhere and at all levels at the same time. *You* just are. You don't need to go to the 127<sup>th</sup> level to contact Me.

ME: *Hang on. I thought there were just 100 levels.*

SE/B: There are only 100; it was a figure of speech. However, an individual may want to split the levels up so that he/she is able to take the evolutionary level jump at an easier pace.

ME: *O.K. You were talking about the core essence.*

SE/B: Yes, the core essence is the real you. It is your essence in the fullest sense of the word. The core star can be considered as a database of all your experience and existence—all that you have done, will do, and are doing. Once you access this, you will fully understand and believe that the material world really is the great illusion. You will understand that you are energy and that you can manipulate energy. In being able to realize and fully believe this, it will become your ultimate reality. You will realize that you can manipulate energy in the material world, as well as affect the material world reality.

A master knows and fully understands and believes this, for he is who he really is. This is how a master can do things, like dematerialization, teleportation, and telekinesis, etc.—all the things that will get the attention of the people in the material world, the so-called *hard evidence* of a higher order of things. A master can do this because his belief is unequivocal. He is himself incarnate in the material world together with all the knowledge, understanding, and experience of the universe and God, for he is one with God and the universe, and the universe and God are one with him.

ME: *Thank you. That is both beautiful and interesting.*

SE/B: Of course, it is the nature of everything. All is in balance when understanding is finally achieved, and belief is replaced by knowing. Getting in contact with your core star/core essence allows you to get in contact with the real you. It allows you to access who you really are.

## Removing the Veil of Separation from Our Real Self

ME: *But what happens if we remove the veil that separates us from our real self and what we think is reality? Would this not cause mayhem? People would think that all that they have strived for is to no avail. They would realize that there is life after death and that everything is love and light and that this real reality is infinite. Then they'd come to the conclusion that if everything is love and light, then why not have a good time while they are here on Earth. They would abandon the need to strive and work for the evolution and experiences that they came to Earth to experience in the first place.*

SE/B: That is correct, and that is why a few, and only a few, individuals are able to access both worlds: reality and the material world at the same time. This is because they understand that they are here for a reason and that they must also commit themselves to finish what they started, as well as work with the spirit realms. To do this, they need to be grounded and be able to balance the two worlds of the reality and material.

My thoughts went to the Chinese dynasties of the past.

SE/B: Yes, that is right. They realized that they were going to reincarnate and that life and their real selves were perpetual. Once they had established this, they decided that it was best to have jam today rather than tomorrow, so they abandoned the need to complete their Earthly

45

experiences and delayed evolution until their next incarnation. They chose to have a life of decadence instead. The result was that this belief was perpetuated beyond the normal life and death cycle associated with reincarnation, and they didn't evolve for several lifetimes. In fact, they incurred quite a lot of karma which has taken some of them many lives to work out. Some are still catching up.

ME: *So you really do have to be special to work with the spirit worlds within the material.*

SE/B: Yes, you need to be quite a way up the evolutionary scale and be dedicated to both causes you have taken responsibility for.

## The Role of the Aliens

One Tuesday I opened my chakras and wondered what the subject for today would be. As I thought about discussing aliens, I sensed a presence in my consciousness.

ME: *Who is there? Byron? The Source?*

SE/B: The Source, Byron, both of us, as we are one as we are one with you.

At this time I wasn't concerned with what levels I was on as I now knew that communication was independent of which level I was on. All I needed was the intention and the belief.

ME: *What do aliens have to do in the scheme of things?*

SE/B: They are a part of the bigger picture. They work for the good of the All. Of course, some of them are as ignorant as humans and, therefore, only work towards their own ends. But mainly many of them are highly evolved and are doing everything they can do to support their own evolution and the evolution of others and the universe. They are dedicated to increasing the vibration levels of the universe to bring it back to what

46

it used to be during the time after the separation of My/our self. Humans are part of this because, as you know, independent free will is the great experiment that will allow the universe to evolve faster.

## Byron on the author as an Om

This communication ended as fast as it started, but I was to talk further on the subject the next day with Byron on his own time but with a difference. I was still on the Earth level, but I was talking to Byron via what I visualized as a tube or bypass between the 27th level and the Earth level (level 1).

ME:   *Hi Byron, I am still on the Earth level. How can I talk to you? Are you on the Earth level?*

B:   No, I am still on the 27th level but am communicating to you through a bypass that you have created.

ME:   *Oh, how did I do that?*

B:   I don't know, but it works.

A bit confused as to how I created a bypass without knowing how or even that I had created it, I continued with my intended dialogue.

ME:   *I wanted to talk next about aliens and how I fit in.*

B:   O.K., but I will start with a statement of reality first. You are part of a race of beings called the Om. You are a race of light beings that travel the universe visiting different galaxies.

ME:   *How did I get involved in being here on Earth?*

B:   You were made aware of the work that was going on in the Earth plane and understood how important it was and that it was pivotal to the evolution of the universe. In realizing this, you undertook sacred work under the guidance of the Source Entity to help the occupants of Earth remember the knowledge, the truth.

ME:   *It doesn't seem to have worked very well.*

B:     It has but not in the way you wanted it to. You expected there to be centers of excellence for retaining the knowledge and the truth. This happened, but it was abused by the Egyptians and other notable races that used it to control others. Over a number of lifetimes, you have been able to assist in keeping this knowledge and truth alive in the minds of a few dedicated and aware (awake) individuals, Masters, and believers in the truth.

ME:    *So where are we now?*

B:     You and the Om have assisted in getting the Earth back to the condition where knowledge and truth are becoming known and believed by more and more people. We are now at a point where we almost have the critical mass necessary to allow us to raise the frequency of the Earth back up to the levels that it should be. You have reincarnated into a very important time period.

       The Om are a race of light beings that are one with God. All beings are, of course, one with God, but the Om are higher up the frequencies. When you took on-board the most sacred and important work on Earth, you made a special and massive commitment that has lasted many lifetimes.

ME:    *So what is my work in this lifetime if the critical mass is almost achieved?*

B:     You are to help in the realization process. This is showing the general public the things concerning spirituality that they can relate to and measure. You will show them that this is but just a small part of spiritual matters and that although there is a more physical side to spirituality, this is just for demonstration—to get their attention. Once you have their attention, you will be able to tell and teach them about the reality and truth, the big picture. You will need to be pure of mind, body, and soul, so you had better start cleansing yourself.

## Byron Introduces Hum

The next morning I was grounding myself and opening my chakras when I got the impression that Byron was close to me with there was another entity by his side. He was wearing a silver suit that appeared to have no seams but gave the appearance of a space age pullover type garment. I increased my frequency to that of the 27$^{th}$ level and greeted Byron.

B:       Hello, this is *******.

I couldn't pronounce his name.

B:       You probably can't pronounce his name, so we will call him Hum.
*ME:     O.K. Why is Hum here?*
B:       He is beloved of the Om, as are you, and he will be able to help you in all your questions about alien races in the universe/s. He will also help you communicate with them so that you can further your knowledge.
*ME:     Why does he wear the silver suit?*
B:       That is so you can discriminate me from him. He will help you with the other races.
*ME:     I have to go now.*
B:       That is O.K. The objective was to introduce you to Hum, and this has been done.
*ME:     Thank you both.*

## Byron on Oneness with Our Higher Self

My first morning meditation after coming back to the UK from Crete saw me literally shooting up to the 27$^{th}$ level to see Byron. When I arrived, I felt that I was distanced from myself and was bouncing around like I was on a trampoline.

B:       Your movement up to my level was too fast for your conscious mind to keep up with. That is why you feel

49

at a distance to yourself and see yourself bouncing around.

ME: *This is interesting.*

B: Yes it is. It is one of the ways in which you can contact your higher and true self. You can do this by moving up the frequencies too fast and literally leaving your conscious mind behind. Your conscious mind usually stops you from doing this by making you think of other things, such as those small jobs around the house or garden that you end up doing. You can use this method to get in contact with your higher and true self, which will allow you to operate more in your higher self's consciousness than your physical mind's consciousness.

ME: *I have a question based upon the duality of the two minds. On page 259 of Adrian Divirs' book X3, Healing Entities and Aliens, the author mentions that the physical mind and the higher self mind operate in parallel. The higher self mind has a copy of all that's experienced and recorded by the physical mind and adds it to the larger memories and past life knowings of the higher self and Spirit. When the physical body dies, the physical memories die, and the memories that were recorded by the higher self mind are retained. I find it really disturbing that the person that I currently am appears to really die and that what is retained is just a copy. (My mind went to Arnold Schwarzenegger's film The 6th Day where people were having their memories preserved and transferred to a clone.) This appeared to give the individual immortality until a clone was released before the original was dead, which illustrated the fact that they were really two people with two memories and not one memory being transferred from one body to another.*

B: Yes, that is mostly true and is correct for the general population of incarnate entities who are never aware of their higher selves. However, when you are truly in contact with your higher self, you are in total control of who you really are and tend to focus your attention more and more within your higher self's consciousness. You are totally able to access all your previous lives' memories and information accumulated in your higher self's mind. When this happens, you see the human body for what it is—a vehicle for evolution and not who you really are. Because your attention is now in the higher self rather than the physical self, you experience yourself as your higher self. Your attention is shifted from one part of you to another, the real you. The only problem here is that the individual must try to stay grounded when in this state; otherwise, he/she will appear to become distant (or spaced out) from the physical body. Then it will lose control of it. When your attention is focused on the higher self, you will not experience the feeling and fear of this kind of mental duality. You will be able to move your consciousness freely between the physical and higher self, effectively creating one mind, one set of new cumulative higher self and physical memories and thus perpetuating a feeling of oneness. The greater picture is that once you can do this, you will be able to interface and integrate with the other parts of yourself that are either incarnate or in spirit experiencing the total oneness of your true, true self as a multidimensional being experiencing many things and many incarnations on many planets and many dimensions all at the same time.

ME:   *Wow! Thanks a lot. Now I understand.*

B:   Not bad for a six minute meditation, but, of course, time is different when meditating. And don't forget that concepts, knowledge, and understanding are transmitted in more than the spoken or written word.

## Byron on Accessing Higher Self Memories

The next day I again went to see Byron on the 27$^{th}$ level and decided to prove the comments he made about moving too fast through the frequency levels. I moved through the levels bouncing around from the 27$^{th}$ to the 15$^{th}$ to the 30$^{th}$ to the 50$^{th}$ to the 100$^{th}$ and down again. I moved so fast that I (my physical mind) was starting to lose sight of my higher self's mind. I moved from galaxy to galaxy in the blink of an eye.

B:      You're losing me, too. I can't keep up with you!

I then moved back up to the 100$^{th}$ level where I saw another galaxy form. This I recognized as the Source Entity. He/She/It spoke to me.

SE:     Remember who you are!

I then experienced something totally unexpected. I received impressions of many, many, many lives being lived. I gained glimpses and impressions of pictures and feelings of where I was and where I had been. I was a Byzantine warrior, a Roman, an Egyptian. I saw an aircraft go over my head in Atlantis, I saw structures of buildings on another planet, and I met up with the Om and embraced them.

I received the impression that there was far too much for my physical consciousness to comprehend so only fleeting impressions were received and interpreted. Mere snapshots of what was being given to me were grabbed by my physical consciousness and relayed to me. As I write this, I feel that I have been given a gift. When I de-focused my attention from my physical mind to my higher self-mind via core star mediations or simply moved too fast through the frequency levels for my physical consciousness to keep up, I effectively diffused the concentration of physical consciousness to the more diffuse requirement of the spiritual or higher self-consciousness. In effect, I raised my vibration level and expanded my consciousness to encompass the wider corners of self by expanding the horizon of my awareness through diffusion of concentration. In eyesight terms, it would be like fully using your peripheral vision. I was told that this technique would allow me to focus on my higher self's consciousness to access my higher self's memories.

## The Om on Concentration, Focus, and Meditation

My morning meditation was proving to be difficult with my mind wandering onto more Earthly pursuits. After I finally managed to calm my mind down, I projected myself up to the 20th level again and looked around. The gap between the 20th and 21st was narrow, so I expanded it so that it was more comfortable. I saw the usual black/grey appearance of this level and then decided that I would expand my awareness to what the real appearance of the 20th level was. It instantly went into a bright white light and at the same time two of the Om came to greet me. They were pleased that I had been able to see what the real 20th level environment looked like. In contrast they looked like wispy black entities, but I perceived that this was only in comparison to the very, very iridescent bright light of the 20th. They told me that this light was pure celestial light. They then said they would give me a lesson in concentration. I thought this was very appropriate.

I suddenly found myself on a tight rope (without stabilizers) crossing a canyon in the US with the knowledge that I had to concentrate 100% on the task at hand or risk losing my life. I felt the level of concentration as being total engrossment. I was one with the wire I was walking on and knew exactly where to place my feet and how to distribute my weight. There was nothing else in the universe that mattered; I wasn't even interested in the wonderful view or the birds that flew by me. I was totally focused on the task at hand.

53

Afterwards, I returned to the 7$^{th}$ Earth plane levels. What an excellent example of concentration and focus! This experience helped me tremendously to understand this concept.

The next day I started my meditation and closed all of the doors off on the downwards spiral staircase that represented my thoughts. Each door represented a different thought and, therefore, a different distraction. I opened up all my chakras and rose up to the 20th level pulling up some friends (who I assumed were some of the Om, who were on the 14th level) at the same time. They then re-emphasized the previous day's lesson on concentration. They stipulated that the tightrope walker was an excellent example of pure 100% concentration. The level of concentration was such that nothing outside of doing the task at hand was important. A tightrope walker needs to dedicate those minutes of his life purely to walking the rope. He/she cannot allow any outside influences to intrude or distract his concentration.

This is the level of concentration that is necessary when meditating.

Om:     You must be dedicated enough to allow the short period of time to be used in the meditation process and nothing else.

I then had a fleeting thought about looking at my watch to find out what time it was since I had to go to work soon. The Om picked up on this instantly and said that this is exactly what they were talking about. Even this minute distraction was enough to cause a downward spiral of lack of concentration.

Om:     The ten or so minutes of meditation should be considered sacred, and no other thoughts should be allowed to interfere with it. The distractions are only the conscious mind's desire to take control again. It feels that when you are accessing the higher self-mind, it is somehow losing control and is frightened that it somehow may not get it back.

## The Source Entity on Preparing for Meditation

SE: A number of different ways can be used to still the mind as a prelude to meditation. One is to count the heart beats; the other is to concentrate on the breathing rhythm. A further method is to imagine you are stroking a favorite animal or throwing a ball for a dog. All of these focus the mind on one thing only. You could also think of a big yellow ball above your head and then imagine your spirit rising up to join with it. This also works.

Concentration can also be considered a vital part of meditation, and, even classed as meditation in its own right. When you meditate, you need to focus on the meditation and not the idle chatter of your mind that wants to continue to control you and prevent you from accessing your real self. Only when you are fully focused can you meditate properly; focusing requires you to concentrate on the meditation process and only that. Give yourself a little mental note to know when your meditation/concentration is wandering and drag yourself back into focus. Concentrating on something simple is the best route.

## Celestial Light

With this lesson well and truly learned, I commented on the bright light that was the 20th level, and the Om again said this was celestial light. It was not the same as the celestial love experienced on the 6th level. It was the light of all things and nothing, all places and no place, all universes and no particular universe, all times and no time, all dimensions/frequencies and no dimensions/frequencies, all beings in all times, dimensions, frequencies, and universes all at the same time. This is what made the light so bright; everything and everyone was burning so very brightly. I then saw some bright spots that moved around, and I was told that these were other beings that were specifically aligned with the 20th level. That's why they were brighter than the ambient light. My fellow beings looked dark in lieu of all this brilliant ambient light. On the Earth plane they would look like brilliant white/golden light, but here they looked dull in comparison. I wanted to embrace them all and thank them for the lesson and their patience in teaching me. I felt them smile, and I sensed that it really was time to hit the road and go to work.

## Mixed Remembrance of Memories and Abilities

At my next mediation I was more focused and determined not to be distracted. I opened up my first seven chakras to associate myself with the auric levels and then swooped up to the higher levels. When I arrived at the 14$^{th}$ level, I noticed the tube (bypass) that I had put in place to allow the Om to pass up to the 20$^{th}$ level. Upon my arrival, I felt the presence of another being who I assumed was one of the Om.

Om: We are impressed with your ingenuity; you are remembering.

*ME:* *Thank you. I am starting to remember stuff but not remember it in the way that I want to.*

Om: Define.

*ME:* *Well, I just know that I can do things, such as constructing the link between the 14$^{th}$ and 20$^{th}$ levels, but I can't remember past lives or the places/planets/galaxies/ dimensions where I used to live or even my previous time with the Om.*

Om: It is interesting that you mention the time before. You really must be next to a computer when you are meditating so that you can write our discourse straight away, but if you can't, we will make sure that you can remember what we say to you.

*ME:* *How will you do that?*

56

Om: We will program you with a long term memory function so that you can download what was communicated to you.

This dialogue was typed a few hours after the meditation. The conversation flowed back from my mind and into the keyboard. It felt like I was having total recall!

## The Om on an Image of Om as a Ball of Light

I then decided that I wanted to see the celestial light of the 20th level and that I wanted to see the image of the Om.

ME: *Oh, you look almost human (angelic) to me.*

Om: That is because this is all your mind is able to cope with in its existing incarnate form.

ME: *Can I see what you are?*

Om: Yes, but you will only see us as something you can translate into your current limited understanding, but, you will SEE later.

ME: *I see you as a ball of light energy.*

Om: Yes, this is a good example and one that your mind can use as a translation substitute for something that it can't directly place into a recognizable context. You need some form of reference point, a datum from which to work. If you don't have the experience in this incarnation of what an energy being looks like, your brain will use a substitute, one that you can understand as meaning "This is an energy being."

## Seeing an Energy Being

ME: *Oh, do I have to see an energy being, or do I only need to sense or communicate with one?*

Om: There are energy beings that you will not be able to *see* because the energy is not visible. It is too refined, too fine to be picked up even with spiritual eyes. You don't really need to see them anyway for you will know their presence and be able to communicate with them, albeit in a limited way.

ME:     *Thank you. I must go now.*

During these meditations and subsequent recalls, especially when I am typing up the text that forms the dialogue, I am constantly thinking that I am deluding myself, that I am only talking to myself. But it is the speed and subject matter of the information that comes through that tells me that this is more than just talking to myself. Also, some of the information is said in such a way that it is foreign to me. It is then that I know this is not the Earthly me speaking.

## The Source Entity on Intuition and Common Sense

ME:     *I have had a number of occurrences over the years when the correct answer to a question has popped into my head before I have had chance to work out the answer by logic and calculation.*

SE:     Yes, I have seen you do this. You must learn to trust intuition and use it as much as possible. When you use this faculty often enough, it will become second nature to you and will lead you to instant communication with the higher self. Intuition is the higher self's way of giving you **in**ternal guidance. It is the way that the higher self (the larger part of you that is still in the energetic) tries to train you to start using the information that is not available by logic or from your Earth experience/s but from your higher self. It makes you trust your feelings by putting you into a situation where the intuitive information is correct, and this was only apparent when you have arrived at the same conclusion by Earthly logic. Hence, you learn to trust your intuition as you see more and more evidence that the information given is both correct and accurate.

Using one's *common sense* is similar.

When people say "Why don't you use your common sense?" they don't actually know what they are saying. The *common sense* is actually all the total learning and experience of all incarnate spirits in the universe, a true reservoir of knowledge. Thus, when people use their *common* sense, they intuitively tap into the wealth of knowledge that is available to them via the universe. For example, when individuals use their common sense for servicing their car, they might not actually have the knowledge and experience themselves, but they are able to do the work when they intuitively tap into universal knowledge. They might not actually need to have experience of the learning themselves but can benefit from the learning of others. This is also true of an evolved and aware spirit who may need the knowledge of a great inventor or leader of people but doesn't have the time or need to go through a whole life to gain the experience or knowledge to help him address a certain life issue.

Common sense can also apply to recently gained knowledge, i.e., what a spirit learns two minutes ago, could be used as common sense by another at the same time or two minutes later.

## The Source Entity on the Twelve Source Entities

The next day I was again outside the universe and talking to the Source Entity, one of twelve entities that were split off from another larger entity, the Origin. Of course, the objective of Their creation is to find out as much about Themselves and the universe as possible and report back to the Origin for Its and Their collective learning and knowledge.

ME:   *So how many of You are there?*
SE:   There are twelve of Us.
ME:   *And your purpose is to learn.*

59

SE:    Yes, this is the purpose of all beings given individuality from the Origin.

*ME:*   *So what are the others doing?*

SE:    They are doing the same as Me and you, trying to find out about Themselves and give the collective knowledge to the Whole, so that the Whole can progress.

*ME:*   *So how are the others doing this?*

SE:    Each of Us has decided upon a different route of evolution. I have chosen to split into two with one side of Me being whole and the other being many billions of souls in a number of universes in a finite (but nevertheless infinite to you) number of dimensions. Each has its own individuality and collectivity. Another has decided to be one and contemplate the reasons for self on Its own. Another has split Itself into four, whereas another has split Itself into a billion souls totally, etc.

*ME:*   *So why are there only twelve of you?*

SE:    Why not? That is the number of entities the Origin decided to split off from Itself.

*ME:*   *The number twelve seems significant! Weren't there twelve apostles and twelve ascended masters and even a council of twelve?*

SE:    Yes, and this is all due to the other Sources visiting My area of responsibility, including Myself. Each ascended master was a Source Entity trying to learn outside Its own area of responsibility. You will also find that there are only twelve dimensions used in My universe although in reality they are infinitely finite (finite but infinite to you).

*ME:*   *So when do you expect the learning to finish and You twelve return to the Origin?*

SE:    Who knows? There is no plan.

# Part 2:

# The History of God

Chapter 4:

# *The History of God*

## Meeting the Origin

During a morning meditation, I found myself asking the question about whether or not the material I was taking down as a result of countless meditations was worth publishing. Bearing in mind that many others had already written these sort of books, and they numbered in the thousands, I felt that another book of the same genre would not make enough impact to progress this "good" work to another level of awareness/discussion. I, therefore, needed direction on which way to go.

I had previously found that I could explore different levels of consciousness up to and past 100 levels. Each level was a frequency level equal to that experienced by healers who have the ability to sense the seven frequency levels of the human aura (based on current popular understanding). After some thought on this, I found myself focusing on the frequency that led me to the Source Entity (an energy being that I had previously been in contact with during a number of meditations and subsequent channeling opportunities) and zoomed up past the 100th level to talk to Him/Her/It.

ME:  *I want some direction on what I should be writing about for my book.*
SE:  You should write about the history of God.
ME:  *What?!*
SE:  This has not been done yet since most people who are

in contact are actually in contact with Me and not the
Origin.

## Who Is the Origin?

*ME:*   *Who is the Origin?*

SE:    The Origin is the entity that I am part of; it is the one
that we twelve are split away from to understand what
I/We are.

*ME:*   *I have not been in contact with the Origin yet?*

SE:    You have but only fleetingly.

*ME:*   *Should I be speaking with It/Him/Her?*

SE:    Yes, it is the best place to begin.

I then called the Origin in my mind hoping that he would speak
to me. At this time I found myself outside the multiverse
controlled by the Source Entity I associated with as God and
looked further afield. In the distance I saw a coalescence of
light.

*ME:*   *Origin, can I speak to you?*

O:    You may.

*ME:*   *Where are you?*

O:    Everywhere and nowhere.

*ME:*   *I want to know about the history of you.*

O:    Do you have the time and patience?

*ME:*   *I think so.*

O:    Then I will begin.

I chuckled to myself. This all sounded a bit "story tellerish" to
me . . .

# Chapter 5:
## *In the Beginning*

## The Origin on Creating Greater Awareness of Self Via the Twelve

O: In the beginning I was not aware that I was aware and just existed. You can consider this by just "being" and listening to everything that is going on around you without making any judgements about anything or trying to work out what is going on. At some point over the millennia, I decided that I was aware of wanting to know more about what was going on around and in Me.

ME: *Were there any other lifeforms around then?*

O: Where there is energy, there is eventually consciousness and there is life, but consciousness is not true life until it is aware. There was lots of life at what you would call the "vegetable level of consciousness," but this to Me was only like the cells that are in your body. You know they are there, but you can't communicate with them since they don't yet have that level of awareness, and neither do you. As I further reflected on this need for awareness, I decided that I would split Myself into thirteen, one being Me and the other twelve being other smaller parts of Me that had individual consciousness and awareness, plus an inherent need to search and learn about consciousness and awareness. How They did this was up to Them, but They were charged with returning to me with an answer of some kind.

ME: *So You became aware and wanted to know more?*

O: Yes, that's right. The task for the other twelve parts of Me was to find out more about the environment that

65

was Me.

ME:    *Are there others like You? I only sense You.*

O:    That is because you are within Me now.

ME:    *There must be an end to the number of times I can go up to see other higher beings, and You must be it because I can't imagine any more than Your level.*

O:    That is because of your limited point of view.

ME:    *Are there more? Is there a higher level?*

I tried to look further and suddenly found myself in another environment where there were more Origins. This was freaky, and I was feeling very spaced out.

## A Starting Point Where Everything Just Is

ME:    *There has to be an end somewhere?*

O:    Yes, there is, but you will not accept it when it happens because your brain considers that there must be something bigger. How can I explain that there has to be a start, a point where everything just is until it becomes aware?

ME:    *I have real difficulty with this. I feel like my brain is about to explode under the strain.*

O:    I can see.

ME:    *So if there are many entities that are controlling the multiverses to learn about what awareness means and to experience different things, how can They call themselves God when a person like me or some other person says they are in contact with God?*

O:    That is because we are all part of the total. If you call the total a name and that name is "God," then We are all God. We know We are God because We are in contact with the total and Ourselves all at the same time. We don't know any different because We are not "cut-off" from God like you are; therefore, We call ourselves God because that is who We are. We are all one entity; We are all God.

## The Origin Looks Within Self

Me: *So how did You become aware and decide that You wanted to know more about Yourself?*

O: When I became aware that I was, I decided to look into Myself and see what I was. I was surprised to see that I was many things.

ME: *How did You do this? It must have been a massive task?*

O: It was ... Consider yourself as the sea and imagine the wonder that I had when I found out that the equivalent of fish and crustaceans were also part of Me.

I then found myself looking into me, looking at the very heart of myself. Suddenly I felt as if I was floating in space and looking at things as small as cells and bacteria and wondering at the diversity of life within me that I had no prior realization about on the personal experience level.

O: Yes, that's it, except that what I saw was different types of energy in different densities and different frequencies, and some were only present on certain dimensional levels. Some of them spread across many dimensions and changed in their appearance when they were present in different dimensions. All of them behaved differently, depending on the dimension they were in or how many they were linked to.

ME: *So did they also have awareness?*

O: No, but some parts were developing rudimentary consciousness, which is the first step towards awareness. The task was so big that it literally took millennia to go through every part of My "different levels." To move around within Myself, I would focus my attention, and I would be there instantaneously traveling within Myself and able to create within

67

Myself anything that I wanted without barriers or limitations.

## The Origin as the End

I then suddenly saw the truth. The Origin was the end, and everything was taking place within the Origin. All of the other twelve "Source entities" were split off from the Origin but were still contained within the Origin. They even appeared to pass around the outer edge of the Origin. This is where I was getting confused and muddled up. I could see the others and their own experiments happening in front of me, and around me was the environment that was the Origin.

O: It was fantastic to see different parts of me doing things that I had absolutely no knowledge about. Eventually I got to the point that I needed to dig deeper and deeper within Myself to see what was going on. As I was doing this, I noticed the lower dimensions or frequencies and realized it was possible to have different frequency levels in a single dimension.

*ME:* *You mean dimensions within dimensions?*

O: Yes, I noticed that at some level I was much slower and had difficulty in accessing the rest of Myself.

## The Origin Breaks Off Twelve Parts of Itself

*ME:* *Would this be the physical levels?*

O: Yes, and others like it. It was at this point that I thought it would be interesting to discover how I would react if I was in a position where I was totally cut off from Myself. This I did for a certain indiscernible amount of time but discovered that I actually didn't learn much since I didn't have a task to do. I then decided that I would create the others and give these other parts of Me the opportunity to do the same but with both of Us observing and learning/experiencing what was occurring. Your level is the lowest and most difficult and most fruitful in terms of the learning experience.

ME: *So what made you decide upon the number 12 as the number of different parts of yourself to split off?*

O: This was based upon distinction in the different levels of the dimensions within Me. I noticed that there was a specific difference, and that this was in twelve parts. So when I decided that I wanted to know more about Myself, I decided it would be a good idea to have parts of Me focus its attention on each one of these twelve dimensional zones. As I delved further into Myself, I also noticed that these twelve zones were also divided by twelve with each zone being separated by twelve dimensional octaves with each octave being a group of three dimensions.

Me: *Wouldn't you be better calling it a tritave?*

O: Possibly, but I decided that octave sounded better and could be more easily understood by you in your current level of incarnation and ability to access the common knowledge base whilst using your conscious mind.

## The 12 x 12 x 12 x 3 Different Dimensional Levels

ME: *So in effect you have 12 x 12 x 12 x 3 different dimensional levels. That is 5,184 dimensions.*

O: Yes, and each is divisible by the major dimension or an octave. This is why the numbers 12, 4 and 3 are important. 12 = a dozen (a baker's dozen = 13, the 12 plus 1 Me!) the twelve disciples and 1 – Jesus – Me! 3 days for the spirit to totally leave a dead body, 4 octaves to a dimension (the three physical planes in your case, plus 1 "time") Also, you can make any number you like out of the manipulation of the numbers 4, 3, and 1.

I tried it, and He/She/It was right. You could make any number.

*ME:*   *What about different frequency levels?*

O:   The dimensions and the frequencies are, in effect, the same thing; however, one is separate whereas the other is together.

*ME:*   *Can you explain?*

O:   With a frequency change, the matter (spiritual or physical) is further apart from its lower frequency self; whereas, with a higher dimensional level, the matter (spiritual or physical) is in the same place as its lower dimensional part. A dimension is, therefore, overlaid by time rather than frequency, which is separated by a molecule's speed and the space it occupies.

I tried to see how this would look, and my head started to hurt with the stretching of my mental boundaries.

O:   You are trying too hard. Try to think of it in these terms. Each of the twelve *Mes* was assigned to work within a certain range of dimensions; these were split into twelve levels. There are twelve more levels separating the levels between each of these levels, and these were split again by 3 to bring the structure down to the lowest dimensional or frequency level. Three of these together create a workable environment that I call an "octave." You humans happen to live in the bottom three frequencies that make up the first dimensional level in a particular Source Entity's area of evolutionary responsibility.

*ME:*   *How does this relate to the existence of different universes?*

O:   As previously stated, each Source created as many universes as He/She/It needed to gain experience and evolve. Simplistically, within each dimensional level there can exist a totally separate universe with each equally important and addressing the issue of evolution in a different manner. Each is independent of the other but equally dependent and interlinked with one another.

ME: *So this linking is why it is possible to travel through other dimensions or use other dimensions for traveling instantaneously in our dimension?*

O: Yes, as I said before, you have to have a back door.

ME: *So why did You allow all of the Source Entities to split the dimensions into the octave parts?*

O: To allow Me to experience everything about Myself right down to the quark level, as you would put it, and below. I felt the need to do this when I found that parts of Me lost contact when they were at the lower levels. This is what you experience as humans incarnate and are projected into the very lowest levels. You start to lose contact with the rest of your higher selves and develop individual consciousness and even limited awareness that is separate from the rest of yourselves. Your higher self was, of course, aware of what was being experienced at the lower levels, but that part of you that is actually in these lower levels loses the ability to communicate because of the limitations that present themselves in these lower frequencies. It is like a worm that is cut in two but is still connected by its skin. The worm develops as two separate worms and eventually becomes two, but you don't because that skin that holds you together, the aura, never withers and dies. The information accrued in the physical is in both zones, so when the physical dies, the information contained in the "physical consciousness" is still maintained in the spiritual consciousness, and your attention is presented back to the spirit rather than the physical. This is the reason why you should not be afraid of dying in the physical because your projected consciousness is withdrawn and not lost, unlike the worm's body that eventually becomes separated from the original when the skin withers and dies.

71

## The Origin on the Purpose for Humanity's Incarnating

I decided to ask the main reasons for our incarnations.

ME:   *What is the main reason for us being here on Earth?*

O:   To experience and learn from those experiences and in the process evolve whilst contributing to the whole.

ME:   *What do I have to do?*

O:   You have to do a number of things, and the fact that your discussions with me are limited to small amounts of time means that you are experiencing many things, which is good.

ME:   *So what is one of things that I have to learn?*

O:   What is your pleasure?

ME:   *What?*

O:   What is your pleasure? You need to experience pleasure and joy. This is one of the things that you really haven't grasped yet. Sometimes it is best to just sit back, be, enjoy the fruits of your hard work, and feel the pleasure and joy that comes with relaxation. Try to ensure that you aren't too engrossed in striving for more or trying to be better because as a result you are never happy with what you have.

ME:   *I can relate to that. I think I know exactly what you mean.*

O:   Do you? You are still not grasping the nettle [See Glossary for clarification]!

## The Twelve Sources Varied Approaches to Learning

ME:   *So the twelve Sources have different approaches to the way They learn about Themselves and Their environment, YOU.*

O:   That's correct; the Source Entity that you are working with decided to duplicate the way that I split Myself up

72

into twelve.

*ME:*    *Is that why we have 12 x 12 x 12 x 3 dimensions?*

O:     Yes, that's right. If you look at one of the other Source Entities structures, you will find that They are 12 x 4 x 12 x 3 with the multiplication by 4 that comes from the number of times They have divided Themselves, i.e., the number of universes that They have decided to use as the medium that They are using to work out all about Themselves.

*ME:*    *Looking at the number of universes created by my Source Entity and the position that we humans are working in, I would say that we are right at the bottom of the universe, dimension, and frequency pile.*

O:     Yes, you are, but that is where you score the most evolutionary points, so to speak. As I have said before, you, or at least part of you, is totally cut off from the rest of yourself, so you have to do an awful lot without your higher functions. It's a bit like what I explained before; it's your equivalent of having no eyes, ears, touch, smell, or taste and still trying to build the Eiffel Tower.

*ME:*    *It's an almost impossible task.*

O:     That's right, but somehow all of you manage to succeed.

## The Origin on The Author's Writing about the History of God

*ME:*    *How do you want me to tell the world about the history of God?*

O:     That is entirely up to you. You can write it as twelve or thirteen books with each book dealing with the works of each of the Source Entities and, of course, Me. Or you can write one book with thirteen chapters, each with a summarized version of the story of each Source and Me. This would give you and your audience a taste of what is to come and give them an appetite for buying other books.

*ME:*    *But which one should I write first?*

O:     You could write about Me and the Source Entity that looks after your universes first. This will be the most popular. The other books will only be popular with those people who want to know the truth about the rest of Me, but people will read them. I can hear your thoughts now. No, they don't need to be massive novels. Just write enough to make people feel that they are getting value for money and big enough for you to convey what you need to convey.


## The Origin on Its Sphere of Twelve and the Termination of Our Universe

## The Source Entity as Independent and Yet Integral with The Origin

My mind suddenly saw the rest of the Source Entities, and then I just as suddenly zoomed into the memory of the Source Entity that looks after the universes that the Earth plane is within. I suddenly had the feeling of joy and awe associated with realizing that a part of it now had focused consciousness; it was independent but still integral with the Origin. It was a strange overwhelming feeling that came over me. One that was all encompassing.

I looked back again at the Origin and saw that the configuration of the different Source Entities was not as I had previously seen them: as individual spheres within the sphere of the Origin. They looked like the sphere of the Origin that had been segmented into twelve.

*Me:*    *Why has this changed?*

O:     Because you are now able to understand what happened to a greater depth. Look at your own Source Entity; it is a direct copy of My own division.

I looked at the Source Entity that we refer to as God and saw that this was true. Each of Its twelve divisions was also layered into the twelve dimensions. They appeared like the individual veins of a set of retractable blinds, each one signifying another plane of existence, another dimensional level. Each one occupied the same space and time but did not interfere with the other. Each plane of existence split into the three levels that allowed the 3rd dimensional world approach that we are aware of with each three levels together representing a single dimensional octave in Origin space. It was beautiful.

*ME:*   *I have been thinking about the universe and the popular belief that there will be an end to the universe. What can you tell me about that?*

O:   Well, the answer to the question that there might be an end to your universe is the choice of the Source Entity who created your universe.

## The End of Earth's Universe

*ME:*   *Do you think It would end the universe?*

O:   That would depend upon the circumstances of what It's trying to achieve. Remember, I created the Source Entities to help Me explore Myself and to know more about Myself on all levels. The Source Entities created Their own versions of Me in order to duplicate the effort behind the exercise of knowing Myself. They had free will in how They chose to achieve it. If that means that They disassemble the environments that They have created, then that is up to Them.

*ME:*   *Why would They disassemble the environments They have created?*

O:   That is a question that you would need to answer by asking all of Them yourself. In essence, They would only disassemble the environment They have constructed if it had finished the job it was constructed to do, if it was not meeting its objectives (and, therefore, needed to be modified in some way), or if a complete change of direction was required to make the exploration process more efficient.

ME: *What would happen to the other entities like me, for instance, if the Source Entity that controls our universe decided It had either completed Its job or It was so far off track that It needed to be broken up and started again?*

O: You are part of It. All of you are, just as all of Them are part of Me. Once you are given sentience, you are considered separate. A return to the Source Entity is not something that is enforced upon a sentient being. It is something that the being either strives to achieve or believes that it is happy in its singularity. Everything is down to free will. However, once you return to the Source, you are not stuck there. You can break away and experience whatever you want to experience on your own at any time. You do not lose your individuality by becoming part of the whole again. In essence, you never really had your own singularity because you are always part of something bigger, the Source Entity/Me, but by the Source Entity allowing you to have your own energy system, you achieve complete singularity by association with a local nucleus. This nucleus is the singularity which allows the energy that is you to stay together. It is in a similar way that the universe is held together. So you become your own entity whilst being part of a bigger entity. Together with this is the ability to group together to solve problems or experience different things, as well as return to your creator, the Source Entity, when you desire. This gives you the ultimate flexibility of being a singular part of a smaller whole or part of the greater whole, Me.

## Grouping to Create

*ME:*   *I just got a picture in my mind's eye showing lots of entities clumped together to make a bigger entity than they could ever make on their own.*

O:   Yes, this is a common occurrence and one that is useful to the entities taking part in the *grouping* because together they can achieve much more than they could in ones and twos. In essence, they are able to create a smaller version of the Source Entities by being in *concert* together. Remember the old saying that *birds of a feather stick together.* Well, there is not a truer saying, for all those entities grouped together in concert that you saw in your mind's eye were of the same opinion.

*ME:*   *What were they doing?*

O:   They were solving a problem.

*ME:*   *What was the problem they were solving?*

O:   Inter-dimensional connectivity between the universes created by the twelve Source Entities. They are trying to understand the mechanics of how it all stays together as a singularity and a whole. They are also interested in why entities that are integral to the universe that a specific Source Entity has created have not yet migrated from their environment to another Source Entity's environment, especially as it is not only possible but desirable from an evolutionary and experience point of view. The cross-fertilization of entities created by another entity experiencing existence in a universe that is alien to their creation is a most interesting opportunity for in-depth evolution.

*ME:*   *Could it be that we, as our own entity, are happy to be within our own environment and not move into another? After all, the universe created by my Source Entity has more than one universe and a heck of a lot of dimensions and frequencies. It must be a really large place to exist. So large, in fact, that I can imagine it is quite a thing to meet another entity at all—let alone have enough around you to inhabit a planet.*

O: Good observation. This is one of the reasons why your Source Entity is not likely to end this universe quite yet. There is so much to do and so little populace to do it with. There are several eternities yet before the time comes for the disassembly of your universe. In any event, now that you have your own nucleus and surrounding energy to exist on your own as a single entity, you will not just disappear when the Source Entity disassembles the universe if and when the time comes to do so. You will still be present and held within the space that is part of the Source Entity that is not associated with a dimension-spatial environment. You will be waiting patiently to occupy the new environment when it is constructed. I guess this is the question you wanted to ask, i.e., will we exist past the end of the universe? Well, as I have explained above, the answer is yes. Of course, a Source Entity may create entities that are not singular like you and, as such, these entities would, in fact, return to their base energetic condition when a universe is disassembled. However, that is the choice of the Source in question for He/She/It has the free will to create and change at will.

ME: *Would an entity from my Source Entity be disassembled if it was visiting the universe of another Source Entity which was disassembled?*

O: This has not happened yet because there has not been migration between the different Source Entities' environments. But if this did happen, then that entity would be transported back to its environment of origin by the Source Entity making the universal change, for all Source Entities know which entity is one of Theirs and which is not.

## The Origin on Dimensions, Frequencies, and Space

Another meditation led me to being in contact with the Origin again, and I received a short lecture on mass and frequency. I had just gone through the frequency barrier that I see leading up to the 100th level and into the mass of *stars* that represent all of the returning souls when I found myself outside of the *sphere* that I knew represented the Origin in Its entirety.

*ME:*   *Why can I see you as the sphere? Why is there darkness all around?*

O:   You are tapping into the ability to see beyond yourself/Me. The darkness that you see is merely a reflection of you/Me and is not real dimensional/ "frequentic" space.

My mind then turned to the dimensions and frequencies. I wondered if I would occupy the same *space* if I was accelerated up to the next frequency/dimension.

O:   You would, of course, occupy the same space. Dimensional increase and frequency increase do not affect the area occupied by a being.

*ME:*   *But what about the increase in frequency that ice has to be turned into steam? This increases the area in which it exists because of the increase in energy and the resultant movement of the molecules.*

O:   This is only true for some matter (matter not associated with a soul or being). The law of the universe is totally different from that currently known and understood by man. A person accelerated up to the next level would occupy the same area because of the *will* or *intention* of the being to exist in the same area. This is an automatic function of all beings, no matter what their evolutionary experience and is, therefore, a universal law.

# Chapter 6:
## *The Source Entities Become Aware of Themselves and Their Environment*

## The Source Entity on the Twelve Source Entities' Initial Experiences

During another meditation, I moved from talking to the Origin to talking with the Source Entity Who created the universe in which the Earth plane is located. The Source Entity shared "the early days/millennia" of the creations of the twelve Source Entities.

SE:    We were whooshing around all over the place for ages when we were first created by the Origin. Having a part of the Origin to ourselves and having singular and connective consciousness was fantastic.

*ME:    What else were You doing?*

SE:    We were fascinated with the different dimensions and the shadows that were created by things in one dimension that had their origins in another dimension.

*ME:    You mean that for everything that is in my dimension there is something else manifested in all the other dimensions?*

SE:    Yes. This is the link between all of the dimensions that were recognized as being the Origin.

*ME:    Is this correct for everything?*

SE:    Yes, even down to the smallest item.

*ME:    So why can't I see many things in my dimension?*

81

SE: Because your dimension is rock bottom in the frequency pile. No, sorry, I mustn't get you confused. You already know that dimension and frequency can exist mutually and independently. I shall not use frequency again to describe the level of functionality and manifestation of existence between the dimensions because this is misleading. Suffice to say, your dimension is at the bottom and has a limited capability to show the shadows manifest from other dimensions. It is more likely for your dimension to have many shadows in the higher dimensions. These, of course, diminish as you go up the dimensional levels.

## Shadows in Earth's Dimension

ME: *So there are some shadows in my dimension?*

SE: Yes, but you can only perceive them and not see them with your physical eyes. Some animals can see them, however, because they have not shut down their connection to the universe. Have you not seen cats look up and track the movement of something that you cannot see?

ME: *Yes.*

SE: Well, they are looking at the shadow (or what you might call "spirit" if it's the shadow of a being).

ME: *I thought all beings higher than our dimension could move in our dimension?*

SE: Not all of them, but some actually live in your dimension but at a higher frequency.

ME: *O.K., now can I get the frequency/dimension stuff sorted later? Can we talk about the history of what you did when first created?*

SE: Yes, of course. You only need log into Me and ask the question.

## The Source Entities' First Creation Experiences

*ME:*    *So what were You doing when You were first created?*

SE:    We were all so new and everything was so wonderful. We were whizzing up and down the frequencies and experiencing everything that was Us. We knew that everything We experienced and learnt from was being passed on to the Origin and between Ourselves, so to make the best of this, We did absolutely everything We could think of.

*ME:*    *O.K., we can talk about what you did specifically later. What made you decide to divide yourself into twelve as the Origin had?*

SE:    When We all got over the joy of everything, We got together and decided on the best way to begin the task at hand—that of experiencing the Origin and Ourselves and everything that was. I copied the Origin and added to the division, whereas the Others chose different ways. We were all so impressed by what We could do with the energies! We found that We were enthralled for ages (literally)!

*ME:*    *What do you mean?*

SE:    We saw that We could manipulate the way that matter manifested itself when We gave an area of matter in a specific dimension more or less energy. We were impressed by the shapes and patterns We could make. When We looked more closely at these shapes, We could see that We had made what you call *galaxies*, and that within these galaxies there were many little balls that burned.

*ME:*    *Suns?*

SE:    Yes, suns. We noticed that these would live longer or shorter if We gave them more or less energy and that this depended upon their size and how they interacted with other dimensions.

*ME:*    *The suns interact with other dimensions?*

SE:    Yes, of course they do. They have to because of the

83

level of change that is happening at a quantum level to make them burn like they do.

ME: *O.K., what about planets?*

SE: Yes, We also found that after some time other objects became visible and that this was a result of the un-burned matter or that matter that was not sucked up by the burning balls.

ME: *What else did you notice?*

SE: We noticed that We could affect the outcome of the movement of certain chemicals when We used certain energies to move them or view/scan them.

ME: *How do you mean?*

SE: Some of the chemicals paired up together. Chemicals and molecules that were totally unrelated appeared to have a level of attraction that was most interesting, especially when the chemicals were manifested on the lowest frequency possible.

## The Building Blocks of Biological Life

ME: *What?! Do you mean that there are chemicals and molecules on other dimensions as well?*

SE: Of course, everything is manifested in every dimension in some way; the building blocks of biological life and other life are not exempt from this process.

ME: *You mean that you actually experienced the process that started biological life?*

SE: Yes, in the most basic sense of the word; all that We were seeing was the first basic life forms of viruses and amoeba. This was particularly seen in areas of dense matter.

ME: *You mean planets?*

SE: Yes, but also in areas that you would call *stellar clouds* and other dense matter areas, such as gravity wells (black holes).

ME: *There was life in black holes?*

SE: Yes, of course. There is life everywhere.

ME:    *Were you actually creating life by changing the energy flow of certain physical and non-physical matter?*

SE:    Yes, it was great fun to see things become animate and take on a life of their own.

ME:    *Did these animate objects have souls?  Were they immortal as we are in our energy state?*

SE:    No, these entities were only as rough forms.  They did not have the grace of God in them.

ME:    *So they lived and died?*

SE:    Yes, although it is not death as you know it because they were never really alive in the first place, just thought given form.

ME:    *So when did you decide to split yourself out like the Origin?*

SE:    Oh, much, much later. There were many more things that We went through and experienced before We went our separate ways for seeking knowledge about the Origin.

## The Earth's Source Entity's Experience of a Sense of Self

ME:    *So what was it like when You first noticed that you had your own "oneness"?  That You were no longer part of something bigger?  That You now had your own sense of self?*

SE:    Strange.  We were so used to not having the focus of attention on Ourselves, of being part of something bigger, much bigger and not being able to ascertain who or what We were, that to suddenly have Our own consciousness and know what We were like before and after the Origin separated Us out was amazing, even for Us. We had received our Own thought processes and Our own ability to reason. Seeing what We were before Our individualization was strange and a little frightening.

ME:    *So what was it like to be part of a whole without your own individuality?*

SE: Strange. I don't think that you can understand the feeling in your current focus of self.

*ME: Try me!*

SE: Well, it's like being able to focus on one thing rather than being focused on all things at the same time. It's like you are constrained to a point where you know that you are smaller but still part of the whole. It felt very small.

*ME: I still don't get the feeling of being nothing but everything and then something but still able to access everything out of you!*

SE: You have described the transition phase perfectly. The being nothing but everything was as if We were not in existence but were in existence because We were part of the whole. When the Origin split Us off from Our/Itself, We felt a focus that coalesced Us into awareness of the focused self. The self was that part of the Origin's energy that It had decided to be "set to one side." Don't get Me wrong. We did not have what you would call "consciousness" straight away. We had to develop/evolve our own awareness over billions of years. Some of Us took longer than others. This was all part of the great experiment that the Origin was performing.

## The Origin on Observing the Evolution of the Twelve Entities

I then moved my attention back to the Origin.

*ME: So You split Yourself into twelve parts to find out more about Your Self.*

O: Twelve points plus Myself, to be precise.

*ME: Was the intention to give the twelve points intelligence straight away, or were You waiting to see what would happen?*

O:  The intention was to give the others the same "start" in existence that I had experienced Myself. I wanted to see whether or not they would follow the same path. The outcome was interesting.

ME:  *What do You mean?*

O:  Well, in previous communications I have explained a little bit of what happened and even let the part that is now the Source Entity (SE) for your multiverse talk to you about what it felt, but I have not explained it all because you have not asked all of the questions.

ME:  *O.K., so tell me.*

O:  I just let them be. The idea was to see if They would evolve Their own individuality and awareness and how they would take to *awaken*. I wondered how long it would take Them to realize that They were part of a bigger picture, so to speak, and whether They would want to return to the whole. I found it rather interesting from my Own perspective at first because I felt like there was more of Me that was able to think. It was like the parallel processing that you use in your computers but on a much larger scale. I will further explain this if you wish.

ME:  *Yes, please.*

O:  As I said, it was interesting to see the speed at which They became aware. Some took millennia after millennia whilst others took a fraction of the time. After some millennia of being aware, One even came back to the source (Me) and found that It still retained Its individual memories of self even though It was back in the whole. It then decided to go back into self again. A couple of others even duplicated the experiment that I had done with them. Later They expanded the idea beyond what I had envisioned them capable of expanding. Your Source Entity is one of those that did, and that is why you are in existence. I am delighted that even in your restricted states, you are able to contact the Whole to some extent. It was very interesting seeing them play with their forms and awareness of selves on all the dimensional and frequency levels.

## The Origin on the Twelve Spherical Source Entities

*ME:* *What did They do and what did They look like?*
O:      I will show you.

I then got an image of the parts of Itself and what They were doing.

*ME:* *They are spherical.*
O:      Yes, all energy is spherical in physical appearance and energetic cohesion. This is consistent throughout the dimensions and frequencies.

I then saw more. They were literally playing with Themselves on all frequencies on all dimensions. One of Them was squashing Itself really flat and thin whilst another was extending parts of Itself into nodules with very, very thin links to them from Its main body. This reminded me of the description of what happens when we squeeze ourselves into our physical bodies, and the link is just the so-called "silver cord." This link is so small that we have very, very limited access to ourselves, so much so that we can't access our higher selves even with our extreme concentration. I then got a quick thought from the SE that I was correct, and that It was a very good comparison.

The images of what I saw in my mind's eye are illustrated below:

ME: *So how long did the new Source Entities mess around with Themselves?*

O: Many, many millennia, more time than you can appreciate in your current physical state. You do not have a concept for the amount of time that they spent just being Themselves and exploring what They could do with Their energies.

ME: *Why not give me a chance?*

O: The amount of time is infinitesimally larger than the largest amount of time that your scientists have conceived. They can only think in terms of the amount of time that the area of space they call the "universe" has been in existence.

ME: *You mean the Big Bang?*

O: It wasn't a big bang. You will find this out when you start to dialogue with your Source Entity, but it is a good reference point for you.

ME: *When did you decide to get the Source Entities together and give Them the task of experiencing everything down to the Nth degree so that You could understand Yourself more?*

O: I didn't.

ME: *What?*

O: I didn't. That was the whole point of the exercise. The exercise was to create Them and then see what happened.

Just at that point I got a quick image of one of the SEs that didn't do anything. It just sort of withered and died away stuck in some sort of limbo state.

O: That's interesting. I am very surprised that you picked that up.

ME: *I thought that all of the SEs were successful in some way or other.*

O:      That is correct. They were all successful.

*ME:    But I just got the image of an SE that appeared to have failed!*

O:      It didn't fail; it hasn't failed.

*ME:    So It managed to get out of that state?*

O:      Oh no, It's still there.

*ME:    Then It has failed!*

O:      No, It hasn't. It merely hasn't moved on to Its next experience yet.

*ME:    So It will move on and experience more.*

O:      Who knows?

*ME:    Surely You must know, You of all entities. You told me Yourself that you exist on all levels of frequency/time/dimensions/space all at the same time, so You must know.*

O:      Of course, I know, but the best part is in sometimes not knowing. That is why you were created by your Source Entity. Not knowing makes it so much more fun.

*ME:    It makes it more frustrating in my mind!*

O:      Maybe, but it is the achievement of doing something that you want to do without knowing what is around the next corner and succeeding against the odds that make the achievement all the more worthwhile. This is one of the things that your immortal spirit was created for, and, this is one of the most important things you are experiencing and feeding back to your Source Entity and Me. Moving forward without knowing the future with all but the very rudimentary senses available to you from a physical form is one of the hardest things that any entity can do. It is a very noble act that you are all doing to limit yourselves so much in order to enable you and the rest of your peers to progress, evolve, experience and teach Us more about Ourselves.

*ME:    Oh, thank you!*

91

## The Source Entity on the Fun of Creation and Manipulation

Later I was thinking about getting my head around this idea of being able to touch all dimensions and spaces and times simultaneously whilst thinking of the Source Entity during its first few millennia. The Source Entity decided to comment.

SE:    Oh, yes, you can't believe the fun we had in those first few millennia when We realized Who and what We were. We were twisting and manipulating time/space and dimensions all over the place.

*ME:*    *My mind has a bit of trouble trying to visualize this.*

SE:    You will. Your ability to grasp such concepts or realities is significantly reduced whilst you are incarnate in the physical without the ability to access most of your true self.

I then had a picture of a sphere. The sphere had many, many levels like a sphere within a sphere within a sphere etc., etc., until there were 10s of dimensions. I then saw that if you squeezed the sphere hard enough you could get one end to touch the other, and, at the same time all of the dimensions touched at the same point. They were all in contact with each other!!!!! You could travel from one dimension to another really easy; galaxies could be "transversed" easily, too.

SE:    Yes, yes, that is a good way of understanding it. Well done!

I then had an image of the link between the points on the same dimension and the others being a conduit to them. The picture/film I then had in my head was like traveling down a wormhole in a science fiction film.

SE:    Ha, ha, ha, that is just fanciful thinking. The actuality is much more boring, and the travel is instantaneous. There is no travel down a colorful "hole." That is just artistic licence to fill a few film minutes.

*ME:    Oh.*

SE:    Don't sound so "put out." You do it all of the time when you are back in spirit. You are free to travel the whole of the Origin and the fragments of It, Me / Us, the 12.

*ME:    So how do I do it?*

SE:    With ease.

## The Source Entity on the Loss of Connectedness in the Lower Dimensions

Later dialogue gave further clarification on the loss of connectedness with the total being when probing into the lower dimensions.

SE:    We found the lower dimensions very interesting.

*ME:    Why?*

SE:    Because when We probed into the lower dimensions, We felt that We had lost part of Ourselves. It was like your leg going numb. I had to literally *pull out* that part of Myself that was protruding into the lower dimension as I could not communicate with it.

*ME:    You couldn't communicate with it?*

SE:    No, I could talk to it. I could hear it, but it could not hear me. And when I left that part of Me in the lower dimensions for a long time, say a millennia, it developed its own personality as it felt that it was cut off from its self. It did not remember being part of a whole and had to fend for itself in the energies of the lower levels the best it could. I/We found this an interesting learning experience as I have previously told you.

I then got an image in my head of how the Source Entity looked as It was delving into the lower dimensional levels. It was like a blob of paint dripping ever lower and lower and then the thickness of the paint between the blob and the major part of It became thinner and thinner so that It was hardly discernable.

SE: We experimented with this several times and found that We could actually protect that part that was projected into the lower levels by placing an intermediary dimensional field around it. That allowed the protrusion to both experience the lower levels and be in direct communication with the rest of Me and the Origin. A similar method of using differing energy frequencies surrounding their crafts has been developed mechanically recently by some of the beings that live in other dimensions.

ME: *So how did You make the change from delving into the lower dimensions/frequencies Yourselves and breaking Yourself up into smaller parts, Us?*

SE: Once We had all tried this a few million times, We decided to experiment with differing ways to investigate Ourselves. My way was to replicate the segmentation that the Origin had done and then break it down even further into billions upon billions of little Mes. I thought that it would be interesting to see what would happen if They were left to Their own devices, especially if They were allowed to project Themselves into the lower dimensions.

Specifically, I was interested in knowing the answers to these queries:

1. How long would it take them to get back to the higher dimensions?
2. How long would it take them to be in contact with the higher dimensions whilst still in the lower?
3. What diversity of experiences would they have?

4.  What could they pass on to Us and the Origin about
    Itself as a result of their experiences?

We were so very interested in the way that different densities
of matter acted depending on which dimension or frequency
they were projected into.

*ME:*   *What do you mean, how they acted?*
SE:   The lower the dimension or frequency, the more they
      coalesced.
*ME:*   *They made planets and suns, of course.*
SE:   Yes, but it was new to us. We were used to seeing
      things on the higher frequencies. As we looked into the
      lower frequencies and dimensions, things responded
      differently. Things "came together."

## The Source Entity on Coalescence in the Lower Frequencies and the Creation of Humankind

*ME:*   *We understand this as gravity, an attractive force*
      *caused by the mass of one particle or object relative to*
      *another.*
SE:   Mmm, this is not the case though; gravity is not an
      attractive force in its own right.
*ME:*   *So what causes the attraction of one mass to another?*
SE:   It's all to do with the distortion in local space. In all
      dimensions and frequencies, this occurs but to differing
      levels. This creates a sort of curved space around the
      object. Let's use three dimensions for this example.
      Once another object is caught in the curved space, its
      direction of movement gets changed due the
      intersection of the line of movement with the amount of
      space curved. Speed is also important because if the
      speed of the object intersecting the curved space is slow
      enough, it will be distracted enough to get closer and
      closer to the object distorting the local space. If the
      object is faster than that required to affect the line of

95

movement, it will either be un-affected or its direction will be changed but not stopped. Your astrophysicists know this as the "sling shot effect."

ME: *So this is due to curved space rather than attraction due to mass.*

SE: Yes, and you can prove this by performing a simple experiment in two dimensions.

ME: *You can prove this in two dimensions?*

SE: Yes, it's simple. All you need is an area of water like a large bucket or a pool. Put one large ball in filled with some water to increase the weight (mass) and a smaller ball in at the same time. With the water perfectly still, the local area around the large ball will be distorted by the mass of the ball. This locally curves the surface of the water (2D). The curve is more severe the closer to the ball you get and less severe the further away you get. But nevertheless the curve in the surface (this represents space) is enough to change the direction of movement of the smaller ball, which (if the speed of the small ball is right) is attracted to the larger ball. This is attraction due to mass curving space and is not due to attraction due to size or mass. Attraction due to curved space is gravity not attractivity due to mass. This is what we found to be interesting.

ME: *So space must be "locally curved" all over the place.*

SE: Yes, and small objects can curve space more than some larger objects.

ME: *Yes, I think we know that.*

SE: We were particularly interested in the way that molecules of the same type started to group together.

ME: *How does that happen?*

SE: Each molecule has a "key," so to speak, that only allows molecules of the same type to join together. This is well known by your chemical engineers, but this was the first time We saw this since it is a physical level phenomena. We saw this with all sorts of molecules, argon, neon, krypton, gold, iridium, etc., including thousands upon thousands of other materials in solid, semi-solid, and gas forms that you have not yet discovered. We also found that we could collect these "same" molecules ourselves by applying Our own "influence and intention."

ME: *This must have been quite interesting.*

SE: Of course. Don't forget that We were only just "aware" of who We were ourselves since the Origin had only separated Itself into Us plus Itself recently. So all this was new as was Our mission to understand more of Ourselves and Our environment. As the planets started to form from all of the molecules collecting together, which included those "hybrid" molecules that had keys to more than one molecule and, therefore, allowed bigger molecular constructs to grow (hence the planets and star systems), We decided that We needed to experience what it was like to exist on that dimensional level in its entirety.

ME: *So how did You do that?*

SE: We had to develop something that would both house a part of the energetic side of Us and allow Us to experience the physical dimension exactly as it was. This needed to exist long enough for Us to make the transition into this dimension worthwhile. It had to be self-sustaining, repairing, and able to have all the possible sensory opportunities that were available.

ME: *Are you talking about creating human beings?*

SE: No, not at first. We had simpler vehicles at first, and it was only as We became more adept at the design process that We eventually got to the point where the vehicle is as you are currently experiencing.

ME: *Does this include animals and plants?*

SE: And the mineral world as well. We very quickly discovered that We needed to have a vehicle that could be more flexible and able to experience the dimension that we had projected ourselves into. This required a lot

97

of thought and development over a long period of time.

ME: *So what were You developing?*

SE: A vehicle that, as I stated previously, was self-sustaining and self-repairing. We later found out that the vehicle must be able to take on more of the spirit to be useful in this dimension and that needed to be of a certain design to be useful. This meant that We had to design something bigger. Also, the vehicle We made was dependent on this dimension so much that it couldn't survive on "Spiritual" Energy on its own. It had to be able to process energy from the most basic level to survive long enough to be useful.

ME: *You mean eating plants, etc.*

SE: Exactly, We changed the design of the vehicle so that it took what it could from the energy of the spirit world and augmented it with the energy that could be taken from the dimension We were working in, thus making the vehicle dependent on two energy sources: one that was readily available in the dimension it operated in and the other that it could attract from receptors that protruded into the lowest of the spiritual dimensions.

ME: *Chakras?*

SE: Yes, that is your description/name for them. As with the physical vehicle, We needed to change the design of these to fine tune them to work the most efficiently. You have two energy systems operating within the human body. One works with the cardiac system of distributing the denser physically-based energy that is distributed by the blood. This is primarily to feed the physical part of the vehicle. The other is an energy-based cardiac system (for want of a better word) to distribute the "spiritual" higher dimensional energy that is required by the other interfacing bodies that you have. To allow the communication (albeit limited) between your real selves and that part of you that is projected into this small physical body. There are also other smaller distribution points for the energy system

98

that you call "meridians." These are smaller chakras and are mainly used to act as distribution points to the other areas of the spiritual bodies that need energy. These smaller chakras are important as they can be used to transmit energy away from the body as well as distribute it around the body. Hence, you can use this energy to do other external things such as healing, transmutation, transmigration of objects, psychometry, and energy sensing, to name just a few things.

ME: *So you are talking about humankind.*

SE: Of course, but the first humans were nowhere near what you would call "human."

ME: *What do you mean—different?*

SE: We have modified the size, shape and complexity over the ages to account for the changes in the dimensional structure that you exist within.

ME: *So what are the auric levels for?*

SE: They are there to act as an interface between the reducing levels of consciousness and communication with the true self. We had to gradually scale down the interaction between the projected self and the true self at different levels of frequency so that a level of translation could occur between levels that could be recognizable between the higher and lower level. It's a sort of reduction in the available language going from the use of six words that basically mean the same thing but have a different emphasis, down to one word that can be used to describe all of them in a general sense.

ME: *So the lower down the vibration levels, the more general the level of communication used to act as an interface between the levels.*

SE: Yes, that is correct.

ME: *But wouldn't that mean that there was a lot of difficulty communicating between the 7$^{th}$ and 1$^{st}$ levels?*

SE: Of course, and that is why We have such a poor level of explanation when we use "mediums" to channel information to you.

ME: *Does this also happen from an energetic point of view?*

SE: Yes, of course. You have heard people say that energy is finer the higher up the levels you go?

ME: *Yes.*

SE: Well, that is because the energy is more narrow band. As you go down the levels, the frequencies are not available, so We have to use one lower frequency to translate a number of higher frequencies. For example, on the 7th level We may have ten frequency bands that are reduced down to 1 on the 6th. We may then get a further reduction from ten frequency bands down to one from the 6th to the 5th. With this continuing down to the 1st level (the physical), you can understand that the frequencies are pretty coarse at this level because the resolution of the frequencies has been reduced by a factor of $10^{-7}$, or to put it into context, we have gone from 10,000,000 frequencies that can be used down to 1. It's hardly surprising that you can't communicate with yourself if you only have access to 1 in 10,000,000 frequency channels! Especially if that one channel is supposed to represent the functions of all the other 10,000,000 channels!

# Chapter 7:
# *The Source Entity on Creating Its Universes*

## The Mirroring Effects of Creating in the Physical

A later meditation had me going back to the time that the Origin's children, the Source Entities, were looking at the mirroring effects of producing a physical environment. In particular, I was interested in communicating with the Source Entity that had created our universe. The others, I decided, would wait until I had enough material to dedicate a sizeable portion of the book I was now sure I was writing.

We talked further of the birth and experimentations with the energies that It had created as part of Its experiment in trying to understand what It and the Origin was.

SE: The lower the vibrations, the more dense the material I was observing and creating.

*ME: You were creating on the lower levels as well?*

SE: Of course. It was more cumbersome but nevertheless interesting.

*ME: Why was it interesting?*

SE: There were things happening as a result of my creating differing physical dimensions that I had not expected. I would have expected them had I given Myself the time to look into the right level of the time line.

*ME: I thought you didn't use the term "time."*

SE: I do it for you. In reality it was that I didn't focus my attention on the events that would have been completed had I thought about it, i.e., I wanted to experience what you call "wonder," the wonder of not knowing. This is why all of you queue up to incarnate in the physical planes for now. You desire to experience the wonder of achieving things without knowing what is going to happen. What can happen if I change my mind, and what will ultimately happen? I simply didn't focus on the *after* part of the event because I was too interested in what was happening.

ME: *So tell me, what was happening that got you so interested?*

SE: I noticed that as I created on the macro level, this creation was reproduced on the micro and sub-micro levels.

ME: *What! You mean that everything was duplicated?*

SE: Yes. It was like a small universe was being created every time the quantum level was such that this could take place.

ME: *Some of our scientists believe that once you get beyond the level below the quark level, the energy that makes up the larger objects of the quark components is so fine that it is made up of objects so small that they effectively could be classed as a universe trapped in the sphere that makes up the quark.*

SE: Well done. This is not too far from reality on the physical planes. These *smaller* universes also exist in other dimensions, and it was this that I found interesting. What was really interesting was that the duplication went right down to the point where physical matter met with the first of the dimensions that are higher than this one, the "third" as you call it.

ME: *So how many times did this reproduction occur?*

SE: Three times.

ME: *Did you find* life *on these levels the same as* life *on this level?*

SE: No. Don't forget that all bio life has been created by Me and some of My helpers, the first souls that I created.

ME: *So they are barren of life then?*

SE: Not quite. There is energy given form but nothing to the level of complexity that is available at this level. It is simply energy that has coalesced and is attracted to other energies. You might call them "clouds of energy."

## Lower Energy Beings (Animals)

ME:    *I mentioned life on/in the micro mirrored levels of our universe, and you said that it was energy given form. But aren't we energy given form?*

SE:    Yes, of course, but the major difference is that you are energy given form and *intelligence* in a more dramatic sort of way, for you are all smaller parts of Me and because of this, you have intelligence. I have followed that which the Origin did when He created Me and My 11 other counterparts in so much as I have created a universe and decided to populate it with trillions of smaller Mes. To do this, I gave up over half of my *bulk* and divided it until each part was at the lowest level that it could be before it stopped being part of me and the Origin.

ME:    *So there is a level lower than us?*

SE:    Yes, the spirit energy of animals and trees and rocks are successively lower levels of spirit than you are. They, therefore, have lesser abilities.

ME:    *Is it possible for these lower energy level spirits to cross over into our levels?*

SE:    Yes, but only in extreme circumstances where there has been a lot of energy given by a higher energy level spirit to an individual lower level energy for a protracted period. Since some of the entities on Earth are gifts to you to learn how to cherish and act in selflessness, some of these are also allowed to turn into a physical vehicle. Your dogs and cats are examples of this.

ME:    *So in this instance, if a particular energy has been given the ability to absorb this higher energy on a protracted and consistent basis, then it has the ability to cross over to our level and become one with You?*

SE:     Again, yes. But I say they are also one with Me but at a residual level rather than micro level. They simply don't have enough *bulk*, so they coalesce together to experience Me/you and the rest of the higher energies in order to try to increase their *bulk*.

ME:     *Is this where the theory of animals having group souls comes from?*

SE:     Yes, and the coalition sends out many tendrils at a time to allow those tendrils to be placed in physical vessels to maximize their opportunities and to experience your energy when you are in a position of rapid evolutionary opportunity, i.e., when you are incarnate.

ME:     *So does the whole coalition cross over to our level, or is it just the tendril?*

SE:     Generally it is the whole but in even rarer cases the tendril can also gather its own *bulk* and over time can cross over on its own. Your Sooty (our black cat) is one such tendril that is about to do so, and it has only been possible in this life.

## The Further Development of the Universes, Dimensions, and Frequencies

In another meditation I asked about the start of the development of the universe that our Source Entity controls for its own evolution. I wished to learn a bit more about this.

ME:     *So at what point did You decide to create Your own universe(s) to aid in Your evolution?*

SE:     When it was apparent that everything I could learn from being in the same *space*, the Origin needed my own input to allow further progression.

ME:     *How did you decide that?*

SE:     When I and the other eleven entities that the Origin had created had explored all that They/We could in the environment where We found Ourselves. We were confined to all the dimensions and frequencies that were available to Us as part of the Origin but needed to seek other stimulus to fulfil the task that the Origin had placed upon Us.

*ME:*   *Can you remind me on what that was?*

SE:   To learn as much about Myself so that through me the Origin could learn about Itself faster and in more detail than It would have on Its own.

*ME:*   *O.K., so let's continue with your story.*

SE:   As part of the work that I had done with the other eleven SEs, I had established the number of dimensions that I wished to explore and the subsequent number of frequencies within each dimension.

*ME:*   *Yes, I remember talking about the octaves of dimensions/frequencies.*

SE:   So with the experience that I had established by experimenting, I decided that I could evolve/learn the fastest by creating a number of universes and dimensions that allowed a duplicate of what the Origin was while also being contained within the Origin.

*ME:*   *I get a picture of a sort of bubble within a bubble.*

SE:   Yes, that is correct and all that happens within my bubble does not affect what happens in the Origin's bubble.

*ME:*   *So you are saying that the evolutionary opportunities were contained within your bubble and that they would not be experienced by the Origin.*

SE:   The Origin experiences all. It is just that what the Origin does will not affect what is in My bubble if I think it will affect My experiment.

*ME:*   *So how does that work? I am in contact with the Origin at some stage, so I must be    influenced by the Origin, which means that there is a hole in your bubble/filter process.*

SE:   Not so. I have allowed certain levels of communication to be available to parts of Me that have reached certain stages of their own evolution.

ME: *So the more I evolve, the more access to the Origin I get.*

SE: Whilst you are incarnate, and, yes, of course, you have access to the Origin through being in your energy state. But again this is limited to the level of evolution you have achieved.

ME: *Hang on! This all seems a little contradictory. How can you have a bubble that is separate from the Origin but allows things to happen within it without being influenced by the Origin and yet still be in contact with it?*

SE: Consider the levels of access that you are allowed when working with your computer. Some parts you have complete access to because you have administrator rights, but others where you don't have such rights, you can only affect (or manipulate) certain parts.

ME: *So you are saying that access to the Origin is filtered out to those entities, spirits, and souls that have certain rights?*

SE: Yes, and the level of authority is based upon the level of evolution you have achieved.

ME: *But I thought that all spirits have access to you and the Origin?*

SE: They do, but the level at which they can gain full access is entirely up to them and how well they are working on their evolution. Take yourself and the conversation we are having.

ME: *I also have contact with the Origin.*

SE: Yes, taking yourself as an example, you must have reached a certain level of evolution to be able to be having this dialogue. You have reached a point where, even in your physical incarnate state you are aware of something else going on and have decided to dedicate some time to go inwards to the point where you can contact "THE ALL" that is the Origin and all that is part of It. In this instance I am part of it as well, and I have created a series of universes to enable me to evolve further.

ME: *So are you saying that our level of access to everything outside the bubble of your created universes is entirely dependent upon ourselves and our desire to evolve at whatever rate we desire?*

SE: Yes, you are self-governing in that respect. If, for instance, you want to be totally cut off from the rest of yourself and "THE ALL" in order to evolve, then you incarnate into the physical dimensions and the frequencies that are associated with these levels. Some of you (nearly all actually) get engrossed so much with the physical that you totally forget who and what you are to the point of thinking that physical life is all there is. Others get even more engrossed to the point where they still cling to the physical after their physical body has finished its purpose (died). These poor souls hang around at the lower spiritual levels because they feel the association with the physical frequencies more by staying low. They are so engrossed in the sensations that the physical gives them that they are blinded to the fact that they are now back in the energetic or spiritual world/universes. In effect they have regulated their evolution to the point where they are not able to access the reality of their energetic state and the ability to be in contact with their higher selves or communicate with Me and the Origin.

ME: *So our level of awareness and ability to contact the Origin and be aware of what is outside your bubble with all the influences that the Origin has on the inside of your bubble are due to our own level of evolution, which dictates our level of access?*

SE: In a nutshell, yes.

# Chapter 8:
# *The Source Entity on the Theories of Creation*

## Creationists' and Scientists' Views of Creation

*ME:* *In the first part of our dialogue on the creation of the universe, we talked about how you copied to a certain extent what the Origin had done in creating You and the other twelve Source Entities. Like the Origin, you separated yourself into smaller parts, much smaller parts. What can you add to this that would convince the scientific world that the universe was created by a single being? Bear in mind the issues surrounding the Creationists' view that the world was created approximately 10,000 years ago and the scientists' view that the universe was created millions upon millions of years ago by a spontaneous combustion they are currently calling the Big Bang.*

SE: I would say that they are both right. You see, scientists only see what they can quantify by measurement of hard facts that are presented to them by their detecting machines. These machines are limited by the limited thinking of the individual making them and the technology at the point in time in which they are working. Were they working from the energetic levels, they would see a completely different picture. In essence, though, they need to have things explained to them in terms of what can be proven from the evidence furnished by these machines. As a result, they are looking for answers to questions that are not appropriate to the question. You need to ask the right question to get the right answer to the problem you have. From a physical perspective, your particular universe was created by me, the Source Entity, as you call me or God, as the religious leaders would call me although in this context I am not God as such but a part of the larger entity we call the Origin. From the perspective of the religious leaders, I created the universe, and from the perspective of the scientists, the universe created itself, which is not so far from the truth. The only issue here is when was it created? Bear in mind the overwhelming evidence that you have around you that your planet is very much older than 10,000 years. I speak of such evidence as the pyramids, the dinosaurs, and other fossilized remains of animals and buildings created by man that you have discovered and are yet to understand. The Earth cannot be 10,000 years old as the Creationists would have you believe.

I simply did not create this universe that recently!

However, I did create this universe and so in this context, they are right. Even the scientists agree that "something" created the universe, and this is ultimately the key to their understanding, provided they use it to open the door/s presented to them. To create something is the most important thing that an entity can do, especially when that creation has both purpose and function. This universe in all its dimensions and frequencies has both purpose and function. Its purpose is to help in the Origin's understanding of self. I created this universe to help Me in this task, for that is why the Origin created Me and my 11 Co-Source Entities, and I, in turn, created this universe and you. The universe's function is to allow opportunities for entities to evolve singularly as entities in their own right. It is a workshop theater full of all the tools and materials necessary for you to experience all that is from the very highest frequencies/dimensions to the very lowest frequencies/dimensions. This is where you find yourself now, and this workshop theater is so rich with opportunity to evolve and expand.

In creating this universe, I have created the perfect opportunity for all of you, and, in so doing, I have maximized the effectiveness of the purpose and the function. Many times you (humanity in physicality) have risen and fallen only to pick yourselves up from the gutter, dust yourselves off, and start again. Although this is your lowest ebb, you are on the cusp of achieving a higher level of greatness than any series of entities has ever achieved. This could only have happened by your being given the freedom to make up your own minds, to make your own mistakes, and to make your own successes and build upon them. I created this universe countless millions of years ago, in your understanding, to maximize the need to understand the self of the Origin from the point of view of the Origin Itself (Who is still investigating Itself in Its own ways) to the smallest of the contributing entities, yourselves, and the entities that are of the next level down to you.

So was the universe created in six days with one as a rest day? No! It was created in less than a nano second once I knew what I wanted to do to contribute towards the job I was created to do. Did the universe expand? No! It has always been the "dimensions" it currently is. The only thing that has expanded is the understanding *of self* by all the entities that I created when I created this universe.

ME: *So, was it a Big Bang as the scientists think?*

SE: No, it came into existence in a wink, no big bang, no expansion, no binding together of atoms or chemicals, at least not then, and no evolution of biological entities from the primeval soup. Every *thing* was created in perfection to start the job instantly, to hit the ground running, as it were. The only changes are what you and

111

your opposite entities have created, including the human physical vehicle. This is the only change that has happened. This is the only evolution—the evolution through energy-based humankind's desire to understand the self and evolve. It fulfils the promise I gave to the Origin—to help It understand Itself at the fastest possible rate with a maximum of experience.

# Chapter 9:

# The Source Entity on Slipping Between Dimensions

## The Source Entity on Emulating the Creation Process of the Origin

ME: *So let's get back to how you split the (your) universe.*

SE: The idea was that I would try to emulate all that I had experienced as part of the Origin. This means that I wanted to reproduce everything down to the last frequency and dimensional anomaly.

ME: *Dimensional anomaly?*

SE: Yes, these are the rifts that appeared to Me/Us when we looked at more than two dimensions at the same time.

ME: *You can do this, I mean, look at more than one dimension at the same time?*

SE: Of course, and all of you can do this at the same time when you are back in your energetic state.

ME: *So what was/were the anomalies?*

SE: These were what you would call "worm holes" between the dimensions where you could move from one dimension to the other by this link.

ME: *So what is the link?*

SE: It is an area where the dimensional frequency at some part of the dimensional area (you have frequencies within dimensions as well, of course) is close to the dimensional frequency of a neighboring dimension— either up, down, left, right or any rotational distance from the dimension where the area is not as dense.

ME: *I get the image of a sphere with longitude and latitude rather like the Earth mapping system.*

SE: Correct imagery. Each of the crossover points is where

there may be a connection between two or more dimensions, and these points are where the dimensional stability is not as dense (firm) as it should be, allowing the opportunity to slip from one to another easily because they are so alike.

ME: *Is this where we see reports of UFOs suddenly appearing and disappearing.*

SE: Yes, these beings have recognized this anomaly and have developed a way to use this to their advantage. In fact, when they use the crossover points to travel between dimensions, they can use the periphery of the dimension (i.e., the line of dimensional latitude or longitude) to travel to any dimension they please.

ME: *I get the impression that they must follow the lines and crossovers and not go there diagonally. Why is this?*

SE: Because they must use the route of least dimensional resistance, and this is the periphery of the dimension they are traveling in (the line), and because of this, they must travel on either the longitude or latitude and not try to cut the corners.

ME: *Could they try?*

SE: Of course, but it would be like hitting the proverbial dimensional brick wall, and, in doing so, they would damage the vehicle that they are using to traverse the dimensional anomaly.

## The Source Entity on Splitting Its Mass and Creating Entities of Multiple Frequencies

ME: *O.K., so let's get back to the question that I have been trying to ask for the past couple of sessions. Please tell me more about how you split the universe.*

SE: That is easy. I wanted to replicate what the Origin had done.

ME: *In every way.*

SE: Yes, right down to the last dimensional level and right down the lowest frequency. I had to do this, as it would not be a replication experiment if I did not. As I have previously stated, the whole point of it was for Me to create an environment that was exactly the same but separate from the Origin to all but those (to be created) entities that had evolved to the level where they could recognize the greater picture and work accordingly within both the smaller and larger realities of My universes and the Origin's universes. In some respects, it was a bigger experiment than that which was started by the Origin. I effectively split up half of My *mass* to create over 10 billion zillion smaller parts of Me. The only issue here was that when I split, not all of the entities ended up at the same level of quality.

ME: *What do you mean? There is a lower quality of spirit?!*

SE: Yes, in terms of their ability to evolve and navigate the different dimensions and frequencies.

ME: *So what happened to them? How did you categorize them?*

SE: Some of them were as you are now—able to do everything that I wanted to do to achieve the plan of evolution through experience. Others were displaying lower abilities but were, nevertheless, able to exist in some of the dimensions and frequencies. Others were not so good and were only O.K. for much lower frequency work.

ME: *Can you categorize them for me?*

SE: Yes. They are as follows:

- Smaller replications of Me 65% (later these could be projected into the lower frequencies for incarnation purposes).

- Entities that were able to work with these entities as a group but were able to progress to the first level given the right circumstances—later these could be projected into the lower frequencies for incarnation purposes. These would be what you would call the *collective mind* types of entities, your *hive* type of mentality.

- Entities that were able to work with the first entities at a group level—later these could be projected into the lower frequencies for incarnation purposes. These could not incarnate in the more complicated physical bodies, such as the human but on the odd occasion would be able to progress to this level, again with the correct level of circumstances. This would be what you call the *animal* level.

- Entities that could not enter the physical levels but could work with the physical on the energetic level. These would later be called *nature spirits*.

- Entities that could enter a living item but not one that was human-based. These would be plants, trees, etc. This is what you call the *plant* level.

- Entities whose thought processes were so low that they could only gain experience or evolution on a very low scale, and this was by being part of larger objects that appear in all dimensions, such as planets. This is what you would call the *mineral* level.

ME:  *Wow! So that is how we get the plethora of entities here on Earth.*

SE:  Not just on Earth but other planets and in other universes and dimensions. At first I was disappointed in what had happened, but later I saw the beauty of it and the better learning/evolutionary opportunities that had presented themselves.

*ME:* *So how did it happen?*

SE: By not focusing all of My attention on all of Me at the same time, I created what you would call a watering down of the programming due to lack of time I spent doing it.

*ME:* *So you are fallible?*

SE: Fallibility doesn't come into it. This is all part of the evolutionary process.

*ME:* *That sounds like a bit of an excuse to me.*

SE: The Origin would say that excuses are not required. Everything that happens, happens and should be used as an opportunity for learning and, therefore, evolution. The whole point of being is *being*—that is universal law. You humans are so hard on yourself for making mistakes that you make a mistake by taking up more of your time than is necessary to resolve the initial mistake. What you are missing is the evolutionary side of making that mistake. Learning from mistakes is only a small part of the picture. Being able to stand back and see the process that leads to the mistake and seeing the beauty in it is another. Seeing the further process that leads to the resolution is even more beautiful. Once you have all this, you are able (may be able?) to understand the process of cause and effect, which will result in the understanding of cause from a universal point of view where you will realize that it is all part of evolving and is yet another step. Evolution is not just about learning your lessons; it's about applying the principles that turn the event experienced into an evolutionary opportunity. Fallibility, if you want to use that term, is, therefore, an evolutionary opportunity.

*ME:* *This is starting to blow my mind a bit.*

SE: Yes, I can see that you are struggling. You are trying to intellectualize it, trying to apply reason. Reason doesn't come into it.

## The Source Entity Defines Evolution

*ME:* *So what is evolution?*

SE:    Growth!

*ME:* *What?! Is that it?*

SE:    Yes.

*ME:* *Oh. I thought there was more to it than that.*

SE:    No, why should there be? Growth is the best way to describe it. Growth is accepting that everything is what it is. It is going with the flow. It is absorbing knowledge, feeling, passion, pride, love, experience, power, compassion, emotion, understanding. . .

*ME:* *Why have you stopped?*

SE:    Because that's it. There are a whole host of other mental senses that you are not aware of and, therefore, have no words to communicate them, so those specified above will suffice. The words above describe the feelings of experience. Growth is, in short, having wide enough shoulders to accept what is and rejoicing in its wonder. The more you experience, learn, and understand, the more you grow. This is what I intended to do when creating My own universe/s. When I created the other beings, such as you, I also created others that were not of the same quality. This is not failure or fallibility but an opportunity that presented itself for further growth. The process that led to that event in creation was truly beautiful, and experiencing this beauty resulted in my growing and evolving further.

## Different Dimensions and Frequency Levels

*ME:* *What is the next part of the development of the/Your universe You are going to tell me about?*

SE:    Interesting, you had the preconception that we were going to talk about why and what the development for the physical representation of the human form was. This is pre-conception and does not assist us in this dialogue. It is not true channeling. However, you have also seen a picture in your mind's eye of the levels/dimensions that are present in My universes, and so I will discuss this with you.

ME: *Great! So how many are there and why did you create so many?*

SE: There are essentially twelve dimensions and twelve frequencies within each dimension.

ME: *I just looked back at my previous notes, and You mentioned zones and octaves.*

SE: Yes, this is correct. Each zone has twelve dimensions which are split into packets of three dimensions, which you called "tritaves"?

ME: *Yes, I did. But you said that there were twelve zones!*

SE: Well, there are twelve zones in the Origin's universe/self, but I have only created one zone: Mine. Each of My dimensions has twelve frequencies attached to it with each group of three dimensions called a "tritave." Each group of three, therefore, has 36 frequencies within which energies and beings can exist.

ME: *Why did you only create one zone and not copy the whole of the Origin's universe/self?*

SE: What already is—I can't create that which is already there!

ME: *What?!*

SE: I cannot create the Origin. He/She/It is already there, so all that I can do is copy It the best that I can, and that means that I had to be limited to what I could do.

ME: *I just had an image in my mind of what would happen if You did. That image was of a 2 in 1 set up that would even get the Origin a bit confused. A little bit like being schizophrenic?*

SE: More than that. He would get blurred around the edges of all parts of Himself. Everywhere there are rules that We have to follow. You can only work with what you have, and as I have to work within the confines of the Origin because I am part of the Origin, as you are. I

119

have limitations and rules, construction rules, if you call it that.

ME: *So you created a 12<sup>th</sup> of the universe that was the Origin within the Origin that is actually within yourself.*

SE: Well done!

ME: *And the whole point of this was to create a simulacrum of the Origin to allow You to delve into the intricacies of self at a faster rate by creation and division of self-contained parts of yourself.*

SE: Yep.

ME: *Can you next tell me what the role of each of the twelve dimensions is?*

SE: Later, it's time for you to rest.

## The Source Entity on Stephen Hawking's Eleven Dimensions Theory

Quite some time later I was discussing the flagrancies of the universe with a friend of mine at one of my local pubs when he agreed that there must be lots of other dimensions out there. He qualified this by stating that Prof. Stephen Hawking had made some changes to his theory of the universe and had established that there must be eleven dimensions. Moreover, he also thought that he was close to having this whole universe thing sewn up and that he (Hawking) might just do it before he died. I put this to the Source Entity to find out why the great Stephen Hawking was at variance with my channeled information.

ME: *So Professor Hawking believes there are eleven dimensions; you have stated that there are twelve. Why the difference? Who is correct?*

SE: For a start off, our dear spirit Stephen Hawking is very close to gaining a very good personal but limited understanding of the local universe. This he has done with help from his guides in spirit and the ability to think and meditate on unanswered questions for long uninterrupted periods of time, which only a person in his condition has the ability to do. First, the error is a simple one. One forgets that there has to be a base dimension, the one that one exists within. All the others are additional and help to keep the *zone* intact and in keeping with the need for the tritave principle that we discussed earlier. Second, if you consider that the physical universe actually needs the first of the four tritaves to exist, then the question goes the other way. Why does Prof. Hawking have one dimension too many?

ME: *What do you mean? You seem to have turned things around a bit here.*

SE: As I previously stated, the dimensions each have twelve frequencies within them. These frequencies are areas within which you live as energetic and incarnate individuals. To move up the frequencies, you have to live in accordance with the rules. The rules ensure that you don't lose your resonant frequency and start to drop down within your dimension of existence. Once you achieve a high state of frequency, you can move up to the next dimension, provided the area of frequency you position your existence within is close to an area of low frequency in the next dimension. As energetic beings, you can, of course, move around to find these areas and move up and down at will—provided, of course, that you move within your allotted dimensional and frequential range, which your level of evolution has given you permission to do so within.

The first dimensional system, the physical, actually needs three dimensions to exist, including the twelve frequencies of each dimension, that's thirty-six frequencies. The remaining dimensions do not.

ME: *Why not? I thought that they needed to be in threes?*

SE: They do, but they do not need to be in threes to create an environment to exist within.

ME:     *Why not?*
SE:     Because after and including the fourth dimension, everything else is energetic in nature—energetic, that is in comparison to the first three. So in essence you have twelve dimensions of which ten are workable/habitable dimensions, the first three being equal to one.
ME:     *So three plus nine equals ten.*
SE:     That's about the size of it. The other dimensions work as complete dimensions in their own right. This is because they are higher up the frequency ranges.

## The Source Entity on Dimensions' Reliance upon Frequency and How a Multiverse Works

ME:     *Are you saying that dimensions are reliant upon frequency?*
SE:     Of course, frequency is the padding that keeps dimensions inflated. Dimensional relationship is relative to frequency, and frequency bands are collated and collected into dimensions. This is how a multi-dimensional universe works. If we go back a step and look at the dimensions in their own right, we see that as with the first three dimensions, the second three are linked together, The third three are linked together, and the fourth three are linked together, each in its own tritave. Entities that exist in, say the seventh dimension, will be able to move between the seven and eighth (if at the right frequency). Whereas entities that exist in the eighth will be able to move in the seventh and the ninth (if at the right frequency). In essence the dimensions are linked in threes, as follows:

1, 2, 3 are linked;
4, 5, 6 are linked;
7, 8, 9 are linked; and
10, 11, 12 are linked.

So a $7^{th}$ dimensional entity can move in the $7^{th}$, $8^{th}$ dimensions but will not be able to transverse the $6^{th}$ without a construct to assist the entity to transverse to a much lower dimension, nor will it be able to move to the $9^{th}$ as it is too high a jump. This would also be true for a $4^{th}$ or $10^{th}$ dimensional entity.

It is easier to move down the frequencies than up, so an entity that moves into the seventh dimension from the eighth must give up some of his/her/its higher frequencies to move down but also have enough higher frequency in reserve to move back up. In essence, although they can move down to a lower dimension, they can only do so at the detriment of their own frequency, and when moved, they must stay in the highest frequencies of that lower dimension. This same entity will be able to move up to the ninth dimension only with a good level of high frequencies and then he/she/it will only be able to move in the lower frequencies of the higher dimension. Ninth dimensional entities can move into all dimensions within their tritave but would need to surround themselves in a bubble of energy that both permits travel into the lower dimensions and frequencies and protects their intrinsically higher frequencies.

Jumping between tritaves (lower to upper) is a function of evolution. Achieving the reverse requires protection of the sort described above and can lead to de-evolution if care on behalf of the traveling entity is not taken.

ME: *So based upon this, is Prof. Hawking wrong?*

SE: I would say that he is getting there. More importantly he is in a position to promote thought on this question, which is good. As for Stephen, he will understand when the time is right for him to understand because for him to understand, he needs the mathematics to back it up and the mathematics required is not available yet.

## The Source Entity on Further Clarification of Dimensions and Frequency

Later on in the year I was thinking about whether all this held water. I was confused. I believed that what the Source had told me earlier was correct, but I had no real understanding of it. I personally don't like to be in a position where I don't understand a principle because if I don't understand it, how can anyone else reading this text understand it? That is the point of my writing about it! I decided that I needed further clarification on this whole dimensional and frequency subject and contacted the Source with the view to clearing up all of it in an easy to understand way.

ME:   *I am confused with the whole issue of dimensions and frequency. I still can't imagine it in my mind's eye. I can understand how frequencies work, but I can't see how the dimensions work. I understand that You can have many dimensions occupying the same space, but I just can't see the mechanics of it.*

SE:   Mechanics is a good word, for it is simple mechanics that I will use to describe the functionality of dimensional existence. You remember the dialogue we had on the description of frequency where the increase in frequency turns ice into water and then water into a gas? The vibrational frequency of the ice is low so you can both see and touch the ice as a solid object. The water has a slightly higher vibrational frequency and can still be seen and touched, although it is losing its cohesion and is fluidic in nature. The increase in frequency to turn the water into a gas is also small, but it creates a substance that is neither visible nor touchable but is nevertheless present. It's just that you can't identify it with your five basic senses. You understand this because it is basic physics. You know that it has turned into a gas, and a gas has substance that can be detected by machines. This explains how a frequency change removes the object being changed in frequency out of the visible spectrum and out of the physical touch and feel spectrum.

The best way to describe the functionality of dimension is to use the mechanics of radio waves or electricity used for transmission of audio/visual content through copper wires. An analog radio wave, as with electricity, has both amplitude and frequency. The amplitude determines the signal content, and the frequency determines the transmission speed of the content. Information transmitted in this way can be overlapped with other information simply by changing the frequency enough above or below the first frequency not to interfere with the original information transmitted on it. This allows the basis of radio transmission for many radio stations.

If you consider that a frequency high enough to not interfere with the one below or low enough not to interfere with the one above is an environment for energetic life to exist within, then you have a basis for further understanding the use of frequency to create a number of living environments within a known frequency range, but this does not explain dimensional existence. Dimensions exist by the rotation of a frequency range. This can be best described in the use of phasing to increase the amount of information transmitted on the same frequency. If the frequency is also rotated by a single degree of angle, then that frequency is also placed in a position of non-interference with the frequency that is at the, let's say, zero angle of rotation. This gives access to all of the frequency ranges possible in the zero angle of rotation in the 1st degree of rotation as well. This would be the same for 5 degrees of rotation, 15 degrees of rotation or 200 degrees of rotation, thus giving the opportunity for many phases, up to 360 if you use degrees as your angle of phase.

Now if you consider that the degree of rotation equals a different dimensional state then you have an understanding of how a number of different dimensions and subsequent frequencies can exist at the same time in the same space. Simplistically speaking, they are separated by angles of phase. Of course, there are not 360 dimensions. There are twelve with the first three creating the basis for one physical dimension and the remaining nine being higher dimensions in their own right. So the space between the dimensions is large enough to ensure that they do not allow any interference with each other, except by local increase in frequency and phase in areas where the local entities are working at a high level of frequency/phase due to their being in harmony with the universe. Therefore, this allows the opportunity to move up the frequential or dimensional ladder or to decrease in frequency and phase in areas where the local entities are working at a low level of frequency/phase due to their being out of harmony with the universe. Then this allows the opportunity to move down the frequential or dimensional ladder.

ME: *So what you are saying is that dimensional separation is due to an angle of phase.*

SE: Simplistically speaking, yes. Although there are many other ways of achieving the same thing, and these other ways are in use in some of the other universes created by my peers, the eleven other Source Entities. Maybe we can discuss these methods in future dialogues, but right now this helps to briefly explain my construction of this universe.

ME: *I have read a number of science fiction books where the characters in the story line move from one dimension to another by "rotating" out of this dimension. I find that quite bazaar. It's so close to the description that you have just given me that it could be contrived from my memory and not channeled as part of this dialogue.*

SE:     Believe me, it's not. The description used by the science fiction writers all of you allude to is but a word used to make the transition from one dimension to another believable from a storyteller's point of view. The fact that the description is close to the truth is not due to the knowledge of the author but is due to the author's higher self having subconscious access to the reservoir of universal knowledge that every entity has access to. Hence, the use of a word that is close to the truth. The very fact that you have been having trouble understanding the functionality of dimensional existence justifies that fact that the description in this dialogue has come from me and not from your memory of a science fiction book you once read. Does this dialogue make an attempt to help you understand the dimensional function of this universe?

*ME:     Yes, it does. It helps a lot.*

SE:     Then I have succeeded in helping you understand.

## The Source Entity on the Roles of the Twelve Dimensions of Consciousness/Awareness

*ME:     Now, what about the twelve dimensions. I thought that there were an infinite number of dimensions?*

SE:     There are, of course, but I decided that I would apply twelve to the universes that I created. I primarily decided this because there were twelve Source Entities created. It seemed like a good idea at the time.

*ME:     So what are the reasons for the twelve dimensions in an operational sense?*

SE:     Each one is a layer that is closer to the Origin/God, if you like. Each one is special in its own right. They all have a job to do, and as you progress towards the Origin, not only do you progress through the frequencies but you also progress through the dimensions.

As was previously stated by the Origin, each of the dimensions has twelve dimensions associated with it and nested within it. These are grouped in octaves (tritaves) of three dimensions. This is particularly important for the lower dimensions as they are closely associated with the physical levels. Don't forget that the Origin has 12 x 12 x 12 x 3 (tritaves); without this basic structure, they would not be able to function properly.

ME:  *I got the word "work" rather than "function" properly.*

SE:  Don't get confused with this information and the information that I am going to give you. It is different from what the Origin gave you. Also, your own level of reference is so lacking in detail that you won't possibly be able to understand some of it (maybe most of it at times will be right over your head). The difference between work and function is significant, to say the least. Work suggests a task with a pre-set profile, whereas function means that it is . . . functioning. It does not need to have work to do to allow it to function. It just needs to be! In the instance of a dimension, it functions as a dimension; it does not work as a dimension. It just is. Now then, what makes a dimension work is what the entities that exist within that dimension do within it insomuch as how they relate to it and what they do with it. Many entities that have progressed up the dimensional ladder away from where you currently are projected are able to understand their function and work it to their own advantage. This is also correct for entities that have never felt the need to project themselves down to the lowest levels, as you have, to accelerate their evolution. If you considered that water was a dimension, you would see what I am talking about. Water just is, but you use it for all sorts of things. You work with it to create ice, steam, gases, differing concoctions for personal consumption, washing, cooling etc., etc. The list is endless. So you see, a dimension IS, and it is what you make it. The twelve dimensions are not specifically what you think they are.

*ME:* *I would have thought that there are different levels of* dimension *and that they are parallel to each other, just like we are told by our science fiction writers and physicists.*

SE: Mmm, they are sort of correct, but I will explain them below.

| Dimension | Function |
|---|---|
| 1 | Height ($1^{st}$ of the physical dimensions) |
| 2 | Width ($2^{nd}$ of the physical dimensions) |
| 3 | Depth ($3^{rd}$ of the physical dimensions) |
| 4 | Event (Time) ($4^{th}$ of the physical dimensions but bordering on the intangible) |
| 5 | Thought given form (Creation) ($5^{th}$ of the physical dimensions–both tangible and intangible) |
| 6 | Belief (Knowledge that you can do what you can do) |
| 7 | Harmony (Understanding and going with the flow of the universe) |
| 8 | Hope (Transform different ideals into form) |
| 9 | Interconnectedness (Access to other dimensions below dimension 9. The first of the free access dimensions) |
| 10 | Temporal Stability–Static function, the ability to change the universe forever (no turning back) |
| 11 | Universal Creation (The dynamic sphere of creation, ever changing–no stability [Chaos], SE level) |
| 12 | Total Awareness & Constant connection with all dimensions at all times. Oneness with the SE & O |

*ME:* *What! These aren't dimensions!*

SE: Yes, they are. You see, the dimensions are dimensions of consciousness/awareness. These are only available as your level of evolution increases upwards.

*ME:* *But I thought they were like different levels of physicality.*

SE: They are to a point—this point is where you leave the tangible and move into the intangible, i.e., you move away from the levels that manifest themselves in physicality as you know/perceive them and move into the non-physical levels that require perception based upon evolution. Only when you have this do you have the ability to use/move through the other dimensions.

*ME:* *Referring to a conversation I had previously with you, how about aliens and their travel between dimensions—how does this work?*

SE: [It works] because they are working from the 9$^{th}$ dimension and use the bottom five to help them experience things. You also assume that they are ALIENS. They are not. They are just entities dipping into the lower levels to experience certain things to advance their own evolution without the need for the lengthy/complicated process of being incarnated. They don't achieve the same level of inertia in terms of speed of evolution that those who incarnate do because they never experience the "cut-offness" that you experience and feel. But they are nevertheless living, working, moving, and evolving through the dimensions.

*ME:* *So hold on a moment. My understanding is that we are all parts of YOU, and that we are, when we are not incarnate, part of everything that is, including the full suite of dimensions.*

SE: That is correct. You are. However, you have to evolve to a certain level before you can move on. You can do anything you want but that is only truly available to you when you have the experience and wisdom to be able to use the power properly.

ME: *Hang on. This sounds like you are talking about evolution in the physical and not reality!*

SE: It may sound like that, but it is not so. The whole point of you being "individualized" is so that you can all experience things. These experiences are fed back to the Origin and Me for the Origin's benefit, in terms of learning more about Itself and Me because I am interested in achieving the same thing, except by diversifying Myself down into billions of parts. Part of your creation requires you to fully understand yourself as well, in a similar vein to the Origin and Myself. And this only happens through experimentation leading to expanded knowledge and subsequently, evolution. Part of your evolution requires you to understand your limitless limitations, but the limitlessness takes some understanding. For instance, you only know that you can ride a bike when you have learnt how to ride a bike. This is the same for the awareness of the dimensions and your ability to work within and without them and manipulate them at will. Further, your level of evolution allows you to access parts of or all of the dimensions from any particular point. This means that you are able to access the knowledge you have of the manipulation of the energies surrounding and making up the dimensions from any point as well, including that part of you that is projected into the physical. This is the reason why you can communicate with me, and it also justifies the reports of some people's ability to do supposedly fantastic things, such as telekinesis, telepathy, clairvoyance, etc.

ME: *So what you are telling me is that the scientific explanation of dimensions is incorrect?*

SE: Not in the slightest. The physical manifestation of what you are experiencing is, therefore, the datum from which your scientists are working. The answer is that the perception of such dimensions is based upon

131

personal growth, and the descriptions of what the dimensions represent are in the former table. Remember the physical side of the dimensions is but a small part of what they are. The rest is literally intangible to you in your current state unless you are evolved enough to be able to cut through and manipulate what is there. Thus, you are allowed to return to your real state whilst in any state, including the incarnated state. This is what is meant by being one with God; this is what is meant by heaven on Earth because it truly is part of the whole. All you have to do is unlock the doors of perception, and you do this through evolution. The level of evolution you have achieved dictates the level of perception that you can bring with you into the lowest physical levels of energy state. This is only possible when you are highly evolved.

## The Origin's Clarification of the Role of the Dimensions

I was starting to get very confused over the dimensions and what they represented. On the one hand, I was being told that they represented different levels of awareness; whereas, on the other side I was being told that they were levels of division in a holistic sense of the Origin—a division of self that was copied to some extent by the Source Entity that looked after (managed?) our universe/s. I was also being confused by the continual reference within myself to the more physical explanation of the dimensions that human science offers us. For instance, the type of science that I was used to, using "human terms" to explain dimensions and their relationship to each other, is more akin to science fiction with its continual reference to parallel universes and wormholes in space time and assumptions that are continually being updated by new discoveries in quantum mechanics—the research of which seems to be, at least in my mind, spurred on by assumptions made by science fiction writers. As hard science in this area always appears to be "catching up with fiction" (are the authors tapping into the Source/Origin? Mmm. I wonder), I am being told from the highest authority, our GOD, the Source Entity and its creator, THE ORIGIN who is arguably God personified and "in total," that the dimensions are levels of awareness. How could this be? Which is correct? I stood perplexed and even more confused. As a result of this, I resolved to *go to the top* and ask the Origin what the dimensions were. As I type this last sentence, I start to hear the answer already. I prepared myself for the clarity of mind needed to make contact with the Origin, but the contact was already there.

ME:     *O.K.  O.K., so what is the answer then? I can imagine that there are many scientists lining themselves up to shoot me down on this in a couple of years, so it had better be good.*

O:      They would have difficulty in doing so since they don't really understand the data that they are gaining now. They don't have the right reference point to start from, so how can they comment on something that they know nothing about in the most fundamental sense? Remember, they are searching in the dark for something they can't see or feel or even know what it looks like. As a result, when they bend down and pick up a piece of string, they think because they found it in the dark, that it is part of what they are looking for, and, therefore, give it a quantum name, *quantum string,* or *super string.*

ME:     *I got a picture of a banana then. Why did I type "string"?*

O:      I guided you because people would not understand the reference to a *quantum banana* even though the explanation has the same value. Using a name like *Quantum Banana Theory* would not carry the same

133

level of respect within the circles of quantum scientists. Having said that, I have difficulty in giving *string* the same level of respect as well. The reality of the matter is "matter." And this gets in the way of awareness and understanding.

ME: *Why?*

O: Human science is based upon what can be seen, touched, or (more recently) *detected.* The issue here is that the detectors only detect the physical manifestation of the dimensions and the frequencies that operate within them. This is a much, much smaller piece of the picture than they can possibly imagine. However, there is a clue being given here. That is the use of *detectors* to detect and present things or events that the ordinary physical senses of the human body cannot *normally* see, feel, touch, taste, or smell. There are other things happening that scientists were not *AWARE* of.

Now here is an exercise in expansive thought. Because scientists can use mechanical means to detect things that they were not previously able to detect, it gives them physicality. It gives them substance, but more importantly, it gives them the door to the truth and the fact that there is more to what they are experiencing than they can detect by physical means alone. They are, therefore, more aware that there is more and that "the more" may not be in the *quantifiable* physicality of the physical world, and, therefore, must belong somewhere else. That somewhere else is "yet to be defined."

So to put it in a nutshell, the dimensions are, indeed, levels of awareness, and these levels of awareness are relative to aspects of the universe that are accessible as a direct result of the individual's personal evolution.

ME: *O.K., let's talk further about the dimensions and my confusion over what they really are.*

O: As I said before, the dimensions are layers of

awareness.

ME: *You said "levels" last time.*

O: Levels/layers, they're all the same thing. The level of awareness behest/command in the individual dictates their level of awareness. By this I mean what they perceive as reality measured against what they experience as reality is based upon where their "consciousness" is focused. It is difficult for you to grasp in your current state because of the extreme limitations that are placed upon you in this dimension/level of awareness.

Your level of awareness increases as you progress through the frequencies of lightness.

ME: *But . . .*

O: Before you say that I have switched to a physical description, hear me out. In what you call "spirit," you have no form or substance, at least not what you recognize as form and substance. You are part of the whole, ME, your SOURCE and every "thing" that is created by us, and all the other entities I have given form [individual identity]. The level of awareness you have is a direct result of the level of experience of other things, things that have been created by you or others. This gives you a capacity for understanding what is created within creation itself, i.e., what I have created. This removes the limitations of self and mind (spirit) and allows the individual to access information and experience what can only be accessed on the nine physical spiritual levels. The frequencies are levels of physicality whereas the dimensions are levels of awareness—awareness of and experience of the fact that everything is happening all at the same time. Humanity's need for separation of the dimensions into levels or parallelism is a result of a deep down knowing of the greater truth, due to some of the experience and knowledge of the higher self that trickles through the pipe to the subconscious. An inability to intellectualize it is due to a lack of evolution and subsequent awareness.

ME: *So when you have a cluster of dimensions together, i.e., 12, you also have a level or levels of physicality associated with them.*

O: Sort of, except that the levels of physicality are not what you expect, i.e., not at the same level of density.

ME: *So what level of density are we talking about here?*

O: Levels of spiritual density rather than levels of physical density.

ME: *What? You mean there are levels of density in spirit as well!?*

O: Of course.

ME: *Are these frequencies as well?*

O: Yes, of course, but they only apply to the lower levels of dimension (awareness). After these levels there is no density attached to awareness.

ME: *Where are these levels in the scheme of things then?*

O: They are what you might call the upper and lower astral levels—the areas where the interface between the true spiritual levels start and the highest physical frequencies end.

## The Source Entity on Links Between Frequency-Based Universes (Wormholes?)

ME: *One of the things that has bugged scientists and me for some time is the function of a science fiction phenomena turned scientific theory called "wormhole theory," the so-called link between dimensions or frequencies to aid the travel between distances in our universe to the point where it is almost instantaneous. I guess it was once called* hyperspace, *but we have gotten sexier in our use of words.*

SE: I don't think you have gotten sexier but possibly more accessible to the common man with the description of scientific data to aid understanding, and, dare I say, allow those with the research purse strings to get a grip on what they are spending their money. For you are more likely to spend money on what you think you can understand than what you don't feel you will ever understand, hence, the use of more basic nomenclature.

ME: *So is it possible to transverse the frequencies or dimensions? Sorry. Of course, it is. You have explained all of this before.*

SE: I have, but let me explain the function in another way, a way that is in keeping with the *Wormhole Theory*.

If you can consider the universe is made up of many frequencies and that the top frequency allows transition to the next dimension "UP," you will understand that the bottom frequency allows transition to the next dimension "DOWN," so to speak. Now it is possible to travel faster by increasing your vibrations or frequencies to those that are higher or lower than those in which you currently exist. But this requires an entity that is advanced in evolution or the use of a specially designed and manufactured machine to do it for you.

Or . . .

You can use what is naturally occurring in the nature of the frequencies and dimensions. You can use what you call "wormholes."

ME: *So, what are wormholes?*

SE: Well, what I can tell you is that they are neither holes nor worm-shaped, so this will *bugger up* a few theories and science fiction film footage. They are, however, an area of frequential weakness between frequencies.

I shall explain this further.

Imagine that the frequency that you exist within is flat, like a huge blanket all over the universe. Now imagine that the frequencies above and below are not only flat as well but spaced equally above and below the frequency that you exist within. We now have three frequencies, a middle "you," an upper, and a lower, each having its own nominal frequency. Now imagine that we have anomalies within this flat frequential surface where the frequencies are either higher than the nominal or lower than nominal. These are locally higher or lower frequencies that are *still* part of *or in tolerance with* your frequential surface. These would look like dips in the surface or lumps in the surface where the higher frequencies or lumps are representative of the local increases in frequency, and the lower frequencies or dips are representative of the local decreases in frequency. The areas of higher frequency are a product of the entities that work in that area who are generally more evolved and, therefore, working at a higher level or frequency. And the areas of lower frequency are a product of the entities who work in that area that are generally less evolved and, therefore, working at a lower level or frequency. You could relate these to two differing races where one race is working in harmony with each other and their neighbors, whereas the other is at war with their neighbors or in disharmony with each other.

Imagine also that there are dozens or hundreds of areas like this all over the surface, making it more lumpy than flat. The picture you should now be able to visualize is a sheet with lots and lots of lumps and bumps and dips all over it, rather like the surface of a choppy sea. Now imagine that this is also possible in the two frequential planes above and below your plane, and that they also have localized areas of both higher and lower frequencies. You should now have three choppy seas with one above and one below your sea. With the sea, the level of choppiness changes as a direct product of the local wind. As with the sea, the number of and the height and depth of the higher and lower frequency lumps within these other two planes changes as a direct result of the work of the incumbent entities; therefore, the bumps change as does their location. It can, therefore, be seen to undulate in shape.

This *movement* is a result of the migration of entities of higher and lower frequency around the plane of their existence or their rise or fall in evolutionary levels for one reason or another. The product of this is that at certain points at certain times a higher area of the middle frequency (your frequential plane), may touch or overlap that of a part of the higher frequential plane that is both at a lower frequency and in the same spatial area. This allows an entity to translate from one higher part of a lower frequency to the lower part of a higher frequency, effectively translating to an overall higher frequential plane in the process. However, that entity may not find it particularly comfortable because the natural movement of the plane moves upward in frequency as a result of natural evolutionary movement. It may well move too quickly for it.

Similarly, this can also operate in reverse with a lower frequency allowing an entity to translate to a lower frequency and, subsequently, endure a lowering of its own frequencies, which it will also not find particularly comfortable. Both conditions happen on a continual basis up and down the frequencies and, indeed, up and down the dimensions in a similar way.

Interestingly enough, however, it does have to be said that the higher up the frequencies you go, the flatter the surfaces and the more remote the opportunities to transverse up or down the frequential levels. So the appearance of the level of choppiness is reduced the higher up the frequencies you go. This is a general representation of the increase in harmony, resulting in the reduction in the distance between the entity and the Origin.

## Life in Other Dimensions

ME:    *We have talked a lot about dimensions and frequencies, what they are and how they are separated, but we have not talked about life in these* altered states.

SE:    First, they are not *altered states* in terms of an environment for existence although to you they may seem to be. They are states in their own right with their own sets of entities that exist within them.

ME:    *Do they have a physical aspect to them as well?*

SE:    In terms of them having differing frequency levels as well, they do, of course, have physical levels as your own dimension. Remember, everything is duplicated; it is just at a different rotational position of phase. The issue for you is this: do entities in other dimensions incarnate into bodies created to exist in lower frequencies, and if they do, what do they look like?

ME:    *Yes, sort of.*

SE:    Well, the answer is that all but three of the dimensions have entities that exist above the need to be incarnate in physical bodies. They simply do not need to go down to that level.

ME:    *Are they more highly evolved?*

SE:    Not necessarily, it's just that they have not exposed themselves to the experiences that have given you the opportunity to drop down to the physical levels and experience existence at its lowest level of useful frequency.

ME:    *So what do they look like?*

SE:    They are too many and varied to describe in one book, let alone one dialogue, and to be honest, it would not be very useful to you. Humanity has enough imagination to make extremely good guesses at the physiology of physical entities, no matter what dimension they come from. Just look at the creatures you have in your science fiction films. No, it would not be useful to you.

140

However, what I am prepared to share with you is that in every dimension and every frequency, no matter how high, the entities that exist in them have the same level of constraints, physically.

Let Me explain more. In your dimension and frequency, if you touch one another or a door or a table top, you feel resistance. This is because you and the objects around you are all at the same frequency. These are your physical boundaries, your physicality. Now if you use the word physicality to describe this resistance to the point of inability to pass through an object, then you have what is called "substance." The more solid or dense an object or entity, the more substance it has and the less opportunity you have for physical "interfraction." Interfraction is a word I use to describe the ability of two objects of differing frequency to mix and merge in the same space at the same time whilst being manifested in both frequencies at the same time, as well. This means that together they occupy space in two separate frequencies simultaneously. They mix atomically, sub-atomically, and energetically to create a single entity or object but are made from two different and independent entities/objects from two independent and different frequencies. This is a rare occurrence at your frequency, but it happens alot in the higher frequencies, especially with entities that wish to share the same experience at the same time. This, in fact, was a method used by human entities some millennia ago when the physical human body was at a much higher frequency than it is today. And is one of the causes of your demise frequency-wise.

However, let's get back to the interaction between entities of the same frequency. In essence, the boundaries between them are similar to those you experience between yourselves and the world around you, insomuch as you can manipulate them physically.

The main difference with the entities in the other dimensions is that they are able to manipulate the objects around themselves, including themselves, energetically. This means that they don't need to, say, pick things up with an appendage of some sort because they manipulate it with their will just like you do when in spirit or when you are in the lower frequencies and are in complete control of your true abilities. Indeed, to indulge you a little with a description of an entity from an alternative dimension, I will offer the following simple description of an entity that is in one of the other dimensions where the entities are experiencing life in the lower frequencies by choice rather than by karma.

The particular entity I have in mind is physical in appearance in your type of dimensional existence to the point of using a host body, just as you do. However, rather than having a complicated series of energetic and physical levels to work with, it exists independently within each of the levels within which it needs to exist. It is totally fluidic in this sense. As a shape, it is formless but nevertheless physical. The dominant shape is a sphere made of pinky red skin. The organs are entirely designed to take energy from the universe directly rather than by energy transformation, such as the chemical metabolic process of digestion. They are also able to change their structure relative to the needs of the job they have been asked to do by the incumbent spirit. Indeed the whole physical entity could be classed as a single organ that splits itself off to let those parts specialize in certain jobs for the period of time they are required. When they have finished their job, they are re-absorbed back into the whole. Appendages of all shapes and sizes are either grown or manifested when required, as are sensing functions, which are not limited to the five senses that you have in your frequency in your dimension. Its shape and form is purely arbitrary. It is what it needs to be to complete the task it wants to experience. The appendages or limbs that are manifested are created out of the surrounding atomic and sub-atomic material by the direct will of the entity. They are then used for working with substances that are difficult to work with on a physical level with the standard substance that the body is created from.

ME: *So if the entity needs a metal hammer, for instance, it creates one out of thin air.*

SE: Exactly, but not only that, the hammer is physically attached to the entity just as if it had grown there like a hand or a foot. This is the most useful method of using physicality. It is the *energetometabolic* version of a Swiss army knife as bodies go. This "form" affords the energetic entity that incarnates in this body the best opportunity for interaction with the lower frequencies of its dimension and the others that are also experiencing life at the same time.

ME: *Do many entities use this form?*

SE: Billions of them use this form in that dimension. Some of them even use the form to experience life in your dimension, not that you have recognized them because they are on a slightly different frequency level that is different enough to keep them out of your physical human sight but low enough to let them experience your dimension as well.

ME: *I am getting a picture in my mind's eye of a pinky skin shaped blob that is sticking out a tentacle that has grown from the skin instantaneously, rather like the eye of a snail. Its skin is all blotchy, sort of white, very light brown and pink. It has no readily recognizable vision organs or appendages of complexity like humans do. How does it see and sense? What/how does it eat?*

SE: Good. I see that you have been able to tune into that dimension and frequency where this incarnate vehicle shape is at its most prolific. Your questions, however, are rather superfluous as you already know the answers.

They do not need to eat as they take in sustenance directly from the energies surrounding and within the dimension and frequency that they are manifest within. In terms of sensory organs, they are not necessary in the way you are referring to, as they use their normal energetic functions for communication and spatial awareness even though they are incarnate into what is classed as a physical body, but what you would classify as a body that is out of phase with the frequency that is used to experience life within. As a result, it is also able to allow the incarnate entity the opportunity to use its spiritual or energetic functions to their maximum potential. Hence, the vision you had of the blob, as you called it, to instantaneously grow appendages and add what you would call inorganic material to it at will to perform certain desired physical functions. They only create new appendages, however, if it is necessary to use physicality to experience what is required. Generally these entities use the physical vehicle to experience the frequency they are working within at its lowest frequential level.

ME: *But I thought you just said that it was out of phase with the frequency that it is in existence with. If so, how can it be at its lowest frequential level?*

SE: The lowest frequential level is that which can be achieved with the entity's current level of evolution. That basically means that the lowest level that a particular entity may be able to go down to may actually be several frequency levels above the one that you are incarnate now. In essence the very level to which they have evolved restricts the level to which they can travel. So what they think is their lowest possible frequency is actually well above your own incarnate frequency. In terms of being out of phase, that means that the lowest level that that particular entity can travel down to is a level just above the level that it can manifest in. So it appears in both frequencies, one above and one below, and as a result of being out of phase is less dense in the one and slightly more dense in the other.

*ME:*   *So it would appear rather rock-like in the higher frequency since it is denser.*

SE:   No. Density is something that is not applicable in the higher frequencies. Although it would be detectable by those existing in the upper frequency, it would still be transparent, so to speak. This is because the reference to physicality that you keep using is not a law which is in use there; therefore, the "hard" translation of physicality between frequencies is not a natural process in higher frequencies.

Chapter 10:
## *The Source Entity on*
## *the Development of Human Beings*

## The Great Experiment to Help Origin Understand Itself

One of the questions that humanity has asked from time immemorial is "Why are we here?" It's incredible to think that we developed form and sentience out of the primordial soup over a period of millions of years. What are the chances of that happening? Billions, if not trillions, to one! Although I had covered a little bit about why we are here from an energetic entity perspective with the Source Entity of our universes and the Origin, I was intrigued as to what led to us being here in physical form and how the connection between the real us and that bit of us that is squeezed into this physical form interact.

As it was our Source Entity that created us, I decided to contact it rather than the Origin although I was rather surprised to see that the Origin also chipped in later.

ME:   *O.K., so now I am going to ask the big question that most of the world's religions claim to know and preach about, "WHY ARE WE HERE?"*

SE:   That's easy. We, that is, you, Me, all the entities I have created and all the other Sources and the entities They have created are here to help the Origin understand itself. The better question should have been "Why are you here in human physical form?"

ME:   *O.K., so why are we here in physical human form?*

SE:   To help the Origin understand Itself.

ME:   *What?! Now you are talking in riddles.*

SE: Absolutely not. You see, it's all part of the experiment if you want to call it that. Even the lower frequencies and the lower dimensions are part of the Origin. So what better way to understand yourself than to have part of your "self" exist with all its limitations at that level. The Origin has achieved this through Me creating you. As you experience events in your life, so do you evolve. As you experience things in your life, so do I and so does the Origin.

ME: *It sounds to me that it's all being done by remote control.*

SE: That's a reasonable thought process but incorrect. It's incorrect because you are ultimately part of the Origin. As a result of this, It is experiencing Itself through Itself, but that part of Itself, you, has been given individuality and sentience by Me, who, in turn, was given individuality and sentience by the Origin.

ME: *Who gave the Origin sentience?*

SE: It developed it Itself over countless quadroupillions (zillions upon zillions) of years. The Origin is energy, matter, and form given sentience.

ME: *I thought that the Origin wasn't matter?*

SE: Everything is the Origin.

ME: *O.K. We are getting off the track of what I wanted to discuss here a little bit.*

SE: Yes, I see, but it is a relevant discussion and a point to which we will return in good time.

But getting down to it . . .

It was discovered during the Origin's first efforts to understand Itself that the lower down the dimensions and frequencies It went, the more It lost contact with that part of Itself that was projected to that level—even to the point that It forgot that part of Itself was at that lower level. This was ingrained in us (the Sources) when We were created. We were given all the knowledge that the Origin had at that point in time. As a result, We all *had a go* at projecting part of Ourselves to the lower levels to experience it first-hand. When I created all of you, all of you knew that to experience the lower levels meant that you had to be vigilant in making sure that you didn't leave part of yourselves behind. Also, it was discovered that the best way to experience the lower levels was to experience them fully, and that meant in a form that was consistent with the density of the energies at those levels. A vehicle was needed to achieve this, and one had to be developed—one that could accept, house/maintain, and later release without harm an entity whose origin was from a higher level.

## The Source Entity's Role in the Development of the Human Form

ME: *So you actually developed the human form?*

SE: Not Me personally, although I oversaw it. Some of you were involved in the development.

ME: *Us?*

SE: Yes, some of you. You see, you would be the beings that would be projecting yourselves into these lower levels, so who better to develop the vehicle you were going to use than you?

ME: *So how did we do it?*

SE: Over a long time. Seriously it took all of you millennia to develop the human form to what it is now. You went through many, many prototypes.

ME: *So what were the issues?*

SE: Longevity for a start but more importantly the human form had to be able to exist in the physical levels and the lower spiritual levels that would allow communication with the rest of you, the higher self. This required a certain type of physical form and energy system interdependent upon one another for its survival. This required a lot of inventiveness and trial and error.

149

ME:     *I thought that You/we could just think something up, especially if we are evolved enough to access the dimensions of awareness that allow this level of creativity.*

SE:     Thought forms tend to stay in their area/environment of origin, but they also require their creator to give them attention. Hence, for example, poltergeists hang around people who believe in them as they give them form and energy beyond their original creation. In the instance of creating the best form, you wanted to create a vehicle that was, for a period of time, self-perpetuating. It, therefore, needed to operate without the level of attention required to maintain the level of complication that was required to create a thought form in the physical. It needed to be independent of that. This, therefore, resulted in the design of a "living" vehicle that could use the surrounding energy sources to maintain itself.

ME:     *This sounds complicated, and we all know that the human form is a very complicated thing. So how did we start the development?*

SE:     Small at first. You looked at creating small parts that would work with each other and that could be built upon. These needed to be *programmable* from Spirit and work based upon this programming.

ME:     *Are You talking about DNA creating cells?*

SE:     No, lower. I am talking about the RNA being programmed by the Spiritual program. RNA is an interface medium that exists in the higher physical and lower spiritual levels at the same time. It was the first part of the human form to be developed and, therefore, the most difficult to create and the most important. It is the part of the physical that is in contact with the auric fields at all levels.

ME:     *I was under the impression that RNA was the medium that transmitted the programming from DNA to the stem cells to create whatever they are destined to be, such as a liver or a heart.*

## The Role of RNA

SE: That is because you have only one end of the story. Your scientists have only just been able to spot the communication from the DNA to RNA. This is only one way of a two-way communication system and does not take into account the first set of information that was transmitted by the RNA to the DNA. The DNA must feed back to the RNA that it has received the correct information and that it is being passed on to the cell/s that the DNA is held within. Also, RNA is used as a communication medium between cells so they can locate each other and bind together in cells of the same type to create the bodily function they were assigned. You have to consider that many forms of information are being transmitted over RNA and other fluidic mediums, but it is only RNA that is "in contact" with Spirit from a physical point of view. In essence, since RNA is all over the body; the whole body is, therefore, in contact with Spirit, and this is what makes the human form unique. Physical, intermediate/astral, and spiritual—the three-in-one aspect that some of your religions talk about. This is trying to explain something that has been forgotten in the physical. We will discuss this later in another chapter on religion.

ME: *So You are saying that the most important part of the human physiology is the RNA because it allows the body to communicate with Spirit.*

## The Earlier *Lighter* Human Form

SE: Yes, but more importantly it allowed all of you to develop the human form in stages as you looked at what physiology and form worked best for the environment it is in.

ME: *Hang on. Are You suggesting that there are/have been*

151

*different human forms?*

SE:    Of course.

ME:    *Are these the Neanderthals or others?*

SE:    Actually, the Neanderthal form was the last, but one modification the human form had to accommodate due to the increase in density that resulted from the reduction in frequency caused by human free will being introduced. It is free will that has caused the fall in frequencies. It is free will that will make it rise as well. The human form before this was a much lighter construct. In fact, the connection with Spirit was such that the incarnate entity could enter and leave more or less at will.

ME:    *So what did these earlier* lighter humans *look like?*

SE:    You would consider them as waif-like, almost translucent, even glowing "in the dark." They were certainly not the solid robust physical specimens you have today, and they would not be able to survive in the current level of density experienced at this level of frequency—hence, the need to re-develop the form "on the run" as the frequencies changed.

    You have legends about people in Sumeria who were purple in color, and some people born today still display the mark of the Sumerian when they have purple birthmarks. These humans were of a different level of density, and so were the Atlanteans, who were lighter again. These were the times when the Spirit could enter and leave the body at will but not at the same level of ease as the first physical constructs.

## Back to the Development of the Human Form

ME:    *So let's get back to the development of the human form. How did it progress?*

SE:    You developed a medium (RNA) that could aid the programming of the lowest building blocks of the human form (DNA) and was able to create the type of cells required to form the organs of the body that would sustain it in its physical condition long enough to make the incarnating entity have enough time to experience being in the physical. You then set about trying to understand what a self-sustaining physical body needed to work.

ME: *So how did we get to the different organs of the body? How did we know we needed a liver or a pancreas?*

SE: After a few dramatic failures, you started to understand that the construct you made needed to get nourishment from both the physical and the energetic frequencies. The first attempts at making the human form simply died of hunger without knowing it was hungry.

The next objective was to work out how to take nourishment from the environment and turn it into energy that was compatible with your energies as spiritual entities. This meant that you had to develop an energy distribution system that to some extent mirrored the energetic flow. This meant moving the nourishment in a way that it could get to every part of the body and return again if it wasn't used the first time, so you invented the materials to create blood. This in itself wasn't good enough because you needed the blood to accept and give up the nourishment. The area of the body that was doing the work needed its physical energy replenished at the same time as its spiritual energy. Remember, the spiritual energy side of things was a little easier because the energetic side of the human form is mostly energy itself and energy given form to boot! You were starting to develop the metabolic process here and that took time and a lot of trial and error.

ME: *What about the human brain? We put a lot of store in the fact that all of what we are, our personality, our experience are stored in the gray matter.*

SE: Initially there wasn't a brain because the focus of the

incarnated Spirit wasn't so narrow. It was all over the body.

ME: *So why do we need a brain now if we didn't then?*

SE: To have a central control system to control the metabolic process of giving nourishment throughout the rest of the body. It controls the rest of the organs, and it continues to do so today. However, there is a level of "local control programming" in each of the organs to cope with the more mundane operations of the organs.

ME: *So what else happened to create the human form that we have today?*

SE: Once you had established that you had to transmit or circulate the blood around the body in the same way as the spiritual energies are distributed around the spiritual bodies, you then realized that the blood had to be cleaned. It was necessary to remove all of the impurities that are gradually absorbed by the blood cells as part of the metabolic process of giving chemicals to the cells that give them physical as well as spiritual energy. Later, however, you realized that there must be a method where the physical body could replenish those chemicals without external spiritual intervention, i.e., the body had to turn raw material into useable chemical energy.

ME: *Digestion of external organic matter? What made us recognize this need?*

SE: This was recognized because you were having to change the blood every month or so, plus or minus a week. It simply ran out of nutrients to sustain the body's functions.

ME: *I thought that today's human form could only last a month if it had water and if no food was available.*

SE: This is correct but remember that the human body was much different then. It was much *lighter* energetically and was not as reliant on the need for physical energy as it is now. Thus came the need to physically consume organic matter and mix it with gaseous matter of a form

154

that is readily available in the physical universe. You realized that it must be easily replenished as a by-product of inorganic and organic material interaction, as well as contain the basic building blocks of this universe. The other something would have to create a controllable chemical reaction that would result in the creation of basic food blocks as well as reproduce itself in the process.

ME: *You're talking about oxygen and carbon here, I take it?*

SE: Yes, these two gaseous elements are the most freely available in this type of universe. You used them in the metabolic process within the human circulatory system to create its own nutrients to complement the spiritual energies in a way that was independent of spiritual intervention. Thus you created the self-sustaining human form that was ready to go into action—until you found out about how bacteria and viruses affected this system, of course.

ME: *So we had problems with the body getting ill at the very start then.*

SE: Not quite. This happened only when the body needed to operate in a denser environment.

ME: *So why didn't we have problems at the start of development?*

SE: Because as the body was *lighter,* it wasn't affected by the physical as much. Even though it existed primarily in the physical, it was drawing a lot of energy from Spirit and was, therefore, not so susceptible to the maladies of the world where bacteria and viruses existed. Also, don't forget that the human form was relatively new, and the entities that inhabited these forms were at a higher frequency. Still they were not affected energetically by dysfunctional thought processes that create changes in the surrounding energy fields of the higher human form.

ME: *Why was that?*

155

SE:  Simply because the human spirit incarnate had not yet been corrupted by the lures of the physical experience and its ability to seduce the incarnate spirit to the point where it wants to stay in the physical.

ME:  *Why would the Spirit want to stay in the physical when it is so much more in spirit?*

SE:  Simply because of the forgetting that is experienced as a result of projecting oneself into a level where the level of communication is vastly reduced from that normally experienced by individual spirit.

ME:  *So it is a form of forgetting!*

SE:  No, it is just a word to explain the experience a spirit has when it can no longer access all that is. In essence, this is because it can't access all of itself and all of creation anymore. It disregards it mainly because it isn't there so it (the bit that's projected into the physical) quietly forgets about it. As a result of this, it thinks that its incarnate world and all the experiences there is all there is. It, therefore, does things to other incarnated humans that it wouldn't normally do in an effort to make its situation better or improve it. This, in turn, creates thought forms that stick in the energy field and create dysfunction in the physical. Because the physical is linked to the energetic, the physical responds to the dysfunctional energy by trying to reproduce its energetic blueprint in the physical. As the physical body gets denser, the seduction increases the desire to do things to improve the physical experience which then results in dysfunctional energy signatures and subsequent changes to the physical body. Ultimately this means that things that age the physical body— things it would normally be in tune with—are no longer in tune. This then causes friction within the physical functions. In this instance, the virus or bacteria that the body is normally in tune with and works with without issue is now fighting against the body.

ME:  *You said that viruses and bacteria were in tune with the earlier human body. Is that because they were energy life forms in their own right and, therefore, had a role in the universe as well?*

SE:     Yes and no. You see, because the human body was initially a much lighter construct, the denser matter would pass through it or not be able to affect it because it wouldn't have the physicality within which the small life forms, such as bacteria or viruses, needed to grab hold of the human cellular structure and do damage. Also, the higher frequency of the cells would effectively repel the lower frequency of the bacteria by its sheer cleanliness of modulation. This would be a similar effect to that seen when observing magnetic repulsion. Thus, you would have two effects: 1) the lower level frequency bacteria would pass through the human form if the human form was of a high (light) frequency; and 2) there would be a repulsion of bacteria if the frequencies were lower.

## Eating for Longevity

*ME:    So it looks like we sorted it all out with the human form then?*

SE:     Not yet. You see, once you created a system that could work with energy from both the Spirit and the physical worlds, you had to ensure that the energies would mix and work well together.

*ME:    I thought that they worked separately because they had to work with the different energy bodies.*

SE:     No, they have to interact because each energy system is reliant on the one above and below it—hence, the transmission of dysfunction up and down the energy structures when preconceptions were taken for reality or physical ailments or when addictions are prevalent.

You finally established that certain energies work best with the human form, and these were made more desirable to the human palate in the hope that you

157

would eat the right foods in order to get the right energies to ensure optimal efficiency and longevity.

ME: *What do you mean by optimal efficiency and longevity? I thought that longevity isn't an issue with Spirit?*

SE: This is to do with the length of time that a spirit is incarnate in the physical. Obviously you want to get the best value for money for your stay in the physical. The object being to make the most of the short time that the body lasts before it starts to degrade.

ME: *What makes the body degrade?*

SE: Misuse by the incumbent spirit mainly. This is achieved by eating and drinking foods that the body was not designed for in the first place.

ME: *So what is the body designed to eat?*

SE: Root based foods are the best for the human body because the base minerals and the energies associated with them are contained in the root of the plant. Essentially, anything that is grown in the ground is good because it is surrounded by the upper energy field of the earth. Taking energies from root-based plants means that the body's energy levels are replenished with pure energy that is not contaminated by humankind. However, this is more difficult to achieve in today's world where chemicals are used to "preserve" the plant products in an ideal state of presentation. So-called "organic" foods are better but still not what they should be since all root-based plants should be gathered from the "wild" where the surrounding Earth energies are purest.

ME: *So does this mean that eating meat or fish is out?*

SE: No, but it isn't good. The residual energy left in the system is not of the same frequency as that required to replenish and refresh the energies that are normally generated by the root vegetables. Also, they are not in tune with the spiritual body energies. The result of having energies that are not quite in tune with the natural energies associated with the human construct is that it slows the energy down in the areas where the animal meat is passing through. Continued use of energies that are not in tune with the body results in dysfunction over time because the energies change the functions of the messages sent between cells of similar types.

ME: *Are You suggesting that eating meat or fish, a food which is not resonating at the same frequency as the human body, results in cancer?*

SE: Yes.

ME: *Does this also include animal produce, such as milk, cheese, and eggs?*

SE: Yes.

ME: *How about other things like vegetables that are not root-based?*

SE: They are not ideal, but the energies are not so far out of the resonant frequencies of the energies provided by root vegetables that they cause dysfunction. All they do is create lack in the longevity of power given to the body, i.e., how long it lasts in the system.

ME: *So it's like comparing a long-life battery with a normal battery.*

SE: Yes, that's a very good comparison.

ME: *And eating meat or fish is like putting unleaded petrol in a car's engine that is designed for 4 star/high octane fuel.*

SE: Correct. After a few years, the engine is destroyed because it is burning a fuel that burns too hot and doesn't have the inherent lubrication properties that the lead provides in 4 star/high octane fuel.

ME: *So we are killing ourselves by eating the wrong food and drink.*

SE: In essence, yes. But that is up to you. You have been given free will to do anything you like in this physical environment with the premise that the experiences that you have are used to evolve yourself and the other

159

human entities.

ME: *So You don't mind us making a dog's dinner of our lives.*

SE: There is nothing wrong with a dog's dinner if you are a dog. So why should it be wrong for you to do what you are doing with what you have around you to work with? Remember there is no right or wrong, good or bad. There is only experience.

## The Need to Eat

ME: *We previously spoke about the development of the physical human form and the need for physical nourishment resulting from the drop in vibratory level. The human form previously was able to exist on universal energy alone due to the higher vibration level. Do you think we could achieve the level in this physicality where we wouldn't need to eat physical food but could gain our nourishment directly from the universe?*

SE: Not only is this possible, but it is happening on an individual basis right now with some individuals. You see, the human form in its current vibratory level needs both physical food and universal energy. The gathering of universal energy is achieved on an automatic basis due to the lack of personal knowledge of this function by the individual. Full use of universal energy is a function of an entity who is both aware and makes use of universal energy for sustenance and other forms of creativity on a daily basis, thereby, negating the need for the lengthy process of ingesting physical nourishment.

ME: *How does the physical human body gain energy from universal energy?*

SE: Simply by taking the energy that is required to operate normal cellular function/reproduction at the sub-atomic level. You see, everything energetic in the physical is translated from the physical into the energetic by the breaking down of the physicality through the giving of energy. For instance, you need fire to create fire. In order to light a match to create the initial spark, you give energy in the form of friction. The friction removes parts of the match's material at the atomic level by making it unstable in its current atomic arrangement. It, therefore, changes to its next stable state which results in the loss of energy to another separate state. This other conditional transition creates what you see as the flame of the match grows and recedes as the translation increases. Then it decreases as the amount of material required to change is reduced as a result of translation. This translation from the physical to the energetic can be achieved in many other ways. The most common way used by the human body is the giving of energy by the secretion of chemicals. When food is ingested into the stomach, it recognizes that it has a chemical imbalance and secretes the correct mixture of chemicals required to effectively break down the food into the energy it needs to feed the body's cells at the sub-atomic level. The chemicals that are not required are removed from the body as waste. Excess energy of the right type is stored within the body but outside of its immediate functionality. You know this as fat. Since the human body was not designed to deal with synthetic materials, the issue with the body's creation of fat is that preservatives in food are mistaken for translatable material. Subsequently, the body has difficulty in finding the right chemical/s later to break down the preservatives into usable sub-atomic energy. The body, therefore, loses its efficiency in this process and increases its stored food as a result of poor translation and the continued ingestion of the synthetic, i.e., food with preservative content. Additionally, fat that is created from the translation of

161

artificially preserved food is just as difficult to use, so this creates a condition that is difficult to reverse. In fact, it is so difficult to reverse that preservative-free food is then translated into energy when needed in preference to that translated from the preserved; therefore, it is very difficult to remove the fat by natural use. The only real way to remove the fat is to expend more energy than is received by natural un-preserved food than that was created by the preservative-based food.

ME:     *So that is how the body creates sub-atomic energy; it uses a chemical process to separate the energy from the matter.*

SE:     Let Me note here that what I have given you is a very simplistic description.

## The Body's Method/s of Converting Universal Energy

ME:     *Then how does it convert universal energy and with what?*

SE:     The energy used by the physical human body is dependent on the use of certain types of energy and the attraction of such energies. It does this by employing a supplementary energy distribution system, based purely on a direct energy transfer and distribution system. Twelve basic energies are used, and they are collected by all of the major, minor and mini chakras. The minor and mini chakras duplicate the receptivity of the major chakras. Each major chakra has a specific energy to attract and feed into the distribution system. The specific energy a chakra attracts is distributed to the cell/s with the correct sub-atomic signature via a network of energy lines similar to the Earth's ley-lines but operating in three dimensions. No conversion is needed as it is exactly what is required for correct and continued cellular function. It must also be noted here that all chakras have the ability to project energy as well as attract energy—hence their use in direct contact/hands-on and hands-off healing, which uses the minor chakras' abilities to remove incorrect energies gained by the cellular structure. Usually these incorrect energies are a result of un-pure food (preservatives, etc.) and its subsequent conversion into energy, which is then replaced with pure energy collected from the universe and not converted by the human body's chemical process.

ME: *Hang on. I thought that the chakras and their network of energy lines were a primary system.*

SE: No, the primary system is only achieved when the human entity is fully in Spirit. In this instance the human form and the energies required to perpetuate it (the energies of the universe) are one and the same. Humanity can, therefore, be correctly described as energy given individuality.

## Eating Animals versus Vegetables

ME: *How about the eating of animals versus vegetables?*

SE: This is an interesting one, for the human body is not specifically designed to translate the energy of another similar energy-based but incarnate entity, but this is what you ask it to do. Again, this can cause an imbalance in the energy system which results in the need to be healed. Interestingly enough, shamen used to eat animal flesh with the permission of the entity incarnate in the animal chosen. They did this to allow them to take on the energetic characteristic of that animal for many purposes, including transportation, knowledge, wisdom, communication, and physical manifestation of psycho-spiritual and physical skills. It was only done in strict supervision and as a last choice to solve a certain problem.

ME: *Would this explain why many people actually act like*

163

*animals these days?*

SE:    The constant eating of meat would and does have an effect similar to what you are suggesting with added complications: 1) the animal has not given its consent to be used in such a poor way; and 2) the characteristics of the animals' personalities are confused/mixed together as a result of the consumption of many different animal types, including fish.

*ME:    Would this explain why many people who eat meat are intolerant?*

SE:    It explains it only insomuch as the individuals concerned are no longer able to make clear human judgments.

*ME:    You mean they act like animals.*

SE:    That would be detrimental to the animals eaten.

*ME:    What about vegetables and vegetation?*

SE:    They are part of the earth's eco-system and are designed to provide nourishment for those creatures that are not as highly energized as the human species. They are, therefore, a legitimate but not so efficient means of gaining energy for sub-atomic translation. They are also designed to provide various elemental functions for the earth, such as the creation, translation, and nullification of chemicals and gases essential to the earth's function. We have spoken about root vegetables as a foodstuff, and they are a good substitute for universal energy when it cannot for any reason be translated directly, as it is freely available in the earth. Root vegetables tap into this natural energy for growth and because of this are more easily translated by the human digestive system.

Remember this though:

- We are *all* part of the universe;
- The universe is part of us; and
- The universal energy is available to all for the use of all, for the sustenance of all, and for the creativity of all.

If you would give yourselves but a moment to stop and truly experience this wondrous recourse and know what you can do with it, you would not clamber over each other for power, wealth, nourishment, celebrity, or love. You would know that you belong and need for nothing because nothing is needed by those who know and work with the universe in true and full understanding.

## The Body Becomes Denser (The Road to Autonomous Biological Reproduction)

SE: Remember that earlier human forms were much lighter than they are today. Some of your legends tell of humans who could fly, and this is a direct result of them being *lighter* in the surrounding density of the planet, which was also not as dense as it is today. As more and more entities incarnated into the human form as it was then, the number of physical entities needed to increase with the increase in demand. As these entities incarnated, they experienced more of the universe at the denser levels. The more they became entrenched in the experiences they had at these lower levels, the more they evolved when they came back into the levels of "normal" energy-based existence. The entities that had not experienced incarnation observed how fast those who incarnated were evolving and, therefore, saw this as an opportunity for an evolutionary "fast track." This again resulted in the increase in demand for physical bodies.

Since the number of human forms were limited (you had to create them directly from the spiritual energy levels at this point in time), all of you got together to try to work out how to increase the number of bodies without the need to create them yourselves. This meant that the body needed to be able to recreate itself in some way, and that this needed to be designed into the existing model.

ME: *We all know about the birds and the bees, so what can You tell me that I don't already know?*

SE: The birds and the bees, as you know it, is quite a new thing in terms of the length of time that has been spent working on the human form. You see, the information that I have given you about the events that led you to a relatively small understanding about the history of what went on in the moments in time that were used in the development of the human form do not in any way go into the real detail that would adequately describe what humankind in spirit did to achieve the current level of human form. That would require several books and would bore the pants off you, not to mention your potential readers although it may interest some of your scientists. But I will move on.

ME: *How does this link to the human form getting denser?*

SE: Wait and see. The one caused the other.

We have just discussed the fact that there were not enough bodies to go around, so to speak. The entities were queuing up to incarnate when they found out that the chance of incarnating would increase their speed of evolution. Creating the human form from Spirit took a lot of effort so an alternative method had to be found, one that could happen independently of spiritual intervention.

ME: *Reproduction!*

SE: Of course. It sounds simple from where you are

166

standing now, but it took a lot of "time" to sort out. You see, you had to completely redesign the human form so that it could reproduce itself without the need for external intervention. In essence, the male and female sides of the human genome did not exist. You only had a physical biological form that was designed to exist for a set period of time, and once it reached a set period, it stopped working to a greater extent and so became largely un-useable.

ME: *Is this where the three score years and ten legend came from?*

SE: No, no, but I can see why you might make the link with this. Three score years and ten is an average life expectancy that was invented by the author of the Bible called the Old Testament to try to explain why the human form ceased to function after a certain, consistent time after it was created. He called it the life expectancy given by God to humankind provided they followed God's ways—ways that were largely invented by humankind itself.

But back to the story at hand.

The design of the human form was at that time not geared up for reproduction in any way, shape or form, and it took considerable thought and experimentation to get it right. You (humankind in spirit, that is) had several attempts at getting it right.

## The First Attempt at Human Reproduction

ME: *Tell me about some of the attempts we had at getting it right.*

SE: There were three main attempts, the third being what you have now, so I won't go into too much detail on this one.

ME: *So basically we had two prior attempts at making the human body reproduce itself without spiritual intervention.*

SE: Correct. The first version was based upon the reproduction of the original by what you would call "cell division" but on a dual frequency level. The human form was at a higher frequency at this time, thereby making this easier to achieve. In essence the body was able to go "out of phase" with itself to the point where the body was able to create two (or more) versions of the same. One was a body that was half the density of the original. Consider it similar to jpeg compression where you take the data of every, say 3$^{rd}$ or 4$^{th}$ pixel to reproduce the same image but of a drastically reduced file size. In this instance, the reproduction of the human form means that the density of the original body was reduced proportionately by the number of times the body wanted to reproduce.

ME: *So how did the newly reproduced bodies recreate their density to that similar to the original?*

SE: By normal cell division and growth. The biological body was told at RNA/DNA level to increase its cell count if its overall density was lower than that required to perform in the environmental frequency in which it was working before it was reproduced.

ME: *At what age was it pertinent to reproduce using this technique?*

SE: Obviously an age where the body was self-sufficient to the point where it did not rely on others for its continued existence. The decision to reproduce then would not have been made when it was a four year old, for instance, nor would it have been made when it was about to die. At this point in time the human form was ready built to the adult stage, say 16-18 years old in your terms but was still subject to aging due to its need to interface with the lower frequency levels of the physical and the higher frequencies of the spiritual. The shifting of frequencies required for the human form to exist in both the physical, intermediate, and spiritual frequency levels did and still does age the cellular structure of the human form quite dramatically. The only way to slow this process down is to remove some of the physical strains you put on the body that it is not designed to work with, such as smoking, meat, and alcohol. However, even these don't really make a massive amount of difference compared to having the body exist in one frequency plane only.

ME: *Sounds like a good method of reproduction to me.*

SE: It would have been, but the issue was with the continuing drop in frequencies at that time (which incidentally were light years away from where you are now) that resulted in the need for a denser body. In addition, the subsequent loss of continuity in reproduction was caused by the need for massively increased cell division to compensate. This was specifically noticeable when the reproduction resulted in one body creating more than one copy of itself. The more copies that were made, the more diluted the master became. This resulted in cells being reproduced that only had half the information to pass on to the next generation of cells. Thus, there was great deviation from the normal standard human cellular structure, which then created mutations that were a hindrance rather than a help.

ME: *Did this matter that much?*

SE: Usually I would say no because physical mutations on their own are not an issue, but the mutations also affected the manner in which communication with the spiritual messages were received, as well as what they passed on to the other cells in the communication chain—not to mention what was passed back to Spirit.

ME: *How did the messages sent back to Spirit affect Spirit then?*

SE: Simply put, it affected the energy frequencies in a way that created discord (dis-harmony) with the surrounding energies at the various different levels that were being used as the master "plan" for the human form. It created a change to that master which affected all other human forms currently being used in the physical. In effect it caused mutations to appear in all the other humans that were incarnate.

ME: *How could that be? I thought that human beings, incarnate, were all independent?*

SE: They are to a lesser extent now, and that is shown in the variation of your form when you compare each other side by side. You mutate singularly rather than in multiples, but at that point in time you were all the same—clones, you would call them, who were all linked together from a psycho-spiritual/physical perspective whilst allowing the energy of the incarnate spirit the opportunity to be in and out of incarnation at will. As spirits during this time, you were also able to be in contact with your higher selves all the time, and this was a result of the frequency that this human form was based within. However, this was obviously not optimal from a dysfunctional perspective, as any errors that were created as a result of the "back filling" of cells after reproduction or psychological issues caused eddies in the local frequencies that also affected the rest of humanity. It took a long time to see what was happening and to work out a "fix" for the problem because initially all of you thought the errors were part of your basic design for the human form. In essence, you were trying to fix something that wasn't broken, provided the initial thought process of singular divisional reproduction was adhered to. Once you tried to increase this, the errors crept in, and as with any engineering problem, you get "red herrings" that mislead you as to what the problem is.

Suffice to say that the errors that were being created both at the human form level and at the master plan level were such that it was deemed necessary to change the method of reproducing the human race to something more robust. This led to the second method of reproduction, the one before the method you have now.

## The Second Attempt at Human Reproduction

ME: *O.K., so we had a second attempt at reproducing the human race in an autonomous way that did not affect the spiritual energetic realms.*

SE: Not quite. Reproduction on the physical levels always affects the spiritual realms in some way. This is because the physical is still connected to the Spirit, and Spirit is "one" with the universe, Me, and the Origin. You know from basic physics that energy cannot be destroyed, and Sir Isaac Newton stated that every action has an equal and opposite reaction. Newton was not quite right. Physical responses are a "lossy" function with the losses incurred going elsewhere in the universe. Heat, for instance, is a response which is connected to the spiritual realms due to its functional frequency. As it transposes to the spiritual, it is lost in the physical; hence, heat is lost! Lost to the physical energy levels, that is.

In terms of human reproduction or, in fact, any human action, the spirit connected to the physical body is affected in some way. The issue with the first attempt was that the whole of humanity was connected, resulting in the errors seen in one body being transferred to the rest.

This dilemma was so profound that it led to one solution, *to disconnect the physical connection of the group of souls incarnate in the physical.* So with this system of reproduction, the information transmitted through the RNA to the physical and back to the spiritual was limited to dealing with the individual spirit concerned. The method of reproduction was maintained, but the number of reproductions was

171

limited to a 1:1 basis. As one human body was approaching the "worn out" stage, another was created by cell division. Remember, the human body was still manifested on a higher frequency level than it is currently, so this was a much easier job to achieve energetically than it would be today. Also, the incarnate spirit was able to communicate with the rest of itself and the rest of "Spirit" at will—something that humankind at its current frequency level cannot do.

ME: *This looks like it sorted the problems out that You previously had!*

SE: So it would appear. But the issue here was twofold:

1. The physical body had a reduced "life time" due to the optimal time of reproduction; and
2. The physical dysfunctions were not fully worked out.

This meant that over time the errors seen in the reproduction process could mutate significantly as the body re-created itself. During the reproduction cycle, the errors were passed on to next body and the next body and the next body with all the other possible errors creeping in as they did. This was amplified further as the first issue took hold with the reproduction cycle needing to speed up to cope with the reduced life span of the human form. Then there was the need to try and increase the number of physical bodies that could be used for the ever-increasing number of spiritual entities wanting to accelerate their experiences, knowledge, and evolution by experiencing life at its lowest frequencies.

ME: *So it didn't really do the trick then. All that happened was that You were able to remove the association with the rest of the incarnate humans so that the errors caused by reproduction were not spread to the rest of "humanity in spirit," so to speak.*

SE: It didn't really do that either. You see, Spirit is Spirit and it is "one." So even though We/you had removed the major method of communication used in the proliferation of error and energy disharmony, it "snuck in" through the back door.

## Challenges of Human Spirits Sharing Incarnate Bodies

ME:  *How could it have done this? I thought that cutting everyone off from each other in terms of the energetic communications via Spirit and RNA would be total.*

SE:  Yes, in the normal sense it would be, but there was one activity that incarnate spirits liked to engage in that meant that the errors could creep in in another way. With your current method of reproduction, you're all but on your own, apart from when you are evolved enough to get snatches of coherence of the real world (like now), or if you remember, when you are contact with your higher self and other spirits through *astral traveling* during your physical sleep time. But remember, two additional things were still happening to those two above.

1. The errors in reproduction were experienced by the non-incarnate part of the Spirit, affecting it, albeit slightly, by energetic disharmonies.
2. Spirits were able to share bodies or move from one body to another to experience things that another Spirit thought was particularly good.

ME:  *So spirits that were incarnate had the opportunity to "hot swap" between different physical bodies at will.*

SE:  Yes, very much so, and it happened on a massive scale. Moreover, it was not unusual for a human body to have three or four spirits incarnating with it during its lifetime—hence, the proliferation of the errors. In some instances, it was thought to be seen as the solution to the poor availability of human bodies. Why reproduce more human bodies when you can share a body among the four of you? But the errors were created because that human form would have been "custom created," to an extent, to the frequencies of the very first incarnating spirit, which would or could be out of phase with the others who wanted to take advantage of a body share.

ME: *I have heard of similar things happening these days; it is called a* walk-in.

SE: A *walk-in* is a different thing. A walk-in is where the incarnate spirit has literally *had enough* of incarnate life and gives another spirit the opportunity to incarnate by giving up its own body—still a very rare and privileged incarnation opportunity.

ME: *So the errors/energy disharmonies were passed on due to body sharing?*

SE: Yes, very much so.

ME: *So human spirits used to travel from one body to another to experience things that they weren't experiencing in the body they currently inhabited.*

SE: Yes, of course, this was one of the things that you wanted to maintain from the first method of incarnation to the second—the basic ability to remain in contact with the rest of humanity from an energetic point of view. The best way to do this was to be able to move out and away from the physicality that constrained them. However, it was very quickly seen that you could move into another body quite easily. This was mainly possible because there was not the tie with the physical body that is seen in the current method of incarnation, the silver cord.

As the Spirit experienced the energies surrounding and within the physical form, it took these energies, good and/or bad, on-board as an energetic imprint. This was a true full experience of incarnation done at a "rate of knots"/fast speed [see Glossary] because of the ability to share everyone else's

174

experiences without having to do it all oneself. The issue here is that the energy imprints from energies created as a result of cell division errors made in the reproduction method were also passed on to those who wanted to experience other spirits' experiences in the physical. This perpetuated the error not only locally but with all those who had shared a body. Also, it was not unknown for some bodies to have more than one spirit incarnate in a particular body at any one time.

ME: *So this was really a hot bed of evolution with everything happening fast then.*

SE: Yes, it was fast. As a result, spirits from all over the known and local universes gathered together around Earth to line up and experience accelerated evolution. The only issue was that the vessels that were being used for the evolution of these spirits were not optimal in their ability to reproduce. Thus, the errors incurred in the duplication process created further errors/disharmony in the energy flow of those spirits who used bodies for their evolution, i.e., that had been reproduced or were the reproductions of reproductions, etc. This caused great disharmony with everyone who incarnated at that time, and the period of recovery from being incarnate almost outweighed the advantages gained. Yes, the spirit evolved rapidly due to the experiences gained by reducing the amount of "connectivity" and abilities associated with the spiritual energies. However, the fall-out in terms of the amount of care required to help the spirit recover from the energetic dysfunctions that they were picking up as a result of all the other incarnate sprits using the same bodies, meant that they might take thousands of your years to get themselves back to where they were energetically before they incarnated. Remember that this was localized to those spirits who incarnated in a finite number of bodies but experienced the dysfunctions of all the bodies that they incarnated within. If they stayed in one body, then they would not have been too badly affected by the energy disharmonies associated with the previous reproduction/s, but as they were "putting themselves about," they compounded the issue.

This compounding of the energy disharmonies and the long time required for the spirits to "normalize" after a round of incarnations meant that you had to look at revising the methods used for incarnating in a physical body.

These were identified as follows:

- Reduce the number of bodily incarnations to one per spirit;
- Remove the ability of those spirits who incarnate to move around to other bodies once incarnate;
- Remove the connections between spirits whilst incarnate and the memory of such abilities because they won't miss what they can't remember;
- Reinstate full abilities once incarnation is finished; and
- Create a body that is more robust in its reproductive capabilities.

ME:  *This sounds like the recipe for what we have now.*

SE:  It is in its entirety. In fact, it still is the blueprint for evolution via incarnation. You see, the only difference here is that you had to be cut off from each other to ensure that the energetic disharmonies created by the reproduction process did not spread to others as a result of interaction. Once this was known to be effective, and it is, it was then decided to move on to making the reproduction of the human body more robust. This had to be done in a way that was self-contained whilst working with the energies at the boundary line of the physical and spiritual.

## The Design of Modern Human Beings (The Development of the Current Reproduction Method)

ME: *O.K., so in order to stop energetic disharmony across the local energy levels from reproducing the physical body in the way that spread between spirits, we decided to reduce the number of reproductions to one per body. This did not stop the problems entirely because spirits that were incarnate liked to move around from one body to another, so they could experience what other spirits were experiencing in their own bodies. This, in turn, caused problems because the energy disharmonies that were experienced by living in one body were passed on to the next spirit who dropped in for a quick experience of life in the physical from a different angle. This then compounded the issue of spirits returning from "physical living" to spirit because they had to have energy re-alignment therapy, which could take quite a long time, even in spiritual terms.*

*All this resulted in the need to have one incarnate spirit in one body with no movement between bodies whilst incarnate, and what's more, they would have no knowledge of the rest of spirit whilst incarnate. In this way the incarnate spirit would not know what other spirits were experiencing; therefore, they would not feel the need to experience someone else's experience without having to re-incarnate and experience the whole life for themselves. They were to be completely alone for the short number of years they were in their chosen physical body.*

SE: That summarizes it quite nicely. Don't forget that this was a learning process that lasted for millennia in physical terms and one that you, as spirit, could not have foreseen since the whole point of this experiment was to deal with the physical whilst in the physical realms.

## The Physical Realms Encompassing Ten Levels

ME: *I thought the physical realms were purely physical, i.e., as the human body, the Earth, the solar system, and everything else we can see, hear, touch, feel, or taste.*

SE: From a lowest of the frequency levels perspective, you are correct, but the physical realms exist up to the 10th level.

ME: *I expected seven levels because they are related to the human energy field, but you are saying that the other three above the 7th level are also associated to the human physical realms.*

SE: In essence, yes. You see, there are seven levels that interface with the physical/spirituo-physical and seven that interface with the spirituo-physical only. The first three levels are just in the physical with the other four being in the realms where the physical is spiritual in existence. These four are the overlapping levels between the two lots of seven levels. Last are the three higher levels, which make a total of seven in the spirituo-physical but ten levels in total and span the physical and spirituo-physical and represent the higher frequencies of spiritual existence that are associated with the physical from the human perspective. These three levels allow the communication with that part of you (the greater majority) that remains in spirit. They act as a filter insomuch as they translate the thousands upon thousands of senses or experiences used/gained in spirit into a generalized response that can be used by the spirit incarnate in its lowest form, the human form. Whilst it is being employed as a vessel for evolution, i.e., they allow the incarnate being the use of memories and experiences previously encountered in former incarnations or knowledge of activities performed in the spiritual realms that would be of benefit in the physical. More importunately, however, they are the link between the fully spiritual and the spirituo-physical planes.

ME:  *But how can a spiritual plane be physical?*

SE:  By association with the human, and this was My choice. You need to have seven levels to be anywhere close to being fully functional in any realm, especially ones as low in frequency as the human. The seven levels provide a minimum continuity of gradient permissible to allow reasonable communication between infinite existence and finite existence, reasonable insomuch as it provides communication. Any fewer and no communication would happen.

ME:  *Why would no communication happen if the number of levels was less than seven?*

SE:  Because the graduations between each of the frequencies has to be at a certain level for a particular graduation to be on the edge of the phase of that graduation that is higher than it and the next one that is lower to it. It simply takes seven levels of frequency to get from level 10 (and above) to level 4, which is the lowest level you can get to before physical manifestation takes place. Each of these levels acts as a filter. In order to describe what is being fed down the frequencies, each searches for something that is nearest the level being translated to. This is where errors creep in because the data needs to be *generalized* from one level to another seven times to reach the level of vocabulary available at the lowest. Imagine you have 7,000,000 ways to describe a horse with your method of communication. These include touch, smell, taste, speech, sight, and hearing, plus other senses you have but are not aware of having. Then imagine that each sense is not a sense but a communication medium, and you lose at least 10% of the vocabulary associated with each of these communication methods every time you move down the frequencies. Each downward movement results in a 10% reduction which significantly reduces one's ability to describe the horse. Specifically, the methods that disappear first are those that provide the more detailed description opportunity that only comes with higher functionality seen at the higher frequencies. Therefore, the lower you go down the frequencies, the less you are able to say about the horse. Eventually you get down to the five senses you have in the physical and the few things that are associated with them.

ME: *I have just done the mathematics on the 10% reduction through dropping down seven levels, and it doesn't add up.*

SE: The 10% number was used figuratively to demonstrate what could happen. In reality you lose much more in the first levels that you drop. Since the multitudes of senses available at the higher levels are obviously more, you lose more the higher up the frequency ladder you are at the start.

ME: *O.K., so we have ten auric levels then with the last three (going up the levels) being more to do with communication with the rest of Spirit.*

SE: Spot on. Now you have that, so we can move on to the automatic reproduction development of the latest and densest of the human forms.

## Back to Human Reproduction

ME: *So we are going to talk about how we as human beings were developed.*

SE: Yes. When all of you discovered that you couldn't reproduce robustly by the cell division/separation method and the link with Spirit maintained at those levels caused energy disharmonies that spread to other spirits, you decided to try to keep any energy-based issues local to the incarnating spirit. Two major changes were made: 1) to make the human reproduction system work in a way that removed as many reproducing errors as possible; and 2) to remove the link to the rest of Spirit whilst incarnate.

ME: *But I thought that we are always linked to Spirit/the universe.*

SE: Indeed you are, so the best way for this link to be severed without actually removing the link is to make the spirit who is about to incarnate "lose its memory" of what reality is. In this way, it would come into the physical world with a clean sheet, with the exception of one or two rules set in place. These rules are the prompts that are set in place to help you achieve the experiences you want whilst in the physical levels. They are the driving force for your achievements whilst you are incarnate. They are your desire to be a doctor or a businessman, nurse or an architect, to live in a certain way, to succeed in a certain way, etc. With some of you, it is discovering who you really are whilst in the physical. A few of you even re-establish contact with your higher selves and some part of the rest of spirit. Interestingly enough, the forgetting rules are much easier to put in place because the lower levels of frequency are natural inhibitors to communication with that part of you that is connected to the whole because of the greatly reduced communication lines. This is, of course, what the Origin and the other Source Entities discovered in the early days of awareness.

ME: *So how did/do we create the forgetting?*

SE: It is done slowly during the initialization with the physical body, rather like your Alzheimer's but without the trauma. This is done when the fetus is growing in the womb; the link to the physical body is more "pliable" at this stage, allowing the spirit to come and go until the association is complete. The forgetting, although done in stages, is done in such a way so that residual memories don't come to the surface to give the spirit concern by thinking it has forgotten something but can't quite work out what. This is the trauma experienced by Alzheimer's sufferers. The forgetting is only current whilst the spirit is associated with a host body, so when the incarnation is complete, the forgetting is slowly removed. It is completed at a faster rate than the initial forgetting, again to stop any trauma associated with being suddenly bombarded with lots of communication data from all the different senses, including all the memories from past incarnations and experiences when fully connected to Spirit while in spirit. You would be in quite a spin if it happened instantaneously.

ME: *So what about reproduction of the human body? How did we get to the process we have today?*

SE: The method of reproduction you have currently was a bit of a compromise away from the original idea of having a body essentially replace itself with another or derive from itself by splitting itself in two cellularly. Remember, two major errors were being induced as a result of this method: 1) the errors due to the number of reproductions made at any one time (the detail of the body's cellular makeup being watered down in the splitting up of the cells); and 2) these errors worsening and multiplying with each reproduction of a particular body line. So the objective here was to reproduce by growth, growing a body to a known pattern that was free from errors.

ME: *You're saying we designed the perfect human?*

SE: That would be a reasonable assumption although this is not what we have today, as the body is affected by all sorts of things from reactions to diseases, to errors in matching the pattern for growth.

When the experimentation started, the idea was

for the body to grow its own replacement when it reached a certain point in its existence.

ME: *A hermaphrodite?!*

SE: Yes. It was decided to grow the replacement internally due to the vulnerability of the "fetus." As you well know, the fetus is totally unable to do anything for itself, which was totally unlike the previous design which was basically cloning itself as a readymade, ready-to-use human form. This one needed to be looked after for a good chunk of its life.

ME: *So if this was working, how come we have male and female bodies?*

SE: Because it didn't work anywhere nearly as well as it might have because the critical time period between birth and self-sustainability required a significant amount of attention from the host, as you know. Also, the host was particularly vulnerable during the separation (birth) of the replacement, even more so than today from the point of view of predators. Not that there were many in those days since most were in tune with the human species, rather than in fear of it. The main issue here was again in the carrying over of dysfunctional physical material. The problem was that a hermaphroditic reproductive system was basically copying itself in a similar but internal rather than external cell division system—one that started with a small reproduction of itself rather than a full-size reproduction. Therefore all the positive points about a particular body were reproduced, as well as all the negative points. Everything is copied, warts and all. The biggest problem surrounding the hermaphrodite is that one may be immune to a certain virus but another may not. So what we had was a whole bunch of bodies that would suddenly die out if a certain virus was aggressive enough to cause death, whereas a bunch of others would have survived. If these survived a particular virus, another group may well not survive. So what we had was not expansion of the human body, which was the whole point of the exercise. The exercise was to allow more spirits to experience life incarnate, or life in the lowest of the frequencies to allow them to evolve at a faster rate.

Eventually, it was decided to split the reproductive functions of the hermaphrodite into two pieces, a male piece and a female piece. Each piece would be introduced to a body that was designed to deal with each aspects of the job that the hermaphrodite did but in a separate sense. Each one would be allowed access to certain survival traits, *instincts,* and bodily functions that were pre-programmed into the body at a whole body level by spiritual communication to the body via the RNA to ensure that its function was automatic and did not need the intervention of the incarnate spirit. Although the spirit in its normal environment could have coped with some ease with the control of the human body at the molecular level, it would have taken a considerable amount of its concentration quota, as it is quite difficult to control lower frequency level material. Hence, the need for an automatic function.

ME: *So what else was necessary to make a male and female specific body? What made us decide on the method of reproduction we call intercourse?*

SE: The need for the different sexes was two-fold. First, the design of the body could be made simpler and, therefore, more robust from a functionality point of view. Second, the amount of energy needed to hold the "blueprint for creativity" could be shared between two bodies rather than one. This energy is what makes people attracted to each other from a male and female sense. If the two parts of the energy are compatible, i.e., they have the same basic content in terms of frequency and function, then they can reproduce safely without

184

the risk of dysfunction in the reproduction process. What's more, the replacement that is produced is also a simpler job as it only requires one half of the reproductive function to be copied and, therefore, could be reproduced faster and more accurately whilst in the host.

This was an essential change from a design point of view as this gave the opportunity for the positive parts of one body (certain immunities) to be included in the reproduced body, which might not carry the same positive points. The down side of this is that there may well be some negatives (susceptibilities) that are also carried across. However, these susceptibilities would be essentially watered down a bit, as they are being introduced into a body that may have some level of inherent protection against them and, therefore, cancel out the full effect of the negative being introduced.

ME: *So what made us develop the sex organs that we have today?*

SE: This was developed so that the pair of ingredients necessary to unlock the reproduction program to male half and the female half could be commenced in a safe place, one that was free from contamination from airborne infection.

It was also decided that this would be best located in one of the body types, preferably the body that would host the growth of the copy during the time of its critical stage of building. This stage, what you call gestation, is when the most important components of the body are created from the raw materials donated from the host body to create the copy, the replacement, the host for a new spiritual entity. These raw materials are not programmed to be anything other than neutral. This means that they are capable of being anything that they are told to be by the RNA. Each of the raw

185

materials is, for want of a better description, a piece of empty memory but memory with the ability to change itself into anything that it is told to be. When it receives messages from the spiritual energies intersecting the RNA, which then program the DNA, that part of the raw material that is the receiver of the messages is programmed to change into what it is required to be. The DNA then loses and/or relocates certain parts of itself to create the template for the raw material to form itself. This template is on two levels and is represented by two levels of the auric field in adult human beings, level 1 and level 5, one in the physical and one in the spiritual realms/dimensions. It is at this point that the gestation starts to expand and create the copy at its smallest level, the human embryo.

ME: *We have been through this before though.*

SE: Yes, we have, but as with many things in this dialogue, this is so important that it needs to be discussed again.

But let us continue with the reproduction of the human body. As I previously stated, it was found that the best place for the growth to occur was in the host of one of the fully grown human bodies, and that the ingredients for reproduction were to be stored in separate human bodies, these were classified as male and female. The sex organs were developed so that the transfer of the ingredients that were not of the host body, the ones that were to grow the replacement, could be transferred in a way that was safe from contamination, and that the percentage success rate would be at its best. This needed both bodies to be part of each other at the point in time when the opportunity for reproduction was optimal, one inserted inside the other—hence, the design of the sex organs, one fitting inside the other to allow the ingredients to mix and work together in a completely safe environment. As you know from other physical beings that transfer the second part of the ingredients external to the body, such as fish, this is not a guaranteed process. Thus, internal transfer was chosen based upon the analysis of success and a variety of methods, some of which are still used by lower physical entities but ultimately resulting in the use of the current method that human beings use to duplicate themselves.

ME: *Is it as successful as the previous methods? I get the impression that it is not. The other methods at least yielded one replacement for each "current" body being used for evolutionary growth, whereas this method yields one for every two.*

SE: Agreed, it is not the most effective method in terms of the number of host bodies reproduced but it is the most reliable at this point in time, specifically as this is the one that causes the least number of problems in the energetic realms. Essentially, everything is condensed around the one spirit in the one body with neither affecting anything else energetically but themselves in respect to dysfunctional energies.

ME: *So there are still some energies that affect other spirits?*

SE: Yes, but this is relative to the interaction of individual entities and is an energy type that needs to be worked upon to release once attracted. Sometimes this energy takes several incarnations into the physical to clear. The energy is related to something you humans call *karma*.

187

# Chapter 11:
# *Karma*

## Karma as Energy

ME:     *What!? Whoa, hold on here! Are you saying that karma is an energy. I thought it was just a list of issues that you have to work out.*

SE:     I take it you have finished with the evolution of physical human reproduction for the moment.

ME:     *Yes. No. Oh, I don't know!*

SE:     They are one and the same thing. The energy called "karma" is dysfunctional energy that is generated by the association of the spiritual with the physical. It is a natural process of energy attraction based upon dysfunctional interrelationships. This relationship can also be with oneself, from a spirit versus physical entity point of view. Earlier on, I stated that spirits who interacted with each other during the first stage of human beings caused their energies to go out of phase as a result of the sharing and the linking of bodies and spirit whilst incarnate in the less constrained human constructs. This caused individual spiritual entities to affect others in an energetically adverse manner. I did not give a name to this process but I have now, and it is one that you recognize. Surely you can see the link between what you know as karma and the little I have described about the interactions of the spiritual and physical energies and how it relates to the psychological?

ME:     *I am struggling a bit, but I can see some similarity. I just didn't expect it to crop up so early in the story line.*

SE:     Karma has always been in the story. It's just that we haven't named it nor have we focused on its name in this manner. We can go deeper with this subject if you want. Remember we have discussed this already.

ME: *If we must.*

SE: Yes, we must, as this viewpoint on karma is not so well known.

## Scripture Quotations and Karma

On a number of other occasions when I meditated—sometimes only power meditations of 3-5 minutes—there were sentences given to me that I can only describe as quotations from the 10 commandments. The first of these was *Desire not the riches of man but the riches of heaven!* This was given to me whilst I was feeling a bit left out when a colleague of mine was promoted. The second time was when I was admiring the shapely body of a young woman I was behind at work. *Covet not another's wife!* I asked the Origin about this occurrence (similar occurrences were also received by my wife quite independently) to see what the explanation was.

ME: *Why am I getting quotations of Scriptures that sound like they should be one of the Ten Commandments?*

O: Because you are starting to become. When you become, you start to remember the guidelines to a better life.

ME: *I thought that the commandments were rules to live by.*

O: They are not so much rules but guidelines that were/are given to all spirits that take on the burden of incarnation in order to evolve faster.

ME: *So what do they do for the evolving soul?*

O: They allow the soul the opportunity to incarnate and live in the physical world without the need to be affected by the penalties that can be accrued by not following them.

ME: *Are you saying that a spirit incarnate can go through life without collecting karma?*

O: Of course. But most of you are not able to live by these simple guidelines. If you were able to do so, then you would be able to live a life without the need to covet riches or others' belongings or commit crimes, no matter how small and, therefore, experience what you need to experience without getting bogged down with "getting even" or being better, having more than or bigger, or more expensive houses or cars, watches, etc.

ME:   *O.K. Today is more complicated than in Jesus' time.*

O:   Not so much than you would think.

ME:   *So how do we turn the other cheek?*

O:   By not getting draw into conflict.

ME:   *Does this mean arguing and hurting people verbally?*

O:   Of course, the individual has to recognize that there is a potential for conflict and avoid it.

ME:   *Even if it means losing face or looking stupid?*

O:   Of course. The key is to learn from the situation before it turns into conflict and then offer to end it by accepting the other's anger energy and, therefore, dissipating it. This is the true meaning of turning the other cheek.

ME:   *This is hard; people will think that you are weak.*

O:   Not if you accept the situation as a point of learning, a point of growth. When this is apparent (and it will be so very apparent), you will be held in significant light rather than in darkness. Remember, the greatest leaders the world has ever seen had great humility and knew when to learn from a situation rather than to turn it into conflict. No matter how small that conflict is, it still has the potential to attract karma points. The individuals who know these guidelines, know that all people they meet are other souls incarnate doing the best that they can with the limited amount of access to themselves and the universe. They, therefore, have pity and compassion for people who do them wrong rather than reacting in some way that builds up penalty points (karma).

ME:   *I experienced such an example of how dialogue*

191

*between two people can become confrontation the very next day at work. I didn't expect it and so was drawn in. Some part of me wanted to win the discussion/argument at all costs, and another just knew that it was pointless and later illustrated how the conversation and potential for confrontation could have been quashed in just a short sentence.*

O:     Yes, it was a good example.

## Another View of Karma

*ME:     Now you're going to confuse me and the rest of the world. First, my understanding of karma is that it is bad vibes that you accrue as a result of doing wrong to others or even treating them unfairly. Do unto others as you would have them do unto you! To remove bad karma, you have to perform unselfish acts of good for the benefit of others. Second, you tell me that karma is all about the gain or loss of evolutionary "points," and this is all about living in the best way possible so you do not lose these points. The best way to live was given to humankind by the Ten Commandments, which were the ideal way to live without losing these points—points lost need to be re-gained before evolution can be continued. Third, you tell me that karma is energy and not only that, it is dysfunctional energy that is the result of inharmonious spiritual/physical interaction. Which is correct?*

SE:     It is all correct. You said in the first instance that karma is bad vibes. Are vibes not frequency? Is frequency not associated with the resonance of energy, and is the resonance of energy associated with its position in the physical or the spiritual? The slower the resonance, the lower the frequency and the more sluggish is the action or reaction of the individual at that frequency. The faster the resonance and the higher the frequency, the more zestful is the action or reaction of the individual at that frequency.

In the second instance, you said that I mentioned that karma was evolutionary points that we need to keep whilst incarnate or risk being stuck at a certain level. Are not the evolutionary points the individual frequency levels? Consider the loss of a point like a drop from 1700 GHz to 1699 GHz—does this not represent a drop in the frequencies? Isn't the introduction of sluggishness a result of some interaction or other from your being attracted to a course of action that was not in the guidelines of the Ten Commandments for living the karma-free incarnate life?

And third, is not the "loss" of frequency a dysfunction of the use of energy? Remember that energy cannot be lost, so what happens to the energy that *is* lost as a result of your going down the frequencies? It becomes dysfunctional energy, energy with no correct or proper function. So our 1 GHz loss becomes dysfunctional energy with a 1 GHz frequency that is much lower than the frequency that you were and that you now are. Nevertheless, it has an effect on you as a spiritual entity. A 1 GHz loss has an effect that pulls you into a frequency that has no real function even though it is still associated with you. It slows you down and is a drag on your normal high level of function. It is like a weight on one of your ankles. It niggles at you, distracting your attention from the real issues at hand—that of evolving through the experience of things that are not available through the normal spiritual body.

ME:     *So karma is the accumulation of energy without function, energy which is ours anyway but has been removed from us as a result of some wrongdoing or other, some association with something pre-meditated that affects someone else adversely. This energy that is now without direction acts as a drag on my function purely because it is no longer working with me.*

SE: That's a reasonable summary of the function of karma.

*ME: So how do I get this karma energy back and working for me again?*

SE: That gets harder and harder the lower down the frequencies you drop as a result of being attracted to actions that are associated with its levels. It is difficult because the karma energy does not stick together like the normal energy you use. Instead, it stays associated with the action that caused its separation from the main energy source, you, in the first place. So you have two associations for this energy: you as the source and the action that resulted in its separation as the second. The second tries to draw you down the frequencies by making you do other things associated with this energy. The thing you did to cause the separation in the first place causes you to re-offend, so to speak, making the volume of the energy grow. This further augments the spiritual drag on your evolution.

So the antidote is to operate within the Ten Commandments again; do unto others as you would have them do unto you, an eye for an eye or a tooth for a tooth.

*ME: I thought that or "an eye for an eye, a tooth for a tooth" was an aggressive response.*

SE: That is just an uneducated interpretation. In essence it means the same as the "do unto others ..." routine. If you have caused the loss of an eye, you must give up an eye to recover the situation. If you wish to rise upwards through the frequencies and evolve faster, then you should only do unto others that which will cause their frequencies to rise and, therefore, cause them to evolve faster. This is, therefore, resolved in two ways. One allows someone to cause you the same level of "pain" by allowing them to do the same thing to you as you did to them or another spiritual entity.

ME: *I thought that this was specifically tied to the entity who received the wrongdoing.*

SE: No, there is no wrongdoing. There is just "doing," so by definition it can be recovered with the help of another spiritual entity so long as it is pre-conceived in spirit before the incarnation phase.

The second way of recovering the energy is to do "good" or to seek to be of service to the individual you rendered pain.

ME: *What! If there is no bad, how can there be good?!*

SE: Well put. By "good" I mean that you sacrifice yourself in some way that is related to the initial incident in favor of the spiritual entity that you had that incident with in the first place. This has the effect of canceling the disharmony/dysfunction which then causes the energy to remove itself, therefore, allowing it to return to its source, you. This causes you to rise upwards in the frequencies to a level equal to that lost in the first place.

## Recovering Lost Frequencies

ME: *This idea that energy is removed from you when you do something outside of the basic rules for existence in the physical is a completely different way of looking at things like karma.*

SE: It's the only way to look at it. In the physical realms of Earth, karma is not only understood as something negative but something that cannot really be avoided. It is also seen as something that can be put off to the next life, provided you believe that you will get a next life. This is what the Chinese thought, especially the rich and wealthy. Moreover, most people write it off as being too hard to recover from and, therefore, don't bother trying. The crux of the matter is that if you do try to recover lost frequencies (karma), then the rewards are even greater than if you do nothing or didn't accrue karma in the first place as you are "learning" during this process.

ME: *Hold on. Are you saying that you do better evolution-wise if you do someone some harm and then try to recover it? If that was the case, then every incarnate spirit would be doing as much harm as they could with the hope of recovering the situation to get more evolution brownie points.*

SE: Isn't that what people are doing now but without the knowledge of how to recover the situation? Is this not why there is so much turmoil in the world?

Spirits all over the physical universe are trying their best to evolve back to the Origin as fast as they can, and many of them are using the Earth environment to achieve this. The only issue here is that they are lured into doing wrong in the hopes that they can recover and, therefore, evolve faster. This results in them going further down the frequencies and losing their ability to recognize the way back up—meaning that they go even further down the frequencies since they are only remembering that which is associated with those frequencies: doing wrong to other entities. The loss of the higher frequencies is carried over with them when they return to Spirit, creating "drag." That is why they need help from other light workers who have remained in Spirit. In addition, they need to carry over this burden to the next incarnation for recovery.

ME: *Why is it carried over to the next incarnation? Why is it not cleared in Spirit?*

SE: Because of a universal rule. It states that lost frequencies can only be recovered at the frequency at which they were lost.

ME: *Why is this?*

SE: It's a bit like losing a penny on a footpath. The only way to find it is to retrace your steps. You can't find the penny where you discovered you lost it, and you can't find it by walking in the same direction you were going. You have to go back to the point on the footpath at which the loss occurred.

ME: *Is this not linear? I thought that linearity did not exist in Spirit.*

SE: It doesn't. But in the physical frequencies, it does, and because of this, a link is created between the spiritual entity and that frequency, including the event, where frequency was lost.

Of course, how you get back to the event is not linear because as an incarnating spirit, you can choose where and when you want to have the stage set up to recover the frequencies you have lost. You can even go back to that point in time where it happened whilst in the Earth realm and re-incarnate in a different or the same body. Both of these are difficult because of the forgetting factor, the temporary loss of higher self memories. As a result this method rarely pays off and as an incarnation to achieve a means to an end, it is a dreadful waste. There are instances, however, where it has and these are noticeable by profound "overnight" changes to the individual's personality and interaction with others in what you would call a positive way. They have "seen the light," so to speak.

ME: *Tell me more about how frequencies that are lost, karma, slow us down evolution-wise.*

SE: What do you want to know?

## The Physics of Karma

ME: *Hmm.... What will we understand?*

SE: Very little beyond what I have already said as your understanding is limited to your physics

ME: *Karma is based on physics?*

SE: Everything in these universes is based upon physics. Physics is basically the study of the physical through energy, and energy is what we are all composed of. By definition the study of energy is, therefore, a study of the spiritual via the energetic.

ME:   *So explain to me in physical terms this drag that losing frequency has upon a spirit and the attachment of the lost frequencies to the spirit.*

SE:   You have an example forming in your mind even as we speak, and the analogy is close enough to be correct.

Imagine a boat on the sea. This boat is in the air but traversing along the top of the water. The air, which has a higher frequency than water, can meet the water but not be submerged. Any air that is submerged comes to the surface because it is at a higher frequency. It can't naturally exist there. The boat is, therefore, traversing on the interface between two different realms of frequency. If the driver of the boat now throws a sea anchor overboard, which is still attached to the boat, the sea anchor slows the boat down without stopping it altogether unlike the anchor that grips the sea bed and stops it dead. The sea anchor is from a higher frequency, air, but it is in a lower frequency, water, and so it travels much slower than the boat, causing drag. It slows the boat down in its own frequency because part of it, which no longer exists in its natural frequency, is now in a lower frequency whilst still being attached to that part that is in the higher frequencies.

ME:   *So the spirit is the boat and the sea anchor is the karma slowing the speed at which the spirit can move.*

SE:   Yes, and the more karma, the bigger the sea anchor, and thus the slower the boat. What's more, the ability to rise above the surface of the water upwards in the frequencies is stopped dead as the sea anchor, although slowing movement down in the horizontal movement through the higher frequencies stops the vertical transition to higher frequencies totally until the situation is recovered.

ME:   *So you really have to sort out your karma as soon as you can.*

SE: Yes, and the reasons for this are as I have explained previously.

## AS YOU ATTRACT KARMA AND YOUR KARMA INCREASES,

## SO DOES YOUR ABILITY TO ATTRACT MORE KARMA

## WITHOUT TRYING TOO HARD!

*ME:* *Why is that?*

SE: Simply because you get used to being at lower frequency levels. Initially it is uncomfortable, but after time it becomes acceptable and then comfortable. Once you get comfortable at this level, you are in trouble, and you need help, outside help, to construct a workable plan to move upwards and out of the comfort zone associated with the lower frequency where you have found yourself.

You may have noticed that there are some people who are very motivated in their efforts to make achievements, spiritual and non-spiritual. These people are spirits who are trying to increase their frequencies and get closer to where they should be. They also get significant help from lightworkers to keep them on track. They generally appear very driven and single-minded in their approach and only want to do what they are doing. They are single-minded because they know this is their route to liberation from the lower frequencies caused by their constant addition of karma over consecutive incarnations. The issue here, however, is that some incarnates are so determined to succeed that they actually make their situation worse by riding rough shod over others to achieve what they want to achieve. This means that they, in their persistence to succeed, can actually fail.

ME: *So you can try too hard.*

SE: Yes, of course. You know yourself that sometimes you need to go backwards to go forwards. Trying too hard creates resistance in its own right. You can only go as fast as circumstances allow, and the correct circumstances are timed to perfection to be present at the right time and place for a reason.

ME: *That reason being we are ready to make the most of whatever the circumstance presented is.*

SE: Exactly.

ME: *We could write pages and pages on this subject.*

SE: You're right. We could write whole books on the subject, but why labor a point when you have hit the nail on the head in a few hundred words.

## The Drag on Evolution Caused by Lower Frequencies

ME: *Is there another way of describing this drag, one that gives an energetic illustration?*

SE: Imagine you are a ball of energy. This is, in fact, not far from what you really are. Now let's see that that ball of energy lower itself to a point where it is close to the interface of another frequency. The attraction to that frequency is such that you dip part of yourself into the lower frequency. In doing this, you find that part of you, that part that was used to probe the lower frequency, is stuck and cannot be moved out of this "lower level." As you make an effort to move away, the majority of your ball of energy does, in fact, move away, but the part of you in the lower frequency remains connected by a thin tendril. No matter how far away you try to move, you get drawn back towards the lower frequency. The tendril acts like a bungee rope so you can move only so far away without being pulled back. Your association with the lower frequency is maintained until you have extra energy to remove that part of you that is at the lower level. Imagine this like part of you is ice when the rest of you is water. To melt the ice, you need to have enough energy given to you to move the water to steam and the ice to water. Then when the energy given to create the steam is removed, the whole of you stays at the primary energetic level of the majority of you as a entity which, in this example, is water. Thus you can see that to achieve this, you need outside help, enough help to temporarily increase your frequencies to those above your normal position. This takes time to plan in order to get all the correct circumstances in the right place at the right time. It also requires the spirit concerned to be patient and follow the plan.

Another good example of a higher frequency being dragged down to a lower level is hail. Hail is the lower frequency component of a gas, air while rain is the lower frequency component of water. In this instance the higher frequencies of air are affected by lower frequencies to form clouds, which are on the interface frequency between a gas and the higher frequencies of a solid, water. Further external intervention can cause these clouds to lose energy and become water. Further intervention can cause the water to lose further energy, causing the water to tumble even further down the frequencies making it solidify into hail, ice. This ice is now two frequency levels below where it started and now needs a lot of external help from a higher frequency, heat, to help it on its way back up the frequencies to the level from which it started. This is all simple physics and has simple solutions. Unfortunately, it is not so simple for a spiritual entity to achieve, as this has to be done by itself but with gentle nudges in the right direction by its helpers.

ME:   *So how would you use tornados and hurricanes in this example?*

SE:   That is explained when whole groups of spiritual entities/souls get dragged down the frequencies all at the same time. They all affect each other and cause a cascade effect.

# Chapter 12:
## *Galaxies, Solar Systems, Planets, and Creation*

## Creating Earth's Known and Unknown Universe/s

ME: *O.K., we have talked about creating humanity, making humankind reproduce automatically, and creating karma, but we haven't yet talked about the universe as humans see it, here in the physical levels. How was the universe formed, including all the galaxies, solar systems and planets?*

SE: First, the universe that you exist in was created by Me as a direct copy of that part of the Origin you would call "void." Second, it is much more than you can possibly imagine for the universe where you exist is more in the spiritual realms than the physical.

ME: *If you had to put a percentage on it, what would it be?*

SE: Much less than 1%.

ME: *That's not a lot.*

SE: I'm being generous at that. You see, the amount of universe that protrudes into the physical is very little. It's the short end of the spectrum. Most entities just don't go there. It's a bore. It's slow. It's not really exciting, and you have to plan like hell to use it as an evolutionary platform. What's more, you can get stuck.

But . . .

The rewards can be great, and these rewards are why so many entities incarnate. They see it as a short cut. It is a big one, but as you know, it has its problems.

ME: *So why did You create the known universe?*

SE: And the unknown! The need to evolve Myself. Not to

203

mention to find out more about the Origin, which it is all about.

ME: *Hang on; You need to evolve as well?!*

SE: Yes, of course. That is one of the pre-cursors to being created by the Origin as an individual entity.

ME: *Here's me thinking that You twelve were being given free reign to do what You wanted with that part of the Origin that You had been given, but this appears not to be the case. You are governed by rules just the same as us!*

SE: Yes, to a smaller extent. We do have rules to follow as you do, but We can create more, and We do.

ME: *So what do You create?*

SE: Everything that is in the part of the Origin that is allotted to Me and My quest. I create the physical and the dimensional, the temporal and the instantaneous, entities that have collective existence, entities that have autonomous existence, entities that are in existence purely to do work in the physical as maintainers of the balance of existence, and entities that maintain the links between the dimensions and frequencies. I even create entities that look after these entities for Me, and others that in turn look after them. Even the planets and solar systems have entities looking after them, maintaining them, keeping the balance so that the physical experience is kept optimal.

## Reasons the Source Entity Created the Planets, Stars, and Solar Systems

ME: *So why did You create the physical universe with all of its planets, stars, and solar systems?*

SE: I created them to provide a multiple learning/ evolutionary environment for as many entities as possible to experience existence as much as possible, all at the same time. This is achieved in all the available dimensions and frequencies possible to maximize this work and enables the Origin to gather information about itself as fast as possible. The physical bodies that you call solar systems are entities in their own right. They experience life from a different perspective, the perspective of the slow moving, long existence side of the physical dimension while you are affected by the actions of others who use you as a habitation medium. This habitation is not necessarily true for all in the physical either. It can be in higher frequencies that are assigned to a particular planet or the dimensions that it also exists within. Some planets have several groups of entities living in/on the shelter of a planet at the same time with none of them being aware of each other's existence whilst others will co-exist with full knowledge of each other's' presence, and more still having a mixture of both. Your Earth is one of these mixed existence environments.

## The Names of Sentient Entities

*ME:*    *The Earth is said to have the name Gaia.*

SE:    Yes, this is the name it gave itself, one that could be recognized by all entities that shared its environment. All sentient entities give themselves a name, or something to be recognized by. This can be a frequency signature or a favorite form that is adopted when in communication with other entities. Others are simply recognized by their thought processes, but these are those entities that are close to the Origin.

*ME:*    *So all of the planets and stars in our physical universe have names.*

SE:    Yes, to a greater extent.

*ME:*    *Are these the names we would recognize? For instance, would the planet Jupiter be called Jupiter?*

SE:    No, that is a name that humans have given to it, but it, nevertheless, recognizes that it has a name given to it by humans for the use of humans to describe that part of its existence in the physical.

ME:     *So Jupiter exists in other dimensions as well.*

SE:     I would have thought that was obvious as the physical protrusion is gaseous in nature, but yes, it does, as do other planets and stars.

ME:     *So again, planets are sentient entities as well.*

SE:     Yes, they are. In general they are not as miniscule as yourselves in this physical environment. But there are planets that are on a much smaller physical level that operate in a similar way to the ones you recognize but also make up the fabric of physical space as well.

## The Fabric of Physical Space

ME:     *What do you mean when you say they "make up the fabric of physical space"? Are you talking about atoms, quarks, and lower sub-molecular constructs?*

SE:     I talk about the fact that there are whole galaxies, solar systems, and planets that are small, much smaller than the ones that you recognize as everyday planetary systems. These are entities/groups of entities with living beings existing on different levels of dimension and frequency either singularly or all at the same time, just as you are. They are also in existence in your physicality, but, as a result of their sizes, you bear them no heed as they don't show up so readily on your telescopes as "real" planetary systems. In essence, they tend to be together rather than separate though they present themselves as galaxies in the form of what you would call gas clouds or nebulae. They are whole civilizations on the micro level. These gas clouds/nebulae are literally teeming with life on all levels, from the highly intelligent to the benign, each being created as a result of My splitting Myself up.

You also mentioned atomic structure in your question. Was this with a view to asking if they also contained physical or energetic life?

ME:    *Yes, it was. It just seems possible that as physicists find smaller and smaller parts that make up atoms, they must go right down to miniature solar systems and planets.*

## A New Look at Gravity

SE:    I see your thought process, but this is not totally correct as everything is part of life. In this instance, they are, indeed, part of the framework of creation on both the physical and energetic levels. These lower levels of physicality are mainly in place to create the glue that holds the physical universe together. They provide a force that you call "gravity." Gravity is a poor description because it makes you think of one thing, the attraction of physical bodies, but in essence it is much more than that. Gravity is also a communication medium between the different frequencies and dimensions. In what you call "interstellar space." There is nothing but these small microscopic constructs or atoms, and these are used to communicate the form of the universe and how it moves in its environment. They both hold it together and, if you like, provide the communication channels from one part of it to another, instantaneously. Just as electrical messages are sent from one part of the human body to another to move a limb, so are messages via the force you call gravity, sent around the construct called the physical universe. The more important thing to note here is that this happens on all the frequency and dimensional levels as well; hence, gravity is a whole lot more than you are currently aware of.

Gravity is an interesting energy and one that is employed by many of the more highly evolved entities that exist in the physical. It can be used to manipulate the local space and allow access to other parts of the universe via the communication channels created by the

207

gravity network. This is achieved by converting the physical *objects* or energies into "gravitic" energies and converting them back again, thus, effecting a *travel* translation that allows translation from one side of the universe to the other, for example. This is not restricted to linear travel either as it can be used to move the physical out of the linear time frame, which encompasses the basic physical universe, and into another time frame of choice. As I have stated before, there is no such thing as time except in the minds of men, but it does provide a limited understanding of the concept of events in *existence* that is relative enough to be notable as points in time—time being spherically inter-dimensional as a limitation factor to the advanced entity but of no consequence to the highly evolved entity who exists at every level on every dimension simultaneously. Time has been created by men for men to enable them to try to understand the universe from their limited perspective. It has little use elsewhere and is at worst something that can be or must be manipulated.

## Physical or Energetic Life on Atoms??

This does not answer your question about atoms and whether or not there are civilizations of much smaller entities living on them like you live on planet Earth.

ME: *No, and I think I would like a definitive answer that I (and others who read this) can understand.*

SE: Mmmm, I see your problem. You are looking for a definitive answer where in reality there is none.

ME: *What?!*

SE: There is no definitive answer because everything that is, is changing, so what is definitive now, may not be definitive later.

ME: *You're talking in riddles. You are playing with me!*

SE:     Not in the slightest. That is not the point of this channeling. Just to give you a reference though, it is, of course, possible that energetic entities can link themselves to the tiniest of physical manifestations with the view to achieving some sort of greater understanding of what happens when they interact with such *particles*. It's just that it doesn't happen at this level at the moment. They may prefer to see how the interaction of several sub-particles influences a larger particle, just as you do in particle and sub-atomic physics, but they don't currently. Not because they can't, but because it is not important to them in the greater scheme of things. So to answer your question for the here and now, currently there is no life on atoms, electrons, quarks, etc.

## The Origin As Created and Creator

ME:     *O.K., so I need to get back to the creation of the universe and ask another question that has been nagging humankind for centuries. Is there anything that isn't created in the universe/s that we exist within? Is there anything that just is, was, will be in existence without first being created, made, or thought up?*

SE:     Everything that is, is created (by someone or something). Even the Origin is created. The Origin is creation given thought and form.

ME:     *Something created the Origin then?*

SE:     No, the Origin is creation.

ME:     *But you just said that "even the Origin is created"! This tells me that the Origin had a creator to create it in the first place. Now I am confused!*

SE:     The Origin is created and creation as one. To be created does not mean that you must first have a creator. This is thinking in the tense of the human condition, that there is a start and a finish, a beginning and an end, an up and a down, a left and a right, an upper and lower

209

frequency, an upper and lower dimension. Everything that is, exists at the same time. Is this still such a hard concept for you to follow?

ME: *Give me some latitude here so that I can understand once and for all.*

SE: In essence, the Origin was created and creates itself all at that same time. It is continually improving the way It was created and how It creates in order to better Itself and everything that is part of it. To do this well, It needs to also understand Itself better, hence the creation of the twelve source entities.

ME: *If it is continually re-creating Itself, It must re-create us as well. This means that It must un-create to re-create and, therefore, in the process of changing what was once created, It must destroy it. What I am getting to here is that we as individuals must be continually changing as a result of this, and, therefore, everything that I remember must be different to what I previously remembered, i.e., one moment I exist, the next I don't, the next I do, but in another form in another environment.*

SE: This is not the case. If it was, then there would be no "comparator" and, therefore, no method of comparison, nothing to compare the improvement with. To this end, the Origin granted the twelve and what They create, immunity from change created by the Origin. Lessons learnt and discoveries made by Us and Our creations are also experienced by the Origin. They are used to affect changes to Itself. There are some subtle changes that affect Us but none that affect Our individuality and knowledge that is, has, and will be accumulated because they are only allowed to take place once the previous condition has been fully experienced by the Origin and recorded for prosperity.

ME: *You mean the memory of the Origin.*

SE: Not quite. You see, if the Origin had a memory in the style that you know as humans, when It changed or reinvented Itself, It may well have lost what It experienced in the past, present, and future of the specific NOW as a result of changing Itself into Its new self, therefore, creating a new NOW. Like Us, the Origin is trying to experience as much as it can, in as many ways as it can. In doing so, It placed part of Itself outside of the churn of change so that nothing could be lost or forgotten. The Origin basically stores all of Its possibilities, including what the other FREE and independent parts of Itself experience, in a single place in a single area of records.

# Chapter 13:
## *On the Outside*

## The Peace of Going Within Before Going into the World

*ME:*    *In some of my earlier dialogues with you, I have needed to count my way up to a certain level of energy before I could talk with you or the Origin. I now find that I don't need to do this for this type of dialogue but have found consolation in going there recently, especially as I haven't been there for some time. In fact, not since the direct line of communication was apparent.*

*With all of the heavy distractions that I am experiencing at work and home at the moment, I find it quite consoling to raise my energies to that level every morning before I go to work. I like going up to the top frequencies where I go through to the top of the universe and out into the God energies.*

*When I do this, I actually feel that I am becoming lighter, thinner, faster, and more coherent. I feel that I rise out of the fuzzy darkness and move into real jet black darkness before breaking out into the brilliant white light.*

*What is interesting though is that the jet black also feels high in energy and is similar to that of the energy of the white light. When I am in the black, I feel like I am on the outside of a sphere looking at a perfect set of stars, each having perfect intelligence. I feel that I know them, I have always known them, and, that they have always known me. Then when I rotate myself out of the black, I feel that I am everywhere and nowhere all at the same time, that I am all there is and all there is, is me.*

SE: This is wonderful, for you are at the very start of your enlightenment.

The black area you refer to as being "jet black" is the universe that I have created for all of you to evolve within. This is your universe in all its "multi-frequencied," multi-dimensional, multifaceted grandeur. You are on the outside, the very edge, the boundary of the known and unknown universe. This is it—all there is, all there ever will be, all there ever was, all there ever can be.

The perfect stars that you see are the guardians of the universe. Those spirits who have chosen to dedicate themselves to the maintenance of the universe in every way, right down to the lowest frequencies and up to the largest galaxy within the largest universe within this universe.

## Earth—A Universe Within a Universe

*ME:* *You mean we are in a universe within a universe?*

SE: But of course. Does a multiverse not need to be contained in some way, if not for the sake of being tidy? Hence, the spherical shape that you have experienced. Each universe and each galaxy has a job to do in the greater scheme of things. The perfect stars or spirits are perfect because they have reached the highest level of attainment an individualized spirit can reach. Some of these have visited your planet in your frequency. A few have even walked amongst you at your lowest level trying to help you raise your game in the frequency stakes. They, like Me, experience everything that you experience, know all that you ever knew and will ever know and are with you every second of the day and night. Everything you do is known and experienced whether it is in the physical or in the energetic. These spirits are the recorders, the promoters, the recommenders, the changers, the

214

maintainers of the physical and energetic universe. They are forever changing the environment in the most subtle ways possible to increase the efficiency of the universe and its opportunity for promoting evolution of the individualized energy, the spirit.

## The Origin, the White Light

ME: *So what about the white light?*

SE: That is simple. That is the Origin, God, or whatever fashion you want to call it. The Origin is best as it was the Original recognition of self within the vast area of energy that is the great All. It is not surprising that you felt you were part of the All when your consciousness penetrated that area, for it is what you are truly, part of the all. Everyone and everything is part of the all and to be part of this on a level of the lowest consciousness, that which you experience in the Earth plane, is the most exciting of all for this is when you, at your lowest ebb are at last aware. You are aware that you are whole and that you are part of something much, much bigger than that small part of you that is sectioned off to experience the lowest frequencies.

In your newly re-discovered ability to sit at the table of God, in His light, you are well on your way. All you have to do is let His light fully into your life and be truly one with God, for this, in essence is your true heart's desire. This does not mean that you need to join a church, become a Christian, a Muslim or a Buddhist, for these are man's inventions. They are graven images to be worshipped by the gullible, by the weak of mind. They tell of the truth but do not allow you to be in the truth, for they are developed, although with a bit of truth to entice, outside of the truth for the benefit of men who seek power over men and not over themselves.

## Life on Other Planets

ME: *From my previous dialogue with You, I am aware that humanity is part of the greater picture and is, when disincarnate, able to travel the universes and their frequencies. I also know that there is obviously life of the energetic and physical all over the universe as well. But what about those planets close to Earth? Do they have physical life that we have not yet been able to detect? Or . . .*

*Are we as an incarnate race pretty much alone?*

SE: First, you are never alone for the Origin and I are always with you, all of you, all at the same time. Second, life is not specifically physical in nature. So when you say *incarnate life,* that can also include physicality that is semi-energetic, gaseous and liquid in nature. There are also other forms of life that are incarnate that are made of substances that are not yet recognized by humankind but are nevertheless incarnate in function and existence.

I can see you frowning so I will elaborate. Anybody that is able to accept as a host an energetic entity, call it a "spirit" if you want, allows incarnation. Don't forget that the word incarnate is a Latin word and literally means "in the meat." It is a very old word and was used as a bit of joke on Earth by those who first inserted a portion of their energetic self into a vehicle that was best suited to the frequencies of the environment that they wanted to experience. At first the bodies used in the Earth sphere were of a higher frequency, much higher than they are today. As a result they still afforded the energetic entity or spirit the communication it required to maintain contact with the rest of itself and the rest of energetic intelligence throughout the universe I created. With the human vehicle being at this level of frequency, it was more akin to the gaseous nature that exists in and around other planets and allowed longer life and easier movement when long distances were to be travelled.

## Jupiter and Ganymede

I am telling you this as a prelude to what is currently happening in and around the spherical bodies you call "planets" in your own solar system or local universe. Almost all of the planets in your solar system have either supported or continue to support the opportunity to play host to spirits who wish to incarnate into a body that is best suited to experience the predominant environment that a particular planet affords. As you can imagine, Jupiter is a very good host for gaseous bodies and currently hosts over a million entities experiencing life in the magneto gaseous condition. The entities in the gaseous environments of Jupiter like to manipulate the local magnetic forces to create structures for them to gravitate around and art forms for their enjoyment. They have even been known to create planets out of the materials available with certain magnetic properties. Ganymede is one of those planets created for fun and experience. I know you call it a moon, but it was originally created to be a planet in its own right.

## Mars

Mars is good at offering life experience in the mineral biased and atomic level conditions. Mars is good for its contemplative properties as the interaction with the planet in this incarnate condition is, as you can imagine, at a drastically reduced level. However, it does allow the entity to travel around the planet by transferring the intelligence of the entity from one mineral to another, allowing the entity to travel through the rock at an impressive speed. The entities on Mars enjoy playing games and revel in one you might call mineral pinball. They do this by making themselves the pinball itself, by making their energetic level impervious to certain minerals as they speed along making them bounce off the one that they are impervious to. The crystalline is best for them travel-wise as its straight structures allows direct movement, whereas other minerals afford a more "country lane" method of getting from A to B as they bounce off the impurities that are inherent in the rock they exist in. They don't create areas for habitation because they use the whole planet as their environment, not just the surface as humanity on Earth does.

## Venus

Venus offers a mixture of both gaseous and liquid-based incarnation opportunities with both playing host to a couple of 100,000 entities that want to experience life at the frequencies that allow life to occur at these elementary levels. They enjoy the changes in morphology they experience by mixing the gaseous and the liquid together at different dimensional levels as well as frequencies. They create structures out of gas, ice, and liquid by using the magnetic properties inherent with these physical materials, giving them memory so that they can change the shape based upon the time of day or the mood they feel. They have games where they try to get as many structures out of a certain mixture of liquids and gases as they can in a finite time period. They enjoy the variation in structural art that they create as a result.

## In the Heart of Earth's Sun

As with atomic levels of experience being enjoyed by the entities in the Jupiter sphere, so are well over a billion souls enjoying being in the heart of your local star, the Sun. Here they experience what they can do on an atomic and sub-atomic level by mixing the physical atoms with time-, magnetic-, gravity- and frequency-based modifications. They particularly enjoy making elements in this environment that are not native to the Sun and its solar system at this frequency. In addition, they delight in the properties that these new materials could offer a fully physical incarnate entity, such as those on Earth. In fact, these entities are in constant communication with incarnate entities on Earth that are able to understand some of the concepts used to create these new elements that allow them to be re-created in the Earth sphere.

## Other Entities in Earth's Solar System

ME:   *So there are lots of entities in our solar system?*

SE:   There are many others that I haven't mentioned, for every one of the planets that revolves around your sun has some form of entity associated with it.

ME:   *Why is that? Is it because they all have a job to do relative to that planet?*

SE:   Bingo! Yes, it is. But it's more than that. You see, all entities have a role to play in the evolution of themselves and the gathering of knowledge via personal experience. This, as I have stated before, is to help accelerate the Origin's learning about Itself in every way possible. The payoff to the individual entity is that each is given singularity and individual thought to be able to achieve this goal. The opportunity for these particular entities is to learn what it means to attend to the needs of the larger entities that you call planets. Each of these planets has a role to play in the local universe—one that has an effect on many frequency/dimensional levels all at the same time and as a result needs the help of other smaller entities.

Planets provide much in the physical and dimensional universe. First, they provide stability from a gravimetric point of view and a focal point for "loose" matter to coalesce and clean up the physical side of the locale. Second, they provide a locale for entities to work within. Third, they provide a common cause for those entities to work with. Working together for a common cause in the name of the Origin is the most important thing an entity can do in the universe. Fourth, they provide substance for the larger universe since the universe is a being in its own right. Whereas the planets are the substance for the universe, the entities that work on, in, and with the planets tend to the balancing needs of that planet. Essentially they groom and fine tune or make adjustments to the functionality of the planet at every level, ensuring that it functions at peak performance.

## Neptune's Function and Entities

For instance, the entities that are associated with the planet Neptune work on the dimensional and frequency shifts that are necessary to keep the mass of the planet together. The function of Neptune is the attraction and storage of gamma radiation. Keeping such radiation under control is essential to this solar system because it specifically helps maintain the good physical health of the vehicles you call human beings. Without Neptune storing and processing the stray gamma radiation in this area, the physical side of the human entity would dissolve since gamma radiation affects the communication between the DNA and the cellular structure of the body, and, therefore, its desire to maintain cohesion.

## Uranus's Functions

Uranus performs a similar function but with a similar form of energy that is destructive to other physical life forms on the Earth, specifically those who synthesize energy from the particles responsible for illumination in the physical dimensions. This energy is not yet known to humankind and as such should stay unknown because it would provide a formidable weapon resulting in the ruination of crops and forestry.

ME: *So are these entities in Neptune more or less advanced than energetic humanity?*

SE: They are both. Such as is the combination of beings that are in and around the Earth sphere. There are many entities that are associated with Earth as I have stated in previous dialogue. They are classed as nature spirits, animals, plants, and, of course, humans.

ME: *What is the job of Pluto and Mercury? What role do they play in the stability of the solar system and ultimately, I guess, the universe? And what about the entities who work with them?*

## Mercury's Functions and Entities

SE: Let's deal with Mercury first as its closest to the sun. Your scientists have noticed that Mercury, like your moon, always has one side facing the sun. This is an intentional action by the entities that are working with Mercury to establish a balance in environmental conditions that is only possible at the cusp of the hot and cold sections of the planet, the light and dark sides, if you wish. In this "band" around the circumference of the planet exists a special kind of environment that allows the mixing of certain minerals and gases, each of which are not able to be achieved in their native environments of the hot (light) and cold (dark) sides of the planet. This area provides the most unique opportunity for a form of physical life to exist. Thereby, it allows an energetic entity to "incarnate" into a physical form that is not only compatible with the frequencies of this planet but also able to work at its lowest level without destruction due to the extremes of either side. The entities, if you were to see them, would appear to be bubble-like shapes with sensory organs covering the whole of the outside of the "skin" of the bubble. They manipulate the materials around them by using their normal energetic functions of what you call telekinesis as they work directly with the materials at the energetic level. By manipulating the properties of the atomic structures of certain materials that are created within this band, they are able to make the planet locally heavy, which is the way they make the planet face the sun in a non-rotational orbit. Literally, the heavy ring around the periphery of the planet is attracted in preference to the rest of the planet's mass, stopping its normal rotation dead in its tracks.

## Pluto's Functions and Entities

Pluto offers opportunities that most other planets could not, purely because its position is away from the central source of heat, the sun. The entities that work with planets are specifically involved with the ice-based intelligence that exists in the permafrost that surrounds the planet. This intelligence is, of course, linked to the Origin, as all intelligence is, and as a result, it has an energy all of its own in order to exist. There is an interesting correlation with the mineral-based entities that exist on Mars, insomuch as the ice-based intelligence exists within the solid ice only and avoids the more liquid states that the ice sometimes achieves. Even though this liquid ice is something akin to helium or carbon dioxide in essence, it is not and can be better described as a variant of the rarer airborne gases in the Earth's atmosphere, such as argon, krypton, neon, etc. Hence, its white-like appearance even though there is not much light that far out from the sun's natural illumination properties. Ironically, the planet's job in this solar system is to provide warmth for those entities that exist in lower temperatures in and around the outer reaches of the solar system. It acts as a sort of beacon or lighthouse to space-faring entities who are looking to visit this solar system, as it provides an energy that is detectable long distances away as a result of its mixture of so-called rare gaseous elements at super low temperatures.

In essence the entities are the same as you. They are energy-based beings, and they have a place in the workings of the universe the same as you do. They also aim to evolve over time and experience life in as many different ways as they can in order to give the experience they have back to the Origin.

## Sentient and Communicative Planets

ME:  *So what do they experience? It must be significantly different to what human beings experience.*

SE:  It is certainly very different and this is the point; they experience different things than other entities, things in ways that could never be experienced by an entity in a smaller body.

Planets are not just lumps of rock and gas. They are totally sentient in their own right, and they have an incarnate "life span" the same as incarnate humanity does. As with humanity, each entity is able to do whatever it wants as it is one with the universe in every way. However, unlike incarnate humanity, they do not lose their contact with their higher selves because they are more integrated into the system of the universe and are not independent on the structure.

ME:  *So planets are entities that are part of the structure of the universe.*

SE:  In a way yes, a living part of the structure. As you are aware, they have an attractive force you call "gravity," and this is one of the ways that the local parts of the universe are maintained spatially. It also allows the migration of smaller parts of the universe, as the gravity that is produced by the planets is given direction and force. It is not, as you think, spherical to the planet. Each planet can create gravity in any form it likes, and the methods that it uses are relevant to the job it needs to do. For instance, gravity is a function of universal love, and as part of universal love, it has natural attraction. It is the attractive properties that planets use to hold things together from an energetic and physical perspective. It is also used as a communication medium between the planets and suns themselves.

## Gravity as Planetary "Telepathy"

*ME:*   *How do they do that? By pulsing the gravity or by making waves of some kind?*

SE:   Not a bad guess although you're not guessing in totality since you are picking up the information from the universe as we speak. You are dual channeling. Well done, the more work like this you do, the more open to your real capacity you become as you start to open channels of communication that you previously did not use as an incarnate human.

Gravity is not what you think it is, for as a part of the universal love. It is similar in nature to what you would call "telepathy" for it operates in these frequencies, for want of a better word. If you could see the gravity beams spread out with your physical eyes, they would look like a lattice connecting the planets together. The communication between them looks like red/pink flashes that change shape, speed, hue, coalescence, and direction. Communication is instantaneous as the beams are interconnected on many, many levels all at the same time with time having no influence because it doesn't exist and is a result of the level of interconnectivity. Of course, the visual aspects of what I have just described are only one aspect of phenomena that is associated with communication between the entities called planets; communication occurs on as many levels as there are interconnections. The rest are emotional levels of sorts where communication is in feelings gained as a result of experiencing different things on different levels.

## Planet Earth's Love for Humanity

The planets consider the smaller entities that exist within their environments as brothers but are sometimes confused in the way they treat their host, especially the humans. With the way that humanity is treating Earth currently, it is possible to consider humans as a virus, killing Earth with pollution. This pollution is unnecessary for the evolution of the human species but is a necessary learning curve for the current species to go through to understand the problem that pollution causes to the physical manifestation of the planetary being where their physicality exists and the overall effect that they have on themselves by destroying the very environment that was created in perfection for their progression. Even with this misuse of itself, Earth loves all of humanity with all its might.

Don't think that the work of the planets is just at the macro level that you perceive them to be, for whatever they do on the macro affects the micro level as well. This is duplicated on many levels of size that are both too small and too big for humankind's current level of science to recognize. There is size, dimension, and frequency involved in this universe, and all are the playground of the evolving entity. Whatever the planets do in this size is mirrored in the micro-verse. Whatever is done by the planets in the larger macro-verse is mirrored in the minor-verse where you currently exist. Although I have mentioned but three sizes of universes, there are, in effect, many in-between them, each

225

providing an opportunity for the entity to evolve in some way. More importantly, the size of the dimension changes its characteristics and, therefore, increases the opportunity for more entities to incarnate and evolve by experiencing different things.

## The Limitless Universe and Evolution

*ME:*    *I thought that if the size of the universe was smaller, it would be limited by the size of the atoms and molecular structure of where we are now.*

SE:      No, this is a common mistake that scientists make. They base everything on the universe that they exist within and use that as their datum. This is not the case because the universe is not limited by size in a 3-dimensional way; in fact, it is not limited at all.

You see, the physical size of molecules is not appropriate in the construction of objects. Consider your bricks. They might be small in size but together they can build huge buildings. This you can see and understand very easily, and in your minds you give no limitation to how big the building might be simply because you are going from small to big. However, when you go from big to small you are constrained by what you have discovered. The smallest thing that you have discovered to date is the components of the atom you call quarks, such as up, down, top and bottom. You think that these components are the smallest in the universe, but this is not the case. Although energy is without form, it can create objects that are many magnitudes smaller without limits. In fact, there are whole universes that occupy the space of a quark and smaller particles also provide the same opportunities. In this way, an entity can experience many existences within the same physical spaces but at differing sizes, so to speak. In essence, this expands the opportunity for physical incarnation. Also, the interspacing of frequencies between these smaller molecules allows the use of the same base level of molecule used in different dimensions. For instance, you could have ten molecules close to each other but with each one supporting a different dimension. This means that the so-called physical is interacted by different frequencies and, therefore, different dimensions, which ultimately means that a particular solid or physical object is not only part of the universe or dimension that we see it in, but it is also a part of many others at the same time.

I can see that you are struggling with this a bit, so I will explain it in terms that you, as an engineer, will understand. Consider an object in a Computer Aided Engineering (CAE) environment; it is a whole object that is built up of many layers. Each layer represents a certain level of conformity, convention, or function. All these layers not only create the whole object if allowed to be together, but they can be separated out from the whole to create a separate object, an object that exists in its own right but only on one level. Now if you consider the possibility of having parts of that object on that one level also containing parts that are on different levels as well, parts that on their own are meaningless and are without individual function, then you start to see the interconnectedness of the greater object and, therefore, the ability to use that same object on different levels at the same time. This is how the dimensions work. The different levels are the frequencies that separate out into the dimensions. Now, if you consider that the higher the frequency, the smaller the object can be, then you can now appreciate that objects and even whole universes can be much, much smaller than you can ever imagine. This is not to say that it is a rule that the higher the frequency, the smaller the underlying physicality of a universe because a universe of the same size as your current one

227

can also be extremely high. There is no boundary or rule to this; it is entirely dependent on the Source Entity for a particular environment on how it is constructed. I merely comment on the environment I constructed.

ME: *If I read between the lines, what you are saying is that the planets that we know could not only be energy beings in their own right but could also be the smaller part of a larger object or be the larger whole of trillions upon trillions of smaller objects. Not only that, it could exist on many different levels or frequencies all at the same time.*

SE: That is about the size of it.

ME: *So how small can an entity go before it can't be an integral part of a collection of interlaced, multi-dimensional, multi-frequencied physical objects?*

SE: There is no limit. All size issues are based upon the evolutionary level of that individual entity simply because it is a self-defeating thought process. The entity is truly in its rights to not advertise this, as it would create self-doubt. Let Me stress here that self-doubt is only manifested and, therefore, prevalent in the physical. It has no place in the spiritual or even the higher frequencies of the physical since they are close to the spiritual frequencies in nature, and at this level entities know who and what they truly are.

ME: *So are there different spiritual entities for the different sizes of planets or physical entities? What I mean to say, are there limits on the type of spiritual entity to the point that they can only incarnate into a certain size of physicality?*

SE: There is no such limitation, for it is the right of the entity to manipulate its own environment to experience what it want to experience. Suffice to say, there is little difference between the sizes and the evolutionary opportunities that they present from the planetary perspective. There *are* some significant differences from the biological entities' points of view, for they are

228

able to access much finer energies whilst incarnate in these much smaller dimensional/ universal environments. Planetary experience is all about working with the larger points of function within a specific universe. It is not about working on the self although the self does gain from such an experience. Those in the planetary incarnation are working on maintaining the integrity of the very fabric of the universe. They are working specifically for the whole in a wholly selfless manner. This level of service is also seen by entities incarnating in the flesh who think not of themselves but only of the welfare of other incarnates around them. In doing so, they afford themselves access to the greater God (good); they lose all self-doubt in the process and, as a result, accelerate their own progression. This is how the entities who incarnate as planets progress; they only do it for the greater good and not knowingly or meaningfully for their own progression although they, nevertheless, do progress, which is a rightful function of the work they do for, in your particular instance, humanity.

## The Functions and Entities of Nebulae

ME: *You have told me that planets are incarnate entities and so are suns, but what about other universal phenomena, such as nebulae. Are they incarnate in some way?*

SE: No, nebulae are stray matter, coalescent energy that has not been put to use yet. This type of energy can and is used to create planetary systems and other physical and nonphysical objects used for maintenance of the universe. Nebulae do, of course, house many entities who wish to experience the associated energies.

There are entities that have dedicated some part of their existence in helping maintain the universe, and part of that is the "rounding up" of this stray matter and moving it to a convenient location for future use, thus creating what you see as nebulae.

Although this matter has no form or direction, it can be given form and direction by a highly evolved individual giving it intelligence and independent thought. In essence, if that individual wishes, it can give part of itself to energetically create another. This creates an entity that has matter and energy but no form.

ME: *Does it have free will like we do?*

SE: Not at that point of its existence as it is still newly born and in need of direction. It will eventually be capable of individual creativity with its own matter and, therefore, form as it gains more experience. One of its primary goals is to give itself more substance, especially if it is given the opportunity to become a planet or other denser body. In doing so, this newly formed entity performs a vital function for the universe by cleaning up more stray matter, by attracting it to itself, in turn giving it form and direction and the intelligence that it is creating for itself. This is very important as there are many opportunities for evolution in the universe, and the more parts of the universe that can experience evolution, the more the Origin experiences. In essence, the function of this type of entity is to both perform a sort of janitorial role, sweeping up matter that has no direction or cause and at the same time giving it the opportunity to experience that which it is part of—the universe—by being part of a smaller collection of particles and energy that is given intelligence.

ME: *How far can these entities evolve?*

SE: The sky is the limit, so to speak. Evolution has no limitations, and an entity can, over time, go from the very bottom of the evolutionary ladder to the very top of its capability. I see that you are frowning, so I will explain further. In our earlier discussions, I described my creation of this set of universes and of your selves as individual entities via my own separation and division. Some of the entities, those on the edge of my attention during the time of creation, were not endowed with the same qualities as those in the center of my attention; thus, their abilities as individual entities were limited to the level of qualities they received. In essence, they can achieve anything they want within the boundaries set by their qualities. Do not get Me wrong; they are not any lesser entities than those entities who were in my full attention during my period of creation. All are equal in the eyes of God and both Myself and the Origin love all that We have created. When I create, the Origin creates; when you create, both the Origin and I create, for all is together in creation.

## Human Incarnation of Animals and Planets

*ME:* *In a previous dialogue, we discussed the possibility of animal-based entities gaining so much evolution that they could, if they desired and in rare circumstances, cross over to the human levels. Is this possible for these entities of differing qualities to also progress to human levels?*

SE: No. As you said, it is only in very rare circumstances that an animal-based entity is able to progress to this higher level, and this is achieved by the considerable dedication of that entity to the human entity and the constant reciprocal love of the two over a significant period. We are talking hundreds of millennia here with the connection between the two or three being unbroken. Even though the animal may incarnate and live in the protection of another's household, working with another human entity, the link with the former must not be broken to achieve this level of evolutionary jump.

In the case of planetary entities, there is not the closeness of the energy type or the evolutionary function to allow the jump from planetary entity to human entity. Of course, they gain from the interaction they have with different levels of entities, and they evolve in their own way as a result. It's just that they are such a completely different species in so many different ways than the human that it makes an evolutionary crossover impossible. To be honest, it is also not in my plans to have this opportunity available between such differing levels of entities, for I have seen the beauty in the order that has resulted in the creation of this universe. The total opportunity for universe-wide holistic experience can only be achieved at different levels simultaneously with the differentiation that has resulted from this creation. In this sense, the universe is perfect and so is each and every entity that works within it. I have no desire to modify this perfect universe, for to do so would make it less perfect to achieve the role that it was created for. I created a universe to achieve a goal and sent the creative thought out to the Origin and Me to create it. The thought was pure, the response was pure, and the creation was pure; therefore, the created are pure. I will not change that which is created from purity of mind and thought.

# Chapter 14:
## *Other Major Civilizations on Earth*

### Defining a Major Civilization

During my dialogues with the Source Entity, I broached the subject of other major civilizations on Earth other than human beings. I expected these to be dolphins, but I was taken in a completely different direction.

ME:    *So you ARE saying that there is more than one major civilization. What is the definition of a major civilization?*

SE:    One that knows the Origin and Me.

ME:    *Anything else? Technology, for example?*

SE:    Technology is not a good sign of a major civilization. I am aware that humans think in these terms, but this is irrelevant. Technology has been the downfall of many civilizations that could have been great.

ME:    *So* what *is the mark of a great civilization?*

SE:    One that is in tune with the universe. This may seem a bit strange to most people, but this is the real mark of a great civilization. These are incarnates that are both working within the confines of nature and knowingly working with Me to evolve. They are more significant than the major civilizations because they are more aware and are in constant communication with themselves, and, of course, Me. Before you ask the question about being in constant contact with themselves, let me ask you a question. What does this mean?

ME:    *I was about to ask You this.*

SE:    That is why I interjected.

ME:  *Hmm, I would say that being in contact with themselves is pretty obvious as this relates to contact with the higher self and with the rest of their civilization.*

SE:  Good. You see it is not really good enough to just be in contact with yourself, as you yourself are insular and isolated even though you are aware that there is a greater reality and are able to communicate with Me and the Origin. With the really great civilizations, they are in contact with the rest of those who are incarnate, as well as themselves. In essence, they are coadunate but separate. They know what to do individually for the good of the rest. They are not out to do the best for themselves and only themselves as most incarnates on the Earth at the present time are doing. They are all working together to help each other with their experiences and help each other evolve. Everything in this subject is to be done together for the good of the whole, not the individual. This is the mark of a great civilization.

## The Om, a Great Civilization as an Object of Focus with Earth

ME:  *Have there been any really great civilizations on Earth?*

SE:  One. But that civilization is neither resident in this dimension nor is it still fully associated with Earth as an object of focus.

ME:  *What do you mean by "an object of focus"?*

SE:  Home.

ME:  *So where are they now?*

SE:  In a different frequency/dimension and living freely within the universe. You are part of them; they are called the Om! They have outgrown the need to be part of the lower frequencies and work together to maintain this specific universe for the good of all the incarnates, including Me.

234

ME:    *I am part of them! If I am truly part of them, why am I here incarnate in these lower frequencies? Have I been expelled?*

SE:    Far from it. You and a number of others chose to spend a number of incarnations to help those entities who have only just started to incarnate as a means of accelerating their own evolution. They are all trying it together. They are all trying to make the human race a great civilization, but it is taking time.

ME:    *Quite a lot of time from what I can see. The world is in total disarray and disharmony.*

SE:    It appears to be worse than it is from your perspective, but don't forget that I can see everything. I can see where everything is going, including the contributions that you are all making to help make it happen.

ME:    *That sounds nice.*

SE:    It is.

ME:    *So what about the one civilization that is great that came from Earth?*

SE:    They didn't come from Earth. They came from Me just the same as you came from Me.

ME:    *But what did they do?*

## A Civilization That Created Heaven on Earth

SE:    They created heaven on Earth. Everyone worked together in harmony without conflict. They saw areas of improvement from a natural point of view and worked together with nature to make those changes. Nature is that part of Me that is assigned to maintaining the physical universe. Everything they did was aimed at improving their collective situation, that situation being one of physicality. They understood that the best evolutionary way forward was to work together with the universal rules on evolution in the physical. We have already spoken about—the rules for not incurring karma or evolutionary loss of frequency that results in

235

one's being stuck in the physical planes. This problem, I have to say, was very rare indeed with this civilization. They were both very aware and lucky enough to have started to incarnate when the frequencies of Earth and the surrounding universe were very high. Nevertheless, the risks were just as high in terms of being caught in the traps of the physical world.

ME: *You're not being very succinct here. This civilization seems to be of paramount importance to the evolution and experience of the individual and the Origin, as well as Yourself. Yet You are not telling me what they achieved technologically. Did they achieve the ability to move to the stars? Did they invent teleportation? Did they solve medical issues? What where they, what . . . ?*

## Technology as a Red Herring

SE: Stop! You are missing the point. The way to the stars from your perspective is not with machines but with the self. This civilization achieved all that they needed to achieve to move on to the next level of evolution without the need for technology. The need for technology is a red herring, a distraction, a lack of understanding; it is "miss-direction." You see, it is not technology that helps you evolve. It is one's understanding self and the workings of the universe. This is only possible when the individual stops thinking of himself/herself and starts to think of the bigger picture. How can he/she help others? Which opportunities have been presented but not embraced are opportunities missed? These are all things that the enlightened individual is aware of and takes advantage of. This is the trait of the individual incarnates that collectively make up a great civilization.

ME: *I would like to call a point of order. This dialogue is called the* History of God, *and we are talking more about the history of humanity at the moment.*

SE:    It is entirely appropriate that we do so. From your perspective, God is the perpetrator of creation, which is true. Again you are all part of the entity you call God (the Origin), as am I, but all of you refer to Me as God, as I am the creator of the universe that you are part of. My history also includes the creation of many races that are resident in many of the dimensions and frequencies that I have created as a result of My investigations into Myself. I talk to these races as well, as I am talking to many of you now. Some of these races are all totally aware of the greater reality whereas others are similar to you. In this instance, it is more appropriate to talk about the *History of God* relevant to the human race since this is your framework of understanding. You would not be able to understand the *History of God* from another race's point of view because the cultural differences would be far too different. Part of this understanding is learning the forgotten history of your own race, its interaction with Me, and its environment. As a result, try to understand why the human race refers to a higher order that, in general, at this particular point in its evolution, it cannot fully accept that it is part of something bigger because the human race cannot see the facts as they present themselves. This then is the reason for the higher level history lesson since it shows the relationship with the Source and how it has changed over the millennia.

ME:    *O.K., I think I understand now.*

*In the past we have talked about the development of the vehicle we call the human body and how it was and is used for the evolutionary experience of the individual entity. Bearing in mind that we have just been talking about the different civilizations that have troddened Earth and that some are great. Can you describe one of these civilizations?*

237

## Mechanization and Fall of a Great Civilization

SE:     The best example of a civilization that covers all of those criteria is the race that lived in the environment you would classify as Eden. As you are aware from your own legends, the only thing that is known worldwide about this is that there were two people involved, one called Adam and the other called Eve. These were supposed to be the male and female of the human species with the female eating fruit from the forbidden tree, which resulted in the downfall of the Garden of Eden. Prior to this story that has been told in many forms over the millennia, this particular civilization had indeed achieved greatness.

    The name Eden is not the correct name for the area that this civilization was concentrated within, but for the sake of continuity I shall use it as it is easier to relate to. In essence, this civilization can be called great for the following reasons:

- It was in harmony with the natural workings of Earth;
- They were in harmony with each other;
- They understood the demands of each other from an evolutionary point of view, and everyone put everybody else before themselves;
- They were in communication with other entities that worked with Earth and surrounding dimensions and frequencies;
- They were able to tap into the energies that surrounded them and used them for the benefit of the whole, including creating shelter and providing nourishment;
- They were able to commune with the animals that resided on the planet at that time.

ME:     *So why did it not continue? Why are they not here now?*
SE:     They decided to experiment in creativity from a physical point of view. They saw that they could make

creations with energy that would do things for them without having to continually focus on the task at hand themselves.

ME:   *They made machines?*

SE:   They invented something that you would call technology. Yes, you would call them machines, but they are not what you would recognize as machinery. They were made of energies that permeated from between the dimensions or frequencies. They drew in energy from the surrounding area to allow them to do the work automatically that they were created for.

ME:   *So what did they do?*

SE:   They refined the energies that were being used for nutrition of the physical aspects of the food that the humans needed, root vegetables and berries, not to mention the purification of the energies associated with water. Water is a base element that was used a lot in the construction of shelters and food. It was easy to pollute the water even then due to volcanic activity, so they needed to purify it on a regular basis. Also, because the human body is mainly derived from water, they used purified water to heal those parts of the body that were damaged or worn out. Water could be turned into anything by the use of energy. The big issue with all machinery is that the processes they replaced are forgotten because people don't need to do it anymore. It is like using your logarithm tables. Calculators do it all for you now, so there is a whole generation of students who no longer know what a logarithm table looks like, let alone able to use one. This is exactly what happened to this civilization. They created more and more "machines" to do more and more, negating the need for them to do it for themselves. Thereby, they forgot the basics of energy manipulation and control. When the machines eventually started to fail, the knowledge of how to make them in the first place was no longer available, nor did they have the abilities to manipulate the energies required to do the same. The skills were no longer taught since they were no longer considered necessary because the machines would "last forever." No machine lasts forever, even energy-based productions, as their functionality eventually gets diluted as a result of dealing with the energies they are using to create what they are programmed for.

ME:     *So what other machines did they make?*

SE:     First, I need to remind you that these machines were energy-based manifestations and were not the physical devices that you have currently, such as airplanes, motorcars or computers. They were developed by the best minds in the civilization to relieve them from the drudgery of having to concentrate on doing tasks that they needed to do to make their existence on the physical planes easier. As with most machines, they were improved over time by others who also had a good understanding of the functionality of the machines they had created. However, as I just said, once they were perfected to the point where they no longer needed anyone to improve the machines, they were left alone and forgotten about. Once they were forgotten about and the individuals who created and maintained them had left the Earth plane and returned to their energetic state, the knowledge of what to do to create or maintain them was lost. This is something that you recently experienced with this current civilization and have the evidence to prove it insomuch as some of the devices are present now but totally misunderstood. The pyramids are one example of this as are the "Cleopatra's needles" that are dotted all over the world. They still function, but the output of their functionality is not used.

To get on to the question of what the machines did, I will give you a small list of the jobs they performed.

- Purified the watercourses.
- Energized the plants that were used for physical food.
- Corrected energy "tune" for maximizing plant growth.
- Manifested physical forms for use as dwellings, transportation, etc.
- Directed energy to end users for personal use.
- Directed energy for "energy ways" for transportation constructs.
- Used energy for cleaning the energy ways of the human body.
- Employed energy for rejuvenating the physical human body.
- Directed energy for communication lines.
- Purified the atmosphere.
- Directed weather systems for refreshing water supplies.
- Directed Earth's energy systems to cleanse its auric (energy) levels.

These are only the main machines that were created. There were many others around to do less important functions. The upshot of all this is that the civilization actually had the opportunity to relax and find their real selves and communicate with their higher selves. They did this for quite some time, but the problem was that they started to concentrate on the physical side of the vehicle that they were occupying in terms of the sensations (feelings), both physical and emotional. This meant that over a period of time, they lost the need to be in contact with their higher selves as they concentrated on the physical aspects of themselves.

ME: *We concentrate on the story of the forbidden fruit bringing down the Garden of Eden. What is the significance of this story?*

SE: The significance is the severance of the link between

the higher self and the universe as a result of using automated devices that released the need for constant communication with the higher self and the use of energies in everyday life. Hence, mechanization/ automation (in whatever guise) led to delinquency. The link with the forbidden fruit was, therefore, not that the fruit (mechanism/ automation/ technology) was forbidden, but that it led to eventual decay if it was not used wisely.

ME:   *Hold on. You have just given me a fantastic example of a civilization that was, in your words* great, *and now you are telling me that it failed in greatness and became decadent. This is a great contradiction in terms. How can a great civilization that had all the attributes already quoted, cause its own decay through the use of technology?*

SE:   Sorry to confuse you, I gave you an example of a civilization that was not only great but that lost its greatness as a result of a misdirected collective thought process. I should have described the first race we talked about. This was truly great and achieved everything that was set out before them. I do have to say though that this was a time of great height in the frequencies from your perspective. The civilization, the Earth/solar system, the galaxies and universe were young and innocent and untarnished by the mistakes in decision-making and subsequent loss of frequency made by some civilizations. Unfortunately, the human race as a civilization has been successful in making the greatest drop in the frequencies—hence, the attention it is receiving from other civilizations in the surrounding dimensions and frequencies.

Ironically enough, the human race in its current guise was *greater* than it is today. In a parallel to the Eden race, in some smaller way, the human race is doing exactly the same thing as the Eden race did— right now under your very noses. Everybody wants the spoils of technology; they each want the best they can get for a pittance price-wise. Two costs are involved here though: 1) the low price being the cost in currency of the device desired; and 2) the high price to the Earth in terms of the use of the essential resources it needs to monitor and cleanse its own energy systems necessary to allow other physical organisms to exist within its energies. Most of these are being used up by man at break neck speed. A result of the need to use mechanical means to do supposedly mundane tasks is that you lose the skills of tradition and harmony with the Earth/nature; the communication with the spirits that work with Earth to maintain it and with the self, that part of you (the rest of you) that is part of Me, the Source Entity, and ultimately the Origin.

ME: *So greatness can lead to decay.*

SE: Yes, but it can and also does lead to greater greatness. This is what the teachings of the beings that came to this physical plane tried to explain to all of you over the last millennia. But this, unfortunately, has been used lately for self-aggrandisement, and self-aggrandisement also leads to decadence.

ME: *Which beings are these?*

SE: The Beings you have previously discussed with Me: Mohammed, Jesus, and Buddha.

ME: *What other civilizations do you think were significant enough to talk about in terms of their contribution to evolution and their understanding of the universe and of your existence?*

## Atlantis

SE: There are many races that were understood to be great but again fell into decay. There are many more of these than there are races that were totally successful. All progressed to higher frequencies together; therefore, I would choose not to dwell on the point that they failed to progress. There is no such thing as failure, don't forget, only experience, but to look at what they achieved whilst they were on the up. I see in your mind that you would like to talk about the race of man that was centered in the city of Atlantis, but many people have written channeled works on this civilization. From the general point of view, you would not be adding anything new, but I will add a little.

Many channeled works have identified that the Atlanteans were technologists as well, as well as another civilization to be affected by technology-based decay. They concentrated on the use of crystals for projecting and controlling energy to help them manufacture what they needed to survive in the physical. They were also very good with bio-engineering and, using the crystal/energy technology, they were adept at re-designing the human genome to create hybrid human/animal entities. Some of these are the talk of legends even today. They even swapped genes from one animal to another to create fully hybrid animals. Each of these hybrids was created to perform certain jobs or functions within the civilization. Some were for war; others were for manufacturing, whilst some were for sexual pleasure. The worst case for the use of hybrid human animal or even animal/animal bio-engineering was to show social status. Creation of the most diverse creature was a great show of wealth and social standing. Some Atlanteans even had their own brains re-engineered into that of a preferred animal form if they felt that this would give them greater standing within the higher echelons of the community. Again, the stories of talking animals that have been passed down in legends through the millennia are the remnants of what was going on in the decay years that led up to the fall of this once great civilization.

ME:     *So why don't we see such hybrids today, here and now? Surely they must have reproduced and perpetuated themselves.*

SE: True. But this was not a route that I wanted the human race to go down ad infinitum. First, because it did not provide continuity of form, and second, because it would eventually create a much higher level of what you have now between the different races that have evolved in certain parts of the Earth: discrimination! I also wanted the physical gene pool to be cleansed and saw that the decay of this civilization was the ideal time to do that. This was agreed by all those who were still or currently in or recently returned to the energetic levels of their real existence. In essence, the Atlanteans created a Circus Civilization of such a diverse form that you could no longer tell who was of Original blood. Everyone had been altered in some way. More importantly, the reproductive capacity of these hybrids was not as robust as the true human form at that time, and many became sterile. Again, the necessity to create a self-reproducing vehicle to allow my children of energy to experience all of the frequencies presented to them needed to be reinforced, as the ratio of vehicles versus entities was very much out of balance. I, therefore, allowed this civilization to burn itself out, and I cleansed Earth upon the departure of the last entity to the higher frequencies.

*ME: How did you cleanse the area?*

SE: I allowed the Earth to develop a weakness in its surface local to the center of the civilization and covered the area in hot molten lava. This I later cooled with water from the ocean allowing the minerals in the lava and the sea to mix and "steam clean" the remaining land.

*ME: Remaining land. Do you mean that the area that the Atlanteans were on sank to the sea bed?*

SE: It didn't sink. It was covered with water, and the land was uncovered as a result of the water becoming gaseous when in contact with the lava. This created an ecosystem that was high in sulphur for quite some time and meant that the entities that work on the health of the planet (nature spirits) were hard at work clearing the sulphur away from the planet as it was difficult for anything to grow naturally. The remaining minerals were perfect for plant life to exist and so the plant life caught up quickly with the need to support the re-introduction of the human form.

ME: *So what was the civilization that followed the Atlanteans?*

SE: The current one. It was seen as advantageous to have some of the technologies that were developed during the period of time that the Atlanteans were on Earth available to the newly cleansed and re-introduced humans. These skills were given to entities that had the ability to come and go, to return to their energetic state at will. They had the ability to remember everything they needed to be successful whilst in the physical. And, hence, they were able to guide those incarnating entities into a direction that was desired both by Me and the group of more experienced incarnates that were looking to get the best out of Earth's environment.

ME: *You mean you have a committee of humans, in spirit, controlling the destiny of those who are incarnate?*

SE: Yes, and this is what the Akashic are for.

ME: *So what was the name of this newly introduced race who had technology?*

SE: Egyptian.

# Chapter 15:
## *The History of Humanity*

## Cleansing Earth after Atlantis

ME:  *So you and the committee changed the way that humans preferred to see themselves back to what it was originally.*

SE:  Yes. And as I just said, the race of man you called Egyptian was the first civilization to be placed on the Earth plane following the demise of the Atlantean culture.

ME:  *You said previously that you cleansed Earth by creating a volcanic eruption and then washing the area with sea water! This sounds a bit too close to the great flood that Noah is supposed to have built an ark for.*

SE:  Well spotted. I do stress, however, that I didn't create a volcanic eruption as there were no volcanoes on the island that hosted the majority of the Atlanteans. I caused a schism in Earth's crust similar to what you call an earthquake. But this earthquake also allowed molten lava to come to the surface from all over the island, cleansing the surface of all the DNA that was alive enough to allow the re-creation of the human animal hybrids.

ME:  *But you managed to keep a gene pool of all the pure races of humanity and animals.*

SE:  Yes, including plant life. Everything that was required to assist in kick-starting a pure race of human beings for evolutionary purposes was allowed to be saved from the cleansing process.   This process included the following:

- Having a maintenance program for Earth;
- Maintaining the local eco-system (plants and animals, nature spirits); and
- Providing enough learning of what happened in the past to allow progress.

      Those human forms that survived were occupied by entities that were very experienced and had none of their normal energetic abilities removed. This allowed them to boost the start-up of the new race from a cultural, technological, and evolutionary point of view, as well as have an ingrained understanding of the need to work within the natural constraints of the Earth plane.

ME:  *So what did the ark look like? Everyone on Earth expects it to be a large boat as illustrated in our legends and in the Old Testament.*

SE:  The ark was merely a place of safety for the gene pool samples to be kept. In this instance, the gene pool required whole specimens, as the technology and know-how for gene manipulation used by the Atlanteans was to be suppressed to allow other areas of growth to take place. The ark's primary job was, therefore, to allow the animals to survive long enough without mutation and for the land they were going to occupy to be prepared for them to live on naturally. Even with the use of energetic methods to create this land, it took time for it to stabilize. Everything needs time to stabilize in the physical plane. In order for the entities to exist on their own in this plane, it was necessary to give them time to work with their environment in a natural way, one that worked with the energies that permeate this level of frequency. This is the single most important thing about living in the lowest frequencies and dimensions; the entities needed to live with it and in it rather than move around it.

## The Egyptians' Contributions

*ME:*    *So what about the Egyptians, what did they contribute?*

SE:    They were the springboard for the re-generation of the human race in this part of the world.

*ME:*    *Hold on. I just got a picture, a feeling that the flooding of the Mediterranean was the sea you used to cleanse the land that was Atlantis.*

SE:    Yes, well intuited. Now you know where the legend of the flood came from, and you have an idea of where the Atlanteans were located. The area called Egypt was the next best thing to the properties of the land that the Atlanteans enjoyed, and it was the first to become pure enough to work with from a natural point of view. The committee and I were greatly involved in the introduction of those stored in the ark. The Egyptians were infused with the need to respect the energies of Earth and its naturally occurring opportunities given them to re-build human life. Subliminally, they were aware of the entities that controlled these energies, and as a result, they gave them names and forms—forms that they remembered, racewise, from their Atlantean days. Hence, the important entities were given forms/images that resembled what some of them remembered the leaders of Atlantis took to show their importance. Human bodies with the heads of animals were, therefore, used to describe pictorially which energies these entities controlled.

For example:

Ra was called the Sun God, the word God meaning "responsible one," who looked after the power source for this planet on six dimensional levels.

Anubis was the one responsible for naturally occurring things, such as plants, fish, and mammals, and worked with an army of helpers, what you call nature spirits. Some of these had names and forms of their own given to them.

ME: *What else can you tell me about them?*

SE: The land they lived in was lush and fertile. They prospered for millennia in this environment, working with nature. They were taught many skills by the entities that incarnated with all their faculties (evolved entities who took on the role of helpers on the ground level). Some of these involved the capture and employment of the energies that the Atlanteans used. To assist in this, they were taught how to build structures and devices that could harness these energies and store them for future use. These "skills" required purity of heart and cleanliness of thought to be accessed by those not normally used to dealing with such energies on the physical levels. As such a high level of purity was required, only a few capable of such devotion to a life of concentrated selflessness to achieve this level were able to be taught. Consequently, as those who taught the new humans left the Earth plane to return to energetic existence, they left teachers in their place, but the number of suitable individuals dwindled. As the number of suitable individuals dwindled, the worry of to whom to transmit their knowledge increased. In this state of worry and feeling a desperate need to impart their skills, they taught those who were not so pure, which resulted in the growth of a power-based civilization again and ultimately its decay. It has taken over 25,000 years to recover to the point you are now in human physical existence and evolution. And things are far from satisfactory, as you can see. But . . . you are improving slowly. I am enthused by this.

Me: *Tell me more about the Egyptians, especially the pyramids. What did they do, and how were they really built?*

SE: We are getting into more of the history of the human

race here rather than the history of God.

ME: *Yes, I know, but I need to know this. We can go back to you after this dialogue.*

SE: Very well. They were not called Egyptians when they were first introduced to the land that they lived. In fact, they were introduced in an "up and running state."

ME: *What do you mean, "up and running state"? Do you mean that they just suddenly appeared? A readymade civilization? One day they were not there; the next day they were—houses and all!*

SE: Pretty much so. You see, I was eager to get the evolutionary ball rolling again as quickly as possible. So many opportunities had been lost as a result of the Atlanteans going off on a tangent that I was keen to start again as fast as possible. After I had cleansed the area, the best way to do this was to take a chunk of the Atlantean civilization from the beginning of their time on the Earth plane and insert it into another time line. I removed all spherical memory from the race and gave them a few individuals that were totally aware to guide them in the right direction.

ME: *Spherical memory?*

SE: The ability to affect the here and now by remembering those events that will happen later, linearly speaking. Some of you on Earth are starting to remember how to do this already. They are mediums who can tell the future.

ME: *And what about being totally aware? Are you referring to those whom you talked about earlier, those with the ability to return to the Source (Entity) and back at will? Those that have the ability to have access to the Akashic, the committee, and their own higher/energetic selves?*

SE: Correct. It may seem strange to you, but after forty-three attempts at getting the best out of the Earth plane with human types of physio-biological forms, I was starting to get a bit impatient and simply did not want to start from scratch again. So I decided to start with an "oven ready" approach to civilization.

ME: *That would explain something that the archaeologists have not been able to explain: the evidence suggesting that the Egyptians just suddenly appeared on the scene.*

SE: That's because they did just that. They were no more than a few thousand strong when they were implanted into their new environment with everything from houses to shops to agriculture to industry already working and ready to go. The guides, those who were totally aware, were put in prime hierarchical positions so that they could impart knowledge to the many new incarnates and teach them how to use the natural resources that they found around themselves. Of course, they had some level of pre-programmed memory to allow them to do the basics, but those who were showing the promise of being pure of heart were advised about the ways to capture and use the energies that surrounded them in this level.

ME: *What specifically were they shown by the aware ones?*

SE: They were taught the way to tap into their surrounding energies by focused meditation, using purity of thought as an enabler. This was only achievable by a few as it meant total selflessness. They had to show that they had control of the three major attributes that lead to purity.

1. Love
2. Power
3. Wisdom

Each of these can be seductive in its own right. Once mastered, they can be important tools that can be used for the good of others. Mastery of all three is rare and only the individuals that showed that they were capable of this were taught the skills required to manipulate energy.

252

The first things they were shown was how to affect the molecular structure of an object to the point where two things could be achieved:

1. They could change the shape of the object by re-arranging these molecules;
2. They could affect the dimensional stability of the object to the point where it was neither in one dimension nor another, which would then allow them easy manipulation or transportation of objects.

Next they were trained to use these skills to create structures that would harness energies for their personal and collective use in large quantities and store them.

ME:    *You're talking about the pyramids here?*

SE:    And other structures that you have not yet discovered but are, nevertheless, still intact and doing the job for which they were designed and built: to collect, store, and/or re-direct energy. Some of these structures are constantly venting excess energy/energies and, as a result, causing changes to the surrounding Earth. You know these events as earthquakes.

ME:    *I thought that earthquakes are to do with plate tectonics?*

SE:    Yes, but what causes plate tectonics? The Earth doesn't do it on its own; it's not in its own interest.

The structures were used for other things as well, such as energy-based therapy (re-building broken bodies) and the duplication of essential wares—wares that could not be manufactured in any other way than by energy manipulation because the physical technologies and supporting tools were not there to manufacture such things. They were also used for communication purposes. Individuals who were trained correctly could use the energies collected by the structures to communicate with others of the human race that were transplanted in other parts of the universe. As with the Atlanteans, some of these eventually changed the base form of their physical bodies but only to affect a better interface with the environment in which they existed and not for the egotistical, social, or sexual reasons that the Atlanteans changed their bodies. Some of these individuals were so good with the energies that they could roam the stars with their minds. That part of their essence that was captive in the physical was liberated momentarily and allowed to connect with the rest of their energetic form, so long as it returned.

ME: *So the two separate theories that the pyramids were used for collecting energy or were some sort of astrological observational device are both reasonable.*

SE: Yes, they are both true, but not in the way portrayed by so-called experts and theorists.

ME: *You say there have been forty-three civilizations on the Earth with us being part of the 44th. How come we don't see any of their artifacts? Where is the archaeology to back up such a claim?*

SE: You current humans are all so full of yourselves that you think you are the best thing since the combustion engine. Well, let Me tell you this. The human form has been around for much longer than you think with some derivatives having a gap of over 100,000 years, which is pretty close to the length of time of this version since the last, give or take 10,000.

ME: *Hold on. You gave me the impression that there was only 25,000 years in between the Atlanteans and the race of humans noted in history!*

SE: This is true, but you are of the opinion that the Atlanteans are not an iteration of the current version of humankind. This is not true. If you remember, the Atlanteans modified themselves genetically to improve themselves both for physical and social reasons. This does not mean that they were not part of the current civilization of man. Remember again that I cleansed them to allow them to start again. This does not mean that it was the introduction of a new race of humankind. It merely means that this version was given a second chance—a chance to start again and be successful in the direction that the collective committee of incarnate human souls wanted the race to go.

ME: *Does this mean that we should be seeing some sort of physical evidence? That what we regard as the most successful version of humanity has been present here on Earth and had enough technology of the sort that we would recognize?*

SE: You are equating technology to be similar to what you are used to seeing currently. This is not the case, as there has been technology of all sorts over the millennia, from biological to electronic to spatial/dynamic to palatial to spiritual. Many of these and combinations of them have been used—the most productive being the spiritual. However, I have been impressed by the contribution the most current version of humanity has given. This is primarily because you have all been given total freewill, the ability to do what you want without the need to confer with the collective of humankind, but this is a distraction. The evidence that you are seeking does not exist in the way that you would recognize because you are looking for purely physical evidence. You need to look within yourselves for some of the evidence. It is to do with how you interact with your fellow man. This is the real legacy, the real evidence of previous civilization that leads you directly to the Source, Me, and the Origin. For the evidence is to do with total camaraderie, working together for the good of the whole, but if you are looking for evidence of the sort that is quantifiable, you need to look in two areas: first, in the sand near the countries that locate the pyramids, and second, in the snow near the South Pole.

*ME:* *You mean we can see real evidence of civilization of an advanced type in these areas?*

SE: Yes.

*ME:* *Then why do we not know this? Why have we not yet seen this? Why have we not yet had this published, presented on TV, have academic papers in high ranking journals, world revelations, new thoughts on life/technology? Why, why, why!!?*

SE: Why! Because you have so many people in high places who have made their names on the current understanding. Archaeologists have already unearthed some of this evidence, but they have withheld it for a number of reasons: first, because it would ruin their existing careers; second, because if they took the bull by the horns and presented this new data, they would be rubbished by those in high ranking places who have made their careers on the existing understanding; third, some of these people know this information already. There are many individuals in senior positions in religious faiths that would literally kill to have this information and then withhold it by destroying it, so that they could maintain their position and the position of the faith that they are pushing.

*ME:* *You are telling me that there are those among us that know a lot more about our history in this specific incarnation of humankind than we collectively know, and they are willing to hold it back to perpetuate their careers—careers that are based upon an old truth, careers that could be overwhelmingly successful if they presented this information to a civilization who was eager to know more about where they came from and what life is all about.*

SE: Yes. This is what is happening. You see, the people who are in power as a result of current understanding are frightened that they will lose everything. They are not interested in the advancement of the understanding of the human race even though this would ultimately help the human race rise in frequencies and, as a consequence, evolve faster. All they are interested in is the now, what they have now; what they have now is power over the thoughts of others, which gives them more power. They have power in an environment that most people recognize as their only environment, and as such they play along with the façade.

ME:  *So who has this knowledge? Who has been able to take control of the data that has been "dug up"?*

SE:  Senior officials within the locale. They have, in general, an understanding of what this knowledge means. In some cases there is technology at their fingertips that is far beyond their understanding. In other cases the technology is low grade but still of significance. In many cases it would help the poor in the world flourish, and this is another reason for keeping this knowledge covert.

ME:  *So a little knowledge really is a dangerous thing.*

SE:  In this instance, yes. This is really because limited knowledge not only fosters a superiority complex but a high level of fear, fear of the unknown and what it could do. You see, when you have a little knowledge of something that is utterly unknown to you to the point that you consider it to be alien, you become fearful of the forces that created such knowledge. That means that those that are fearful think that others would also be fearful, and so they withhold the information for fear of causing panic. In actuality, the only panic is in their own minds—the fear of change.

# Older Civilizations – Again A Return to Earlier Civilizations

## Physical Evidence of Earlier Civilizations

*ME:* *So let's get back to the issue of older civilizations. I read in a book by Erich Von Daniken many years ago that it was entirely possible for twenty civilizations to rise and fall in the space of 1,000,000 years with 50,000 years in between them and no evidence available to us to prove their existence in anything other than legend. Is this a reasonable statement?*

SE: Entirely so. In fact there have been many more than twenty, as the level of rise and decline is entirely relevant to the extent to which they spread their influence in the world or galaxy/universe. Some achieve greatness in terms of spirituality whilst others achieve greatness in terms of physicality—in fact, it has been physicality that has been the norm. From a physical perspective, it is the relationship between the spiritual and the physical that gives rise to the amount of detritus that a particular civilization leaves behind when it declines into decrepitude.

## Physical Ascension of Former Civilizations

Let's put this into clear perspective. The really great races that have existed on or around the Earth environment did not always leave anything behind. In many cases they took their whole civilization with them, especially if they ascended to higher frequencies. This also included the dwellings in which they lived.

*ME:* *You're saying that whole civilizations can ascend to higher levels and take absolutely everything with them, houses and all.*

SE: If they so wish, yes. You see, ascension is not specifically about pure spirituality in the sense of shedding the need for familiar items of personal protection, such as houses or tools to help manufacture things.

*ME:* *Why?*

SE: Because there are many levels through which the individual can rise before the need or desire for external support is released. Some of these lower levels still accept a similar level of physicality although to the observer in a lower level they are invisible to the physical eye. In fact, the environment at these higher levels is not too dissimilar to what you are experiencing now. The only difference is the dependence on physical technology instead of the usage of their God-given right to use their faculties in the higher spiritual realms. Some of the technology is a combination of physical technology that works with spiritual energies.

*ME:* *Was this where the Atlanteans were?*

SE: Yes, to a certain level although as I have previously mentioned, they were seduced by experiencing the physicality of physical life to the point of distraction.

## Atlantean Architecture Present Today

*ME:* *So why haven't we seen any of their architecture if they were so engrossed in the physical?*

SE: You have. There are many examples of the Atlantean civilization available for all to see. Some of it is hidden by the natural change in the Earth's topography over the past 35,000 years whereas others are visible for all to see, such as the pyramids. There are others just below the surface, such as in Sakura, Egypt. The wear and tear on the surface of the artifacts gives evidence to their actual age. However, your scholars are not able to think out of the box, as you call it, and, therefore, credit them with a tenth of their actual age because they have date data which they believe are correct, but they are not. I give you the example of the Mars probe sent that had two sets of calibration: metric and imperial. The

259

difference was catastrophic as the device crash landed and failed to work. For years, the scientists who worked on the project were convinced that everything was correct. It was only after the probe crashed that they found out what the problem was. This will be the same with the leaders of archaeology and religion. They will only realize their errors when the evidence is there for ALL to see and not just them.

You only have to look at the detail of the artifacts that are left behind to understand the level of civilization required to create them. High quality mass production does not happen on the scale of a cottage industry. It is the detail that gives the game away in terms of what the truth is in the technology that was available to older civilizations.

## "Neanderthal" Civilization

For instance, the race of man you call "Neanderthal" were actually a very highly evolved and spiritually aware race of beings, who made the very best use of their physical bodies to help them evolve and move on up the frequencies. They worked in tune with the land and the animals, which, in turn, helped them. They were also in constant communication with their higher selves. Those who elected to be their guides constantly fed back to Spirit the wonder of working with the universe at this level of frequency, even if it was painfully slow and restrictive. However, they still knew what they could do with their spiritual faculties, and, as a result, worked in harmony with the energies that were found at this level and those other energies that interfaced with this level. With this *common* knowledge, they created their dwellings and devices of convenience to help them in their everyday lives and made physical life more tolerable for those of them who, like your current iteration of man, were not

260

totally in tune with the wider reality.

## Construction of the Pyramids

How do you think the large constructions you call the pyramids were made? It certainly wasn't with logs and rope and soft metal chisels. It was with the use and fundamental understanding of the underlying energies that were available to those who took the time to develop what every one of them was able to do, but few bothered to learn. They worked with the energies they exist within and had command over. It is the ability to use these energies that results in the lack of archaeology that proves the use of technology that was more than would be expected of a human being at a particular point in time, taking into account the technological position of humankind today. This point is humankind's total dependence on physical tools rather than their using the spiritual/energetic tools available to them if only they would open their eyes, and more importantly their hearts, for this is the blockage to man's spiritual growth.

# Chapter 16:
## *Space-faring Humans*

## Early Energetic Humanity's Space Travel in an Environmental Bubble

ME: *As we were ending the previous dialogue, I was thinking of getting back to the backbone of this communication in total, that being the history of God. I got the image of humans in space on a space craft that was, well, flimsy to say the least. From our point of view, we have only just made it across the gap between our planet and its moon and deposited some rather basic hardware there. I have been surprised to note that this is open to abuse by conspiracy theorists.*

SE: Well, the conspiracy theorists are wrong. The moon landings did actually happen, and I was with the spirits of those humans all the way, watching with interest.

In terms of the images you saw in your mind's eye, this is interesting, mainly because most of humanity's journeys between the stars have been in the energetic form. You have picked on possibly the one time when humanity was in a state of flux energetically. They decided to investigate in a more physical level the protuberances into physical space you call planets, which, of course, are entities in their own right. In actual fact, the machines that you saw were not spaceships as you know. Instead they were machines that allowed the energetic side of humanity to exist within the denser energies without losing the communication with that part of themselves that remains with the higher energetic states.

ME: *So who invented/created them?*

SE: Energetic humanity at this time was, as I stated previously, on its way down the frequencies to the point where it was starting to make an impression in the frequency and dimension in which physical humanity now exists and is used as an evolutionary spring board. Collectively, it was thought that it would be interesting to investigate the environment that was presenting itself to them. In order to investigate this new environment of which they were now becoming aware, they established that they needed to create a bubble—an environmental bubble that maintained the frequency they were used to existing in. This bubble (you would call it a spaceship) was able to move in two environments simultaneously and, therefore, allowed the occupants to maintain contact with the rest of energetic humanity—that part of themselves that was fully in spirit and the normal dimensions and frequencies that they exist in when not in an incarnate state.

ME: *If humanity was energetic at this stage, how could they be incarnate?*

SE: They were energetic when compared to your current level of density. Don't forget you are at the rock bottom of the frequency ladder, so anything above your current level would appear energetic. In essence though, although I describe them as energetic humanity, they were in a form of physicality, just not as solid as you are now. This means that if one were to stand next to you right now, you would not be able to see them because they were at a higher level of frequency and phase. However, as they were in flux, dropping down the frequencies, you might just catch them in the corner of your eye. Just like when people claim to see what they think are ghosts.

ME: *So they traveled the physical universe in a ghost space ship!*

SE: A clever play on words. No, not quite. This bubble was a construct that had the properties of both

264

environments. It needed to have this quality to be able to slip in between the two frequencies in such a way that would allow the occupants to exist in both at the same time whilst not being affected by the lower.

ME:    *How was it made? You use the word "construct" alot.*

SE:    It was created by the manipulation of energy and the changing of the "attractivity" of certain energies, so that they created a level of physicality. This was done by a number of individual incarnate entities that were specialists in energy manipulation. Essentially they made the energies slow down or speed up to the point where two or more energies would "stick" together to create a new hybrid energy—one that was slippery in the frequencies that it was required to work within. As with all constructs that are maintained in the higher frequencies, it assumed a spherical shape. This is normal and is replicated by a number of energies in your dense universe. Water is a good example, as are planets, especially those you call suns. They used this and others of the same construct to experience nearly all the environment you call the physical universe; they visited many galaxies to observe, learn, and interact with the physicality. They were specifically interested in the interaction of energies at this level and what they created. In doing this, they brought back to themselves and, therefore, the Origin and Me much learning about these lower frequency levels that We had not experienced or understood Ourselves.

ME:    *I thought You knew everything about everything.*

SE:    (Chuckle.) No, that is why you are all here now!

ME:    *Did they meet other physical entities?*

SE:    Of course. If you remember at the start of this dialogue, I told you that I separated Myself into two halves. One half is that part of the whole of Me that is part of the Origin. This part of Me has created the environment where you exist. The second part is the millions upon millions of entities that I created. They weren't all classified as humanity.

## Entities with Singular or Collective Free Will

ME:   *So just how many physical life forms are there in the universe you created?*

SE:   Do you want Me to count all of the life forms? Surely you only mean those who are what you classify as sentient.

ME:   *What is a sentient being? I am led to believe that all life forms have sentience of some sort.*

SE:   Correct, but I will ask you the question again, as it will reduce the number to one that you can understand.

ME:   *O.K., those entities that have free will, singularly or collectively.*

SE:   Approximately 415,000.

ME:   *That's races of beings?*

SE:   That's races of beings.

## Shape Shifters

ME:   *And each of them is incarnate in the physical?*

SE:   And the surrounding dimensions/frequencies. Don't forget that the act of incarnation is not specific to the fully physical as it can be classified as physical, but in another dimension or frequency. Just because a vessel for incarnation is in a higher frequency, it does not make it any less a vessel for evolutionary purposes. It is the act of experiencing things from a restricted/different perspective that is the objective of your physical existence, for you truly are the sum of all your experiences. I see that you have a number of images in your head of the shape and form of the variety of sentient incarnate vessels.

ME:   *Yes, they seem to range from snakes to apes.*

SE:   Yes, they do. And some of them even change their shapes to one that is best suited for certain jobs they do.

Each shape has its own particular usage and developmental opportunity.

ME: *Shape shifters?! I thought they were the work of science fiction.*

SE: Where do you think the ideas for what you call science fiction come from but the greater reality? These beings are not of your dimension and frequency, of course, as it requires far too much energy to make the changes at this level. Although with the correct level of training, it could be achieved, but it takes dedication and focus of the level that most of you could never achieve. It requires significant dedication, not to mention the mental and physical exercise, to position the human vessel in the frequency required to perform such feats on itself. It will become more possible when the human race eventually rises through the frequencies again.

ME: *So why do these beings have different shapes? Is there not an optimal physical condition?*

SE: Yes, there is and that condition is relative to the environment that the vessel needs to operate within; hence, dolphins have the form they have and you have the form you have. Each sentient race of beings that currently exists on the Earth exists in a different medium or frequency/dimension. There does seem to be a pattern where a certain number of forms are duplicated independently of each other. This is of interest, as once the physical vessel is designed by the energetic parts of the entities, the real entities, the eco-structure of the environment they exist within, changes, adapts, and presents opportunities that didn't previously exist but are, nevertheless, useful from an evolutionary point of view.

## Dolphins, Space-faring and Sea-faring Sentient Beings

ME: *How many sentient races of beings are there on Earth?*

SE:   Three, but soon there is a plan for a fourth.

*ME:   Would I recognize them if I saw them?*

SE:   You think you know one other holistically, but you are not quite sure, as you expect a sentient being to have technology to prove their sentience. Technology is not always proof of sentience nor is a lack of technology proof of a lack of civilization and evolution. Your dolphins are proof of this. You would be shocked to find that dolphins are space-faring beings, as well as sea-faring beings. As a civilization, they are extremely and highly evolved, performing a great service to the well-being of the Earth and its inhabitants.

*ME:   How can dolphins be space-faring? Do they transport water into space in some sort of energetic construct that we have not yet detected on our radar networks?*

SE:   No, they travel the universe with their minds, their energetic selves, their real selves. They are fully in control of their energies and still exist in a higher frequency than humankind. Even though they have suffered significantly at the hand of humankind's slip down the frequencies, they still manage to maintain their own frequency.

*Me:   If dolphins are of a higher frequency than man, why are they visible in our frequency?*

SE:   Being of a higher frequency does not specifically mean that you will wink out of existence from the point of view of the observer from your frequency. This does not happen for several levels. Also, the dolphins prefer to keep themselves visible to you so that you do not feel alone in this frequency, for it can feel very alone being in a place that most of reality just isn't existing in. The dolphin race helps humankind a lot at the energetic level and communicates with the human committee on a constant basis helping to influence humankind's decision process at the group level.

*ME:   How can they do that if they are based in the sea, and humankind is based on the land even though we do go into the sea?*

SE: You forget that they are not of the same frequency. They essentially do what you call astral travel. They arrange a meeting with the committee of man and using their energetic bodies, they leave their dolphin bodies. They are still at the stage where they can come and go. In fact they never lost it like humankind did. They can leave their body at will and travel to wherever they want, and they do this on a regular basis. They also leave the Earth environment on a regular basis to commune with the other energetic races of their level in other parts of the local galaxy and even the universe.

*ME:* *So how come they don't have technology?*

SE: They have, it's just that you don't have the ability to detect it. But again, it's not the sort of technology that you would recognize or understand; it is mainly of energetic origin, and, as such, is of a frequency that is higher than their physical bodies. Technology is not necessarily electrical, mechanical or computerized. True technology uses the natural energies, working with the universe to help it help you.

# Chapter 17:
## *The Second Silver Cord*

We were talking about being highly evolved when I suddenly saw an image in my mind's eye of a human form with two lines of communication to Spirit. I decided to digress in this direction before ultimately returning back to the question of the History of God.

ME: *I got an image of an additional link to Spirit, almost like a second "silver cord," the cord noted by clairvoyants who witness astral traveling.*

SE: That is a good observation.

ME: *So what is it then, an extra line of communication to give extra "bandwidth"?*

SE: Exactly. It takes a certain level of evolution to achieve this level of additional communication, and it is not easy to maintain as it can be lost.

ME: *What do you mean? We can lose it if we have it?*

SE: Yes.

ME: *How do we do that?*

SE: By quite simply not using it. As you say on Earth, *"If you don't use it, you lose it,"* and you lose it by forgetting it is there.

## The Challenges of Having a Second Silver Cord

ME: *How can you forget about something as important as a second silver cord? It seems so fundamentally obvious that this would make your interaction with this level so entirely different to what most people experience that it would stand out like a sore thumb.*

SE: And it does. The issue here is that the information and experiences that you achieve with this additional level

271

of subtle communication are such that when people comment upon what they see (or perceive), know or feel in terms of what is in and around them from the whole universe perspective, they are considered by others who don't experience such things as the ramblings of a mad person. People who experience heightened awareness are either told by their parents when they are young that they can't possibly see what they are seeing, or they get ridiculed by their friends at school. They are classified as having psychiatric disorders, such as schizophrenia, or they are simply condemned as those who fantasize because those who can't see or sense in that way place their attention on what they see around them.

This then draws their attention away from what is going on in, or what they are taking part in, the physical world. As a result, those that are told often enough that they can't possibly see what is not there in the physical begin to believe it or actively shut it off to become "normal" enough to fit in with the rest of society and their friends or to please their parents. Few recover and even fewer are able to use their knowing to its full extent, irrespective of whether they keep using it or re-discover it, like you.

Of those who do use it fully, many become drawn into the clairvoyant/psychic scene that is akin to "tents in fair grounds" or "dark rooms in flats" for a cheap (or not so cheap) reading of their future fortune. Others use it for egotistical or self-promotional purposes and, subsequently, reach a plateau in their abilities to open up and experience more of the universe whilst in this level, another excellent opportunity for evolution that is not taken to its fullest potential.

Only a very, very few recognize it for its true meaning and take on-board the opportunity to enlighten others and to try to help them evolve further. This is a great sadness but one that is slowly being overcome, as more people fight against what they are being told is reality versus what they experience as reality. The more people who experience similar things based upon their abilities to communicate on a higher level bump into each other or get together and share their experiences and knowledge, the more they have their experiences validated, and the more they open up fully to the true communication opportunity. As a consequence, the more they realize that they have to spread the "word" to help others evolve, too.

## Availability/Choice of a Second Silver Cord

*ME:*    *So the second silver cord is only available to those who are evolved enough to be able to potentially use these abilities.*

SE:    Those entities that feel they are able to use them arrange for them to be associated with the physical body they are about to incarnate into.

*ME:*    *But I thought that all entities that are evolved enough would have these cords automatically available, at least that's the impression you have just given me.*

SE:    All entities of the correct level of evolution can use and have access to the additional cord, but there are those who feel that they are not able to make the full use of the chance for extra communication, and, therefore, don't take advantage of the opportunity.

*ME:*    *This all seems a bit wishy-washy. I would have expected that all entities would be dying to take up the opportunity to have enhanced (normal?) communication levels whilst in the physical planes.*

SE:    The opportunities for evolution don't always require the need to be linked further to spirit, and in many cases it is preferred not to have this additional link to make the best of the randomness of freewill without the knowledge that pre-destiny brings.

*ME:*    *Pre-destiny?*

SE: Yes, pre-destiny. It is the ability to focus on the point that results in the completion of the event. The completion of the event that you are destined to make can be called destiny. Knowing what is going to happen is pre-destiny.

ME: *O.K., so you are saying that they prefer not to have the links that give them the ability to look into the future and see what they need to do to make certain events happen.*

SE: In a nutshell, yes.

ME: *So why do entities prefer to have this extra link then?*

SE: Because they think they can accelerate the evolution of others as well as themselves. This is a massive undertaking as it has the ability to affect the whole of local creation.

## Local Creation

ME: *Local creation? What is that? I thought that creation was everything?*

SE: Local creation is that which affects only itself and not the rest of creation. For instance, what is happening on this plane on this planet is local creation. Entities that try to affect the evolution of creation (as well as themselves) no matter how big or small that effect is, create a condition where all the entities that are associated with incarnation on the Earth plane are affected and ultimately elevated. When local creation is elevated, it also affects the rest of what I have created—hence, the interest in this planet and the physical and nonphysical planes associated with it. That means that the entities that have associated themselves with creating are assisting the other Source Entities and the Origin in the process of universal creation on an inclusive scale.

## The Burden/Gift of Having a Second Silver Cord

Hence, the burden on the entities that choose to incarnate and evolve with this extra cord is immense as they live their incarnate lives always in the knowledge that they are part of something big and that they have something significant to do. Some work this out earlier in life; some work it out later in life, and some, of course, never do for whatever reason.

ME:   *I never thought that this would be considered a burden.*

SE:   They don't consider it a burden either when they are deciding what area and era to project themselves into. In fact, they are proud, (delighted, honored?) that they are being given the chance to help the evolution of others who are not so evolved. They are pleased to be of such significant service.

ME:   *Why is this? Why are they honored to serve others?*

SE:   Because as they serve themselves, so do they serve others; in doing so, they serve themselves even more, which increases the level of service to other entities. It's a never ending spiral upwards which, when every entity is AWARE of what is going on, then they are all helping themselves to help others to help themselves. They all rise through the frequencies together more rapidly.

ME:   *So why did you say it was a burden?*

SE:   Because when you are not aware, but you have the nagging feeling that you have something more important to do, you feel dissatisfied with what you are and what you are doing, no matter how successful you are in the material world. In fact, the more successful you are, the more dissatisfied you get.

ME:   *Why would you get more dissatisfied if you are a successful business man, for instance?*

SE:   Because you are only successful in one dimension, the physical, and this is only for yourself and not for the good of others as well.

*ME:*    *But some people are very successful in the physical world and do a lot of good for others, such as people who run charities, such as Save the Children, Oxfam, or even Green Peace.*

SE:    Ah! Yes, but how many of those do it for ego and not for the good of everyone?

*ME:*    *Sorry, what do you mean?*

SE:    What I am saying is that those who use these vehicles for self-aggrandisement are still firmly in the physical. However, those who do good for others and seek no rewards, putting such opportunities to the people they help out of compassion, are working in synchronicity with their plan, whether they are aware or not. Most TRULY AWARE entities work in the background and are not in the front line that attracts vast amounts of publicity, and it is here that the best work is done since it demands no reward. No reward is sought because it is done for the love of the work and not for the love of the ego and all the trappings that go with it.

# Chapter 18:
# *The Records/Database, Akashic and Others*

## Recorded Physical and Spiritual Experiences of Entities

*ME:* *In a previous dialogue you mentioned records! Are you talking about the Akashic Records?*

SE: This is one part of their function but essentially, yes.

*ME:* *It is said that we humans can access these records for our own purposes and for our own learning. They are said to contain the records of all of our lives, all that we have done, and all that we will do.*

SE: This is true but access is limited, especially when you are incarnate in the physical since access to this knowledge will inhibit the learning gained by the physical experience. The part of the records that are "Akashic" are relative only to human existence. Other records are maintained for other entities and are called something else, but they are essentially all part of the same database.

*ME:* *But this database, record, Akashic, also includes the collective experiences of the Origin as well?*

SE: Yes, but as I just stated, the Akashic part of it is only relative to the collective and individual experiences of humankind. This is, of course, not just relative to the physical experience on its own but also includes all of the experiences that your type of entity has accumulated in both the physical and the spiritual realms. Every one of your experiences is recorded in this area of the Origin.

*ME:* *When I am in spirit, can I look at what the Origin has*

277

*experienced as well?*

## Possible Integration of Lives and Experiences of Other Entities Within One's Life

SE:     To a lesser extent, yes, especially if it is considered to be of use to you in your own quest for experience and personal understanding. To this end, it is also possible for you to look into the lives and experiences of other entities and integrate them or part of them into your own area of the Akashic, the one that you carry around with you.

ME:     *What do you mean by our part of the Akashic that we carry around with us?*

SE:     Your own personal memory. You do have a memory, don't you?!

ME:     *Yes?*

## Three Types of Memories

SE:     I can see that I need to clarify again.

You have three memories:

1.  One that is part of the Origin

    -   This memory is that which is part of the Akashic of humankind and is accessible by the Origin, the Source Entities, and all of the spiritual entities that are associated with this universe and its dimensions. Essentially, the Akashic record is for spiritual entities that are associated with all of the different physical manifestations associated with this universe, are kept in separate sub-sections to make it apparent where they came from and to compare the different experiences achieved by the different types of entities. All records are accessible by all entities. All records can be used as experience by another entity when incarnating into the physical.

2. One that is part of your energetic make-up
   - This memory is yours only. It is not inclusive of the ability to access the first memory but contains the cumulative personal experiences that you have undertaken during your total existence. This is only available to you when you are "whole," i.e., when you no longer have part of yourself incarnate in the physical.

3. One that is part of you when you incarnate
   - This is essentially a clean slate from the physical point of view but contains a subliminal number of memories (personal or imported) that are available for use in the physical if a specific task or experience is to be undertaken that requires a little bit of experiential help.

## The Uses of Imported Memories

ME: *You just mentioned imported memories. Do you mean that we can use other peoples' memories to help us solve problems?*

SE: As I said above, "All records can be used as experience by another entity when incarnating into the physical." However, some of these can, under special circumstances, be imported into your own memory for the duration of an incarnation if it is seen as being beneficial to you in your next incarnation (and sometimes during your current incarnation) and your guides during the planning stage.

ME: *And this could also include the memories or experience/experiences that come from entities that we would consider to be alien?*

SE: Yes. This is used specifically when a certain advancement in technology or art is to be or needs to be introduced. It appears to come from nowhere; it is radical, novel, strange, and unbelievable. When it comes from a single person, the person introducing such novel changes is considered to be a genius. When it comes from a group of people, it is because there is too much knowledge for any one of them to cope with on their own, so each has a part of the picture that is essential to the success of the others. This is a "group" genius.

## Use of the Akashic Records to Learn "What If"

ME:   *O.K., so as far as I understand, the Akashic records are a recording of all of the entities associated with the physical universe and its dimensions. It is part of the memories of the Origin and the Source Entities, and it is outside "change" that can be initiated by the Origin. This seems straight forward.*

SE:   There is more to the Akashic than that.

ME:   *Why? What else can there be?*

SE:   It is a much more useful tool than a piece of memory.

ME:   *So what else does it do then?*

SE:   You can study the interactions of events and how each event affects the individual, past, present, and future. For a limited period of time, you can make changes that affect these events to see what happens next. You can use it to plan the events that need to take place to make your incarnate life work out to the best of its expectation, including putting fail-safes in, so that it accounts for a certain amount of change made by other entities doing the same thing.

ME:   *So what you are saying is that the Akashic records can also be used as a giant "what if" scenario.*

SE:   It is much more than that. An individual spirit can insert into its incarnating memory the memory/ memories of other spirits' lives and experiences to see how they would affect its life plan. The spirit may then make adjustments to the memory structures, removing certain experiences or parts of experiences to plan the optimal life experience and outcome. This, of course, is only a projection and is only "current" at a specific point in time, as the incarnating spirit may make a different judgment on a decision than that shown in the Akashic once it is in the physical where it doesn't have the advantage of its second memory to help it make decisions.

The interactions of other incarnates are also affected, and how they respond to the changes in the decision profile will make a difference to their incarnation plans.

ME: *You said that the Akashic is much more.*

SE: Yes, it is. It also gives you the opportunity to dip into the life experiences of other incarnates, past, present, and future whose lives/existence experiences are stored in the Akashic. You can go into these and experience them as if they were your own, even taking what seems to be the same length of "real time" during the experience.

ME: *Hold on. You just said any entities "whose lives/existence experiences are stored in the Akashic." This intimates that there are some life experiences that are not in the Akashic?*

SE: This is true. There are some that are not. These are lives that are of no consequence to the overall effectiveness of total experience, or they are the lives of higher entities that have migrated back to the Source or even the Origin and are, therefore, out of play. They are not lost to the Origin; nothing is lost, ever, as they are placed into Its overall memory. It is just that they are no longer available to those entities who can only access the Akashic memory.

Don't forget that the Akashic is relative to entities that are operating in this particular universe and its dimensions. It is not relative to entities that are

281

operating in the other universes that I and the other Source Entities have created, as they have their own records of what they have experienced/achieved. These have a different name.

ME: *So the Akashic records have a name, "Akashic." What does this mean? Names must have a meaning.*

SE: A name does not need to have a meaning or a function other than a method of putting a tag on something. This is a human requirement and is also specific to other entities that are of a similar level of group evolution. Akashic purely means "Eternal," which is a way of saying forever, never ending, always. The Akashic have always been in existence from your point of view and will always be in existence. As a result, they are the "eternal records" of this universe.

ME: *Tell me more about the "what if scenario" function of the Akashic.*

SE: This is not used by the individual entity. It cannot be as it relies on the interaction of too many souls at the same time. It can be used by large groups of entities who are working together to achieve a collective purpose. You are part of one of these large groups. The group can be external to the Earth-based incarnating entities, such as yours, or they can be from entities that are wholly tied to the Earth for its evolutionary opportunities.

ME: *What do these groups do?*

SE: They help to turn a civilization in a certain direction, that direction being one that will enhance the evolutionary opportunities.

ME: *To do good!*

SE: Evolutionary opportunities do not always mean that an individual has to do what you call "good." Good and bad are a decisive and divisive verbal tools to discriminate between the actions of one individual or another. *Good* is the word that people prefer to use and prefer to be described as, but this does not mean that a good person will evolve faster than a bad person.

Evolution is about experience and the recognition of the evolutionary opportunities that are presented to the individual by certain experiences. For instance, if an entity was continually good in the Earth dimension, he/she would be outcast from his/her local community as being unreal. This experience in itself has its own evolutionary points as there are a whole host of emotions that go with being seen as a goody-goody or a do-gooder. Similarly, doing bad may also have its plus points because at some point doing bad things brings forth the emotions of remorse, which in itself is a powerful emotional and evolutional experience.

You see, to be able to evolve, you have to start at the bottom of the ladder, and this means that you must experience as many things as you can, good and bad. This is so that you can get a balanced view on existence at certain levels and gain experience on what is necessary to allow yourselves and your fellow incarnates to evolve all together. Once you fully understand this, you can then start to work together as a team in both the higher frequencies and the lower incarnate frequencies. This means that you can work together to change the course of civilizations or local groups to help them evolve, and the best place to find the optimal route for this is via the Akashic. The interesting thing is that the entities being influenced by this "what if scenario" whilst being conducted in the Akashic are, if they are currently not incarnate, aware of how they will be affected. This usually means that an audience starts to appear around the Akashic, mainly out of interest but also to offer comment on strategic improvements.

ME: *This must mean that thousands, if not millions, of entities are involved at the same time if a "what if scenario" is being performed.*

SE: It does, and that is why it is not performed very often,

283

as it relies on all of these entities working together at the same time for the good of the scenario. The outcome of the scenario also needs to be approved by the entities affected because it may affect their evolutional progress in some way.

## The Criteria for Using the Akashic Records for a "What If" Scenario

ME:     *Wow! How often is a "What If Scenario" performed?*

SE:     I explained when it happens, but I guess that you are asking what the criteria are for a scenario to be performed?

ME:     *Yes, that's it. You've only described a loose outline of why, but you haven't described an outline of when.*

SE:     We do this level of scenario with the Akashic when we need to make drastic changes to the direction of a civilization in order to either save it from extinction— this is always a waste, especially when it has a part to play in the overall scheme of things—or it is the right time to help the civilization evolve faster or move on to the next level of evolution. I use the word "civilization" here because I am talking about entities that exist in the physical frequencies/dimensions. These are the areas where the scenario is best used, as the incarnates themselves cannot remember what their life plan is, let alone what the plan for the physical vessels they occupy is whilst they are at this level of existence.

ME:     *So what you are really saying is that the "what if scenario" is used sparingly and only with a view to helping entities using the lower frequencies.*

SE:     That about sums it up.

ME:     *So the sum total of all human and other entity existence in this universe is stored in the Akashic, and this can be used to predict the direction of whole civilizations. That direction can be altered by groups of spirits who have designs on where that civilization should be going. The*

*Akashic "what if" scenario function allows them to fine tune what they need to do to gain the desired outcome.*

SE: That is exactly what happens. More importantly, that is what humanity does in times of world crisis. You see, evolution is not left to chance. The human and other incarnate races are continually being monitored and modified to ensure that the evolution process is accelerated, and the opportunities for evolution are increased. Have you ever stopped to wonder why life is so fast on Earth at the moment and why so many inventions are coming into fruition?

*ME: Yes, it seems that we are rushing around so much that we are not able to give ourselves the time to meditate and be in contact with our higher selves or even you.*

SE: Yes, but what's the real reason behind this rushing around?

## Current Experiments on Earth

*ME: I have no idea. Is it part of an experiment?*

SE: The whole of this universe and its dimensions is an experiment, but yes, there is a small experiment or two going on at the moment. The first one is to see who is able to make contact with their higher selves and, therefore, break into the real reality whilst being bombarded by all these new distractions and to help them to teach others how to do the same. The second is to bring the base level of experience up a notch or two, up to the point where you can work together with other incarnate entities and, therefore, increase the evolutionary opportunities for incarnate-kind in total. Additionally, raising yourself a notch or two will increase your base line frequency levels to one where all of you will become more sensitive to the greater reality again, thereby, putting you back to where you should be at this point in your existence.

All this technology is fine, but it masks your real potential by introducing artificial means to solving problems that are created by not being at the frequency humankind should be. With your true abilities, you would not need all these artificial mechanisms around you, and this is something you need to get over and understand as a race. Indeed, it is a race that you are in. In the very real sense of the word, humanity's racing back to the Source, to the Origin.

ME: *Why would it be a race? I thought that an entity's evolution was personal. That the most important thing was experiencing different things that make you grow as an entity and that going back to the Source was a personal choice.*

SE: Going back to the Source *is* a personal choice. It is one that you are free to choose not to take as well if you see fit. It's only a race because most entities actually want to return to the Source to share the feeling of oneness and totality, as well as share their contribution to the Origin—their contribution being what they have learned and experienced about themselves and their environment. This is the ultimate reason for their existence; it helps the Origin know Itself better and faster, and more importantly in a way that It wouldn't have thought of Itself.

ME: *I thought that the Origin would be able to think of everything and experience everything.*

SE: Of course it can, but the benefit here is that you, as smaller entities, are able to experience things in a much more personalized way, even more so than the Origin itself, purely because you are not distracted by bigger things. In essence, you are able to get into details that the Origin would not find interesting from Its perspective. To do this, you need smaller beings. That's why the Origin created Me and I, in turn, created all of you—to get to the details and, to come back with these details as soon as possible. The Akashic is simply a depository of all the combined experiences that humankind has experienced, could experience, or wants to experience, and these choices are based upon free will in a limiting environment.

ME: *OooKaay, but you only mentioned the human race. You previously noted that all incarnate life had past, present and future life information stored in the Akashic.*

SE: You're being pedantic now. Of course, I mean all the life experience of all incarnate entities contained in the physical universe and its dimensions and frequencies are stored in the Akashic. I am focusing on the human race purely because that is where the part of you that is communicating with Me is currently residing. If I were to include where the rest of your incarnate quotient is, you would only get confused.

# Chapter 19:
# *Living Many Incarnations Simultaneously*

ME:  *Whoa! That was a big jump! One minute we are talking about humankind and the Akashic records, the next you drop in the insinuation that we are living more than one life at once.*

SE:  It was the right time to drop it into the conversation. I did so for the following reasons: first, we were starting to go around in circles about the subject of the Akashic. Second, it is the right time to introduce the subject of living many lives concurrently.

ME:  *Why would an entity want to live more than one incarnate life at a time? Living one seems to take up all of my time.*

SE:  The practice of living multiple lives simultaneously is a regular and common strategy of the vast majority of souls in order to accelerate their evolutionary potential.

ME:  *Why do we only think that we are living one life?*

SE:  Because of your limited awareness. Your awareness is specific to that part of you that is projected into this universe and this dimension. If you were able to tap into the experiences that other parts of yourself are having at this moment in time (there is no such thing as time, of course) and were unaware that you could tap into other parts of you that are either incarnate or energetic (as most people are), you would go mad. In fact, there are people incarnate in the Earth plane who are constantly tapping into the experiences that other parts of themselves are having at the same time right now.

289

ME: *Where are these people? Why are they not shouting from the highest treetop about their experiences, telling the rest of humanity that the truth is much more than we perceive with our five senses!?*

SE: Because they are all in mental institutions. They can't cope with what they are experiencing because they don't know what they are experiencing. Worse still, those around or close to them don't know or understand either. Even worse, they are not able to think of a solution to the problem that they are witnessing because it is outside of their framework of understanding. This is compounded by institutional staff who are only trained to deal with psychological issues that are based upon what they have been taught at university or college.

ME: *So are all these people in mental institutions experiencing many lives at the same time?*

SE: No, of course not. Many are not experiencing other lives that other parts of themselves are experiencing but are simply able to tap into the greater reality of other dimensions associated with the Earth plane.

ME: *So they are seeing other entities, other inhabitants of Earth, that most of us can't see or perceive.*

SE: Correct. O.K., we are digressing. The subject of living many incarnations at the same time is an important one to discuss. As I previously stated, it is a common practice and one that has been in constant use almost since the start of human development.

If you remember, earlier in this dialogue we discussed the development of the physical body by energetic humanity and some of the issues surrounding sharing bodies in the early days of the practice of incarnation—that is, the sharing of irregularities of physical and energetic function brought about by incomplete design of the physical/energetic human form. The sharing of physical form caused the spread of energetic dysfunction. This, in a sense, was the

290

precursor to living many lives in parallel. The practice of splitting selves into smaller chunks is a direct correlation with what the Origin and the other Source Entities have found necessary to affect efficient evolutionary progress.

*ME:* *So are we limited to the Earth plane?*

## In Earth's Universe: in Any Dimension, on Any Planet, in Any Galaxy, at Any Time

SE: No, this is the whole point. You are able to and do have several parts of yourselves incarnate all at once in as many physical or dimensional locations as you deem necessary. This can be in any dimension on any planet in any galaxy at any point in time (event) of this universe. In essence, one part of you can be with Me now having this dialogue, being just on the border of awareness, whilst another part of you can be in another dimension as part of another race, either incarnate or disincarnate with full knowledge of who, what, and where the other sum parts of yourself are. And you are able to communicate with them and to relish in the experiences they are having and being fully able to make use of them as evolutionary opportunities in the environment that that part of you is currently experiencing.

*ME:* *So it is quite possible for me as an entity to be a cave man on one world in this universe . . .*

SE: . . . and a trans-dimensional manipulator on another whilst overseeing all of it from your normal energetic environment. Of course!

You see, this was the best way possible for you to experience everything that you wanted to experience in the shortest possible time.

*ME:* *So if some parts of me are able to tap into and experience what other parts of me are experiencing in other parts of this universe, why are there other parts*

291

*of me, like this part communicating with you now, which cannot?*

SE:  That was a matter of your personal choice. Also, you have to take into account the benefit of having such ability and knowledge would give you in the environment that that part of you is projected into. On top of this is the effect such knowledge would have on the credibility of what you are trying to achieve evolutionary-wise in an incarnation that is designed to give its best performance whilst in isolation from the greater reality, maximizing the experience of decision without precognition and the effect that it has on a soul totally immersed in separate oneness borne from the desire to experience singularity.

Another important factor here is the potential to experience life at all levels, and, therefore, understand a civilization on an individual basis from all points of view (i.e., from all levels of affluence, influence, and contribution) within a specific event or era concurrently, thereby maximizing the opportunity to evolve given by incarnation into the physical plane.

ME:  *I am keen to give others who have the opportunity to read this text a clear picture of what this means to them personally. How does this affect them? Should they be concerned? Should they be afraid? Should they be excited?*

SE:  I would not expect anyone who is open to the possibility of greater realities to be anything other than inspired by this knowledge. Those who would be afraid or concerned would not be ready to read such texts and would not be compelled to buy a book containing such details in the first place. However, there is nothing to be gained by going into further detail than we have, as the intricacies will just confuse.

## The Downside of Communicating with Other Parts of Self

ME:    *I just think that it would be interesting for others and myself to understand a little bit more about what it is like to be one of those beings that are both aware of the fact that other parts of their higher selves are living other lives, having other experiences and are able to tap into them to use those experiences for potential use in the environment in which they are incarnate.*

SE:    To many entities, knowing that this is part of the greater reality is enough. They do not desire or need to be in constant contact or communication with the other parts of themselves. They are aware but decide to focus their energies on doing the jobs at hand in the dimension they are projected into. They know that delving into the other lives they are living would be a distraction and would not help them too much in their current incarnation. Consider your own situation. Would being able to tap into a life that another part of you is having, say, in the Middle Ages, be useful to you in your current incarnation?

ME:    *Probably not.*

SE:    Would being able to tap into a life that another part of you is having, say, in a civilization that is not only space and time faring but disincarnate from your perspective, be able to help you in understanding your own experiences and evolution, and how it fits into the whole evolution of the whole being that is you?

ME:    *I would find it interesting but difficult.*

SE:    Yes, you would find it interesting, but it would be a major distraction and one that could negate your learning in the here and now. It is for this reason that it is best to be aware of the concept but not of the details as this sensationalizes the parts of this dialogue that should not be dwelled on too long, other than to present

293

the individual with the opportunity to expand his/her thought processes on what reality is.

# Chapter 20:
## *Illness*


Being trained in a couple of healing techniques, such as Reiki and energy-based healing (Brennan Healing Science) from one of Dr. Barbara Brennan's direct students, who also provided a significant amount of content of the course based upon the work of John and Eva Periakos, I was aware of how dysfunctional thoughts can cause energy-based dysfunction which affects the human body physically. I had also seen how other more open-minded physicians were recognizing and advocating the knowledge that some physical ailments are manifested from energetic or psychologically induced conditions.

I was pondering upon this as I had recently been experiencing a bad back, which was not getting better even after two months! I have to admit though that, as an active person, I was not totally giving it the chance to heal itself, but, nevertheless, I could not attribute the exercise I was doing to the pain I was feeling. Hence, when I was given a book and a DVD by a John E. Sarno, MD who had specifically written about how backache was essentially born from psychological conditions that we have carried with us as a child, and that "child was still with us in our unconscious," I started to take interest. I watched the DVD and read the relevant parts of the book and bingo, my back problem disappeared within a week.

Additionally, I was doing one of my morning meditations before I went to work when I got the message to write a short chapter for this book, one on illness. After a couple of days thinking about it, I did the usual and offered the subject up to the Source Entity for discussion.

SE: Well, I have to say that I am a little bit aghast that we have not already discussed this.

ME: *Well, we have—to a smaller degree. We have talked about physical issues, resulting from the interaction of different entities occupying the same physical body for experiential purposes.*

SE: Indeed we have, but this is such a fundamental issue that I am surprised it is one of the last subjects to be discussed in this book.

ME: *I suppose it is because many other people have already published on the subject.*

## The Role of Pain in Getting Us Back on Track

SE: Mmm, not convinced. O.K., let's look at this from a different angle.

As an energetic entity, you are free to do what you will with no one else interfering with your work. However, as an energetic entity incarnate in a physical body, you are influenced by many lower frequencies that are created by the lower thoughts of others. As a result, you are subject to emotional contradictions, which are so subtle that they are barely detectable with the conscious mind. The sub-conscious and the un-conscious mind is rational thought that is based upon the second and third energy/auric levels and is, therefore, not immediately accessible by the conscious. These two levels of cognitive application are both tied in with the physical body and the conscious mind. Due to their existence on a different energetic level, they are not recognized or accessed by the conscious mind, the lowest cognitive application of you as an energetic entity.

As a result when you experience something, the conscious mind logs the logical response to the activity experienced; the un-conscious and sub-conscious log the emotional aspects of the experience on the higher functions of communication, emotion, and empathy. The conscious mind rationalizes the experiences as desirable (enjoyed) and educational (mundane but, nevertheless, part of the evolutionary process). Notice it's not good or bad; it's merely experiential whist the unconscious and subconscious rationalizes the experience in the more subtle dimensions of necessity and desirability.

It is these two that have the biggest influence on the human body as they carry the greater opportunity for communication between the fully energetic self and the smaller incarnate self. These levels of communication involve functions of the body other than mind, and, as a result, create the *feel good* factor associated with going down the right course of actions at the right time, i.e., not going against the grain or flow. As a result they can be classified as an irrational or illogical autonomic response made by the physical body when a course of action is correct to the *plan* or NOT correct to the *plan*—the *plan* being the evolutionary opportunities and the optimal time for experiencing these opportunities as chosen before the incarnation.

The result of following the correct path with the correct actions is an indescribable (from an incarnate perspective) feeling of well-being. The result of following the wrong path or one that is seen as not optimal will result in the body feeling sluggish and laggard. It will also create emotional conditions, such as fear, which is a direct product of not following the correct path previously drawn up. This is usually manifested as physical discomfort (this is the best way to describe this as it is a most useful way for the energetic self to get the message home to the incarnate self that *something is not going according to plan and that the incarnate opportunity is not going to be maximized*). This is usually very directly aimed at certain areas of activity and the choices associated with them.

The result is that the part of the incarnate entity that is in contact with the energetic part tries its best to alert the conscious mind to address the job at hand. When the job at hand is recognized, the feelings, the emotional content that is associated with the experience, are released causing distress, especially if they are left to store for too long. These distressing feelings are usually too much to experience in the limited incarnate state so they are absorbed energetically by the physical body. As a result of being absorbed, they introduce energetic disharmonies, which affect the underlying energy flow and interaction of the energies associated with the normal function of the organs of the body and the higher energetic interfaces that you call auric levels. This energetic dysfunction causes physical dysfunction and disease/pain as the function of the physical body is fighting against the dysfunctional energies. Try to think of it as trying to receive energy in the shape of a cylinder when it is being forcibly presented to you in the shape of a cube.

## Correcting/Removing Pain

*Me:* *So this is what pain is and how we get it.*

SE: That's it in a nut shell.

*ME:* *So how do we correct it?*

SE: By tuning into the pain and trying to understand why it is there. To do this, you must not dismiss any images that come to you, for the dysfunction may be a couple of minutes old to decades or lifetimes old. Once recognized, the flow of energy is corrected, and it is no longer absorbed by the physical body, thereby relieving the *need* to alert the conscious mind of the abnormality via physical disturbance. Normality is, therefore, resumed, and you go with the flow again moving forward in the physical world without physical pain.

ME:   *And this works.*

SE:   This works! Very well!

ME:   *So what about disease in general?*

SE:   What about it? It applies to the comments above.

## Challenges of Higher Energetic Frequency Individuals in Low Energetic Frequency Environments

ME:   *But there must be other reasons why we get ill other than those created by energetic disharmony.*

SE:   No, it all comes from energy-based harmony issues. Listen, I think I understand what you are getting at now. Illness is always a product of energy dysfunction. However, it is also a product of being in an energy level to which you are not attuned. For instance, if you are in a human vehicle whose energy system is designed to exist in a higher energetic frequency and the ambient frequency that you find yourself in is lower than the desired frequency, then the harmonics between the energetic and physical bodies will be incorrect. The physical body can cope to a certain level with this level of disharmony and will appear to function as normal, i.e., the body's chakras and organs have a tolerance within which they can work. This appearance of correct functionality can exist for years, sometimes tens of years, but eventually the disharmonies will start to take their toll. The organs of the body that are least able to cope with the energies that are at the lower end of the tolerance will start to fail. Consider it like an electric motor being switched on, off, on, off constantly but irregularly. The back EMF (electromotive force) causes damage resulting in degradation of the motor's functionality, which eventually leads to failure. With some organs in the physical human body, this failure can result in its demise.

## Chakra and Organ Transplants

Organ failure can also be attributed to chakra failure when the chakra affecting the energy regulation of the physical organ associated with it no longer performs its function. The physical organ also ceases to perform its function, again resulting in the demise of the physical body. The only way out of this is the transplanting of a new chakra and quite possibly a physical organ at the same time although if caught in time the chakra transplant can reverse the energetic damage of the physical organ. Interestingly enough, the rejection issues your doctors have encountered with some of the more major organs are related to the further energetic disharmonies created by the replacement of a physical organ without the associated original chakra also being transplanted. If this were known by your doctors, they would see the need to work side by side with energy healers who could perform transplants of the correct chakra associated with the donor organ. An added bonus is that they would no longer need to have immuno-suppressant drugs administered to the patients post organ transplant because the organs would not be rejected by the body's energy system, for all would be in harmony.

## The Rule of Longevity

In essence, physical illness and demise is the result of the gradual damage caused by lower frequencies in your environment. The rule of longevity is that the lower the ambient frequency, the shorter the lifespan of the human vehicle. In its current state of creation, the human vehicle is not designed to be used in the lower frequencies that the Earth is currently experiencing. The human body was designed to work within energies of a much higher level, which allowed it to exist for the thousands of years it was originally designed for. The proof of this is in front of your face. Just look for the cities around the world where people are low of spirit, and you will see people of low life spans. Where people exist in areas where they are high in spirit, they live much longer. Raising the frequency of the Earth is the only solution to removing disease, dysfunction, and early demise of the physical form.

## I Am Part of God

*ME:* *So how do I know that I am part of God/the Source/the Origin? I have no one telling me that I am part of God.*

SE: You have Me telling you.

*ME:* *But how do I know You are real? Surely if You were real, everyone would know You intimately.*

SE: It is all about evolution and awareness. Only those who are evolved enough are aware of the greater reality. They know I/they exist together.

## Communicating with the Cells in Our Bodies

*ME:* *But surely a God that is so big would not be able to communicate with Its lower parts. For instance, I cannot talk to the two cells in my liver that are exchanging oxygen and nutrition with the rest of my body. I simply don't know how to do so. I doubt if these two cells know that I exist as their "God."*

SE: One, you could talk to them if you really wanted, and two, they know you exist because they work specifically for the benefit of your physical body.

Cells are more intelligent than you think. Remember, they are created directly from the commands given to the DNA from the RNA, which is in continuous contact with your spiritual energy bodies. They use the RNA to receive commands from Spirit on

301

what to do next and communicate back to Spirit when they have finished their task. As a result of this, they are in contact with Spirit on a continuous basis, which your intellect is not because you are distracted by the other things that go on around you. Hence, your ability to talk to your self is diminished or even ignored.

ME:     *You can't be serious about this! How can I communicate with my body at a cellular level? I can't even see cells with my bare eyes without the use of a microscope.*

## Seeing the Cells in Our Bodies

SE:     I am deadly serious. All you need to do is focus on an area of your body with your mind's eye and zoom into that area. Most of the time your communication will be the same as we are doing here, communicating by talking in your mind. But when you get better at concentrating and shutting out the distractions of the physical world, you will even be able to see these cells and appreciate the surface of them to the point where you can see the communication interactions of the cells and the RNA and how the cell changes its shape, how the color of its outer surface changes, and how it grows/creates different types of tendrils that have different shapes and, therefore, different specialties. You will see these tendrils come and go from the surface of the cell as they are reabsorbed back into the body of the cell when they have finished the job they were doing. You will marvel in the beauty of the work they do and the efficiency in which they perform their work.

ME:     *I just got an image of what you were just describing. It's fantastic. When scientists are studying cells with electron microscopes and other high powered optics, do they see what I just saw and what you were describing?*

302

SE: Sometimes. They tend to see what they want to see and that tends to hold them at a point in time. This means that they only see the cells when they have changed into the communication medium required to perform a job. They don't stay long enough at the level required to see the changes happen with the COMMUNICATION tendrils. They only see the cell RECOGNITION tendrils.

ME: *I thought that they would since they sometimes use film to record cells dividing or mutating.*

SE: Yes, they do, but the tendrils I am talking about are on the sub-atomic levels. This is difficult to see with electron microscopes unless they know what they are looking at, and they have not yet perfected recording what they are seeing moving or changing through an electron microscope.

ME: *This all sounds a bit marginal to me.*

SE: Maybe, but it's true. Remember people who fly in heavier than air machines would have been called witches or heretics 400 years ago, but today it is accepted as an everyday occurrence.

## Cancer Cells

ME: *O.K., O.K. I have a question on cancer cells.*

SE: Go ahead; ask away.

ME: *If cells are constantly in contact with Spirit via the RNA, how do cancer cells form or even exist?*

SE: Even cancer cells are in contact with your spiritual energies, and they do as they are told, the same as so-called "good" cells. However, the difference here is that they are cells that have been told to do the wrong things by Spirit. In essence, the interactions you have within the physical levels affect the frequencies and modulation of spiritual energies in the higher levels. This causes confusion in translation of the commands sent to the cells in question and makes them do things that they wouldn't normally do. In this instance, it could be not disintegrating when it is supposed to or creating more of itself than is required to do a particular job or even attacking known good cells. It's a bit like you getting into your car and driving it straight into a wall. You wouldn't normally do that, would you?

ME: *How could Spirit tell a cell to do the wrong things then? I thought that Spirit was pure!*

SE: The interactions with the physical disrupt the harmonious flow of energies, changing its meaning or intention. This is caused by the part of you that is projected into the human body reacting badly to situations that occur to you. You react badly because you are not in tune with Spirit and cannot, therefore, see the beauty in the process that led up to what has happened, i.e., you don't accept and learn. Instead, you reject and get fed up. This creates disruption in the energy flow if this situation is accepted as a learning opportunity. It then creates dense energy, which blocks the flow or even changes the energy characteristics and, hence, the messages being sent.

ME: *So what you are saying is that I create my own cancer.*

SE: Yes, but you wouldn't create it if you were in tune with universe/Spirit/Me.

## Byron on Another Approach to Self-Healing

Being in tune with universe/Spirit/Origin/Source is all part of our maintaining a state of wholeness and wellness. This leads me to the subject of healing self when that balance has been interrupted.

One Tuesday morning I started my meditation with my usual linking with the Earth energies (Hara) and opened up my chakras. I then zipped up the 27<sup>th</sup> level to see Byron. As I was doing this, my mind wandered to the thought of self-healing. He put his arm over my shoulder, and we walked out of the dark that was my perception of the 27<sup>th</sup> level into a beautiful field with rolling hills and a small wood next to the sea.

B: This is a mental construct I have made especially for you. Since you like all of these things on the Earth plane, I have put them all together for your pleasure.

## Healing at the Etheric Body and Ketheric Template Levels

*ME: Thank you. I have a question. I know that physical dysfunction is a result of a distorted perception starting at the ketheric template level [See the Glossary and Appendix for further information on the ketheric template.], but I have had this thought that self-healing can also be from the physical plane up.*

B: That's right. It can be. To achieve this, the individual needs to tune into the etheric body (the blue matrix) [See the Glossary and Appendix for further information on the etheric body.] and effect repairs from that point.

*ME: So how do you heal yourself from a disease, say asthma?*

B: You heal yourself by repairing the etheric body for the part of the body that is dysfunctional, diseased, or damaged by imagining the energy grid lines of the etheric body for that area being rebuilt or strengthened. Then you follow up by surrounding the area affected in rose-colored light. The distorted perception that created the physical effect can be removed through personal processing by establishing what faults or perceptions/illusions and assumptions are attached to this illness and changing the mindset.

*ME:* *How do you do that?*

B:     Using your example, if you have a problem with asthma when you travel into a city, you may find that the distorted perception is that "living in the city is bad for you." The distortion may have come from a comment that one of your parents may have made when you were a child. This comment about the air being polluted in the city would have programmed your subconscious into thinking that all cities are full of dirt and polluted air—hence, the onset of asthma when you visit a city. If you live in a city, you will always suffer from asthma until this mindset is changed through personal processing and regeneration of the etheric body for the lungs.

*ME:* *So you need to heal yourself on the etheric body level and the higher levels.*

B:     Yes, you need to start at the ketheric level, as this is the first of the higher levels (below the $8^{th}$. There are 10 levels associated with the human body. See Appendix) to be associated with the incarnated physical body.

*ME:* *So will changing the distorted perception heal you on its own?*

B:     Only if it hasn't manifested into physical disease. If there is physical disease, you will need to heal that part of the etheric body that is affected as well.

As Byron talked about this, my perception zoomed into my own etheric body and saw all the blue energy lines in 3-D going inside my body, as well as on the surface.

B:     That's right; you will also find that the energies are subtly different for each of the different organs and other parts of the body.

*ME:* *I can see them as different colors and different shades of colors, depending on the organ or body component I am looking at.*

306

B:      Yes, the different colors are relative to the different frequencies. The DNA of the cells that make up each organ or body part responds to this energy and makes the cell change to that required of it in the frequency it finds itself.

ME:     *You mean the DNA doesn't dictate what a cell's function is? It's the frequency of the etheric body relative to that organ?*

## RNA→Etheric Body Frequency→DNA

B:      That's right; the DNA of the cell waits to be told what it is supposed to do. It waits to receive its programming. It gets this from the frequency of the etheric body it receives via RNA. When it receives this frequency, it switches itself to the correct code for that frequency and makes the cell perform the role required of that organ and the frequency of that organ on the etheric body level.

## Stem Cells

ME:     *Wow! So what would happen if I put a liver cell in the frequency of the heart?*

B:      It would die before its time because it has already received its programming as a liver cell. The DNA is like a onetime programmable (OTP) microprocessor chip, and this is a safety feature of the human body. Once a cell has received its programming, it is stuck in that mode for its life span (which is also determined by the job it has to do). There are cells that are ready to be programmed and that can be inserted into the etheric body frequency of any organ or body part to effect repairs. You call these stem cells. Again, once they have logged into a frequency, the DNA switches the functionality of the cell to that required of the frequency received and required of that cell type for the frequency relating to that organ's functional requirements. However, this is not totally necessary. If an individual can tune into the template frequency of the damaged area, rebuild the etheric template in that area, and initiate the right intentions of overcoming the dis-ease created by the distorted perceptions created at the ketheric level (and its subsequent cascade down the other levels to the physical level) and correct the distortion in perception by understanding what it is and why it arose, the physical dysfunction can be healed.

ME: *I thought that the DNA was the building bricks of life.*

B: True, but the etheric body tells the DNA via the RNA what type of brick it is for the house it is in. It is the energy frequency of the etheric body that calls the shots.

The next day I continued the dialogue after I had discussed it with my wife (who worked at that time with genetic manipulation for treating ovarian cancer).

ME: *My wife told me that some of her colleagues are replacing the DNA in some cells for DNA therapy. She said they think that will do away with the need for stem cells.*

B: It is possible to do this, but the cell receiving the new DNA would not function as efficiently as a stem cell that has not yet been programmed by the energy frequency of the etheric body relative to a specific part of the body, say the heart.

ME: *Why is this? She seems to think it will work.*

## Mismatch Issues of DNA Replacement in Cells

B: As I said, it will but not as well as the newly programmed stem cells. This is because a cell whose DNA has previously been programmed has adapted itself to the job required of that part of the body.

ME: *Do you mean it can't change to something else?*

B: No. It will function because some of the tools it has, such as receptors, sensors, and transmitters for the chemical commands, together with other functionality, are similar to all cells. However, the tools that are specific to the cell functioning as a heart cell if, for instance, it was previously a liver cell, won't be there. The cell will have discarded these tools or functions when its DNA was exposed to the energy frequency of the liver's etheric body. Also, it will have been programmed to live for a certain length of time. A certain amount of degradation will already have taken place which will cause another mismatch issue.

ME: *So why are stem cells better?*

B: Because they have all the tools they will ever need to perform any function in the body ready and waiting for the time that they are told by the etheric energy programming of the DNA what they are going to be. Also, they are considered cumbersome in this state, so when they change to the requirements of their programming, they get rid of all the excess baggage of a universally useful cell to allow them to be efficient as, for instance, liver cells, not heart cells. Additionally and as mentioned above, a programmed cell's life span has already been programmed in. And although cells can live forever, if required, once they have been told their function, their life span is changed to suit the need to renew old tissue. So a liver cell that normally lives a shorter life span than say a heart cell would, in fact, live only as long as a liver cell in a heart environment, which would cause compatibility issues, as the heart cells may be expected to live longer.

## The Effect of Transplanting a Liver Cell into the Diseased Section of a Heart

To summarize, a liver cell can have its DNA changed to that of a heart cell, and it can be transplanted into a diseased area of a heart, but it will not function as well as a stem cell that is introduced into the energetic frequencies of the etheric body of a heart. Although it will survive, it does not contain the tool kit of a heart cell. It contains the tool kit of a liver cell and will try to use these "liver tools" to work in a heart environment, which it can't do effectively, but it will, nevertheless, try to do but poorly. This level of poor efficiency will be noticed by the heart's defense system because some of its tools will not be compatible, and the cell will eventually be removed/forced to die. How fast this happens is determined by how fast the heart's defense system picks up the anomaly. So it will do some good, but it will be limited.

ME: *So this type of genetic manipulation is fruitless.*

B: Yes, but as you say, "Any port in a storm." Some people will think that a poorly operating heart is better than no heart. A partially functional heart is a better port than a port that doesn't have a functioning heart. This type of therapy will have its place but only as a transient therapy until these rules are better understood.

# Chapter 21:
## *Relaxation, Meditation, and the Core Star*

Another morning meditation saw a very short communication with the Source Entity on the subject of relaxation.

SE:  Relaxation promotes recreation.

*ME:  Why is this?*

SE:  Because you have the ability to tap into Spirit when you are relaxed. This is only possible when you don't have a million and one things to do.

## Core Star Meditation

*ME:  How good is core star meditation? [See the Appendix for instructions on how to do a core star meditation.] Does it allow one to contact Spirit any better than normal meditation?*

SE:  Core star meditation is the best way of contacting your "self" and Spirit.

*ME:  Why the two?*

SE:  Because you are Spirit. The core star is the part of your Spirit that is linked to the physical. If you, therefore, focus on your core star long enough, you will inevitably get into contact with the real you. Because the core star is you, you will start to break down the barriers of the physical world. When you do this, you will inevitably raise the frequency of your physical body to those close to the astral, which will allow you to see the other entities around you who exist in this realm or use it for trans-dimensional travel purposes.

You have to understand that all meditation is good, but some is better than others to achieve certain goals. For instance, transcendental meditation is good

311

for practicing astral travel. Other meditation techniques, such as those practiced by Yogi Masters are good for slowing the degradation process of the physical body. Others are good for developing and honing your attention to your intention, which enhances your creativity with energy.

## The Link Between Astral Travel and the Core Star

*ME:* *How is astral travel linked to the core star?*

SE: It is the link with the core star that allows you to be connected and to visit the middle realms, the realms that are neither spirit nor physical. The core star is you, and you are the core star but understand that in all good texts you will see the illustrations of the astral body separating from the physical and still remaining attached to the physical via a silver cord. This silver cord attaches the 4th level of the human aura, the astral body, to the other bodies. This is achieved through the core star, or the real you. When the core star truly leaves the physical body, it dies. Thus you are only allowed to leave your body through one level, the fourth or astral, the one that sits in the middle of both worlds.

# Chapter 22:
## *Souls Returning to the Source Entity*

### At Home with God on the 100th Level

During a meditation I had the impression that I should go to the 100th level and to the Source Entity. When I arrived, I saw in my mind's eye the now familiar galaxy-like image of the entity that was the Source of all of us, the One that many texts refer to as God. As I approached the Source Entity, I saw lots of stars that were so close to each other, they looked like the Source Entity Itself.

SE:    These are all the souls that have returned to God.
*ME:    I thought they would just blend into You.*
SE:    They have, but they have retained their individuality. They are individual and part of the whole at the same time. They are more than just a piece of Me; they bring to the Whole different evolutionary experiences. Some of them will start the long cycle again if they want; others will not.

I then had the image of a wizened old man with a long white beard standing by me. Everything about him was the same color: white.

### The True State of Earth's Source Entity

*ME:    I thought you would show me your true state.*
SE:    I will show you this if that's what you want.

With this the Source Entity then disappeared although I could still communicate with it.

313

ME:   *I can't see you.*

SE:   You did want to see what I was really like; this is it.

ME:   *I think it would be good to have the image of the old man back as it gives me a focal point.*

SE:   As you wish.

He then re-appeared as the old man. I then had the impression that grid lines were present in the vast expanse that was the Source.

ME:   *I see that you have structure, too.*

## Retaining Individuality

SE:   Yes, there is an order to everything, and that is what you have seen. Everything is in its place and has a place with Me. Remember, returning to the Source is not loss of individuality; it is coadunation, being one with the whole whilst being individual. Returning souls/spirits/entities need not fear loss of individuality, for there is no loss.

ME:   *I will ensure this is in the text of one of my books.*

SE:   Please do. It's an important concept to convey.

## The Collective Mind

This was a morning meditation with a "curved ball" surprise from the Origin, one that caught me off guard since I was wondering whether or not I would be able to do any meditation that morning—no matter how short.

O:   The collective mind is nothing to be feared, you know.

I knew that I feared the loss of singularity of mind and, to some extent, I found it both scary and intriguing.

ME:   *You knew that I was worried about losing my singularity.*

O:      That's not surprising as all of you on Earth are in the unique position of having your own focus on intent, your own singularity in total. This is not given in general.

ME:     *What do you mean "in total"?*

O:      By this, I mean that you are all "Gods," for the want of a better word. You are all mini-Mes. You are all capable of doing so much, but this is only achievable at this moment in time if you will meditate on getting back to Source and ignore the distractions.

I thought about the things I like: cycling, diving, etc.

O:      Yes, these are the sort of distractions. Meditate upon being part of the whole and don't be afraid. Even in a collective mind, those parts of Me that have been singular retain singularity; it's just a larger, **much larger** singularity.

## Coadunation and Expansiveness

One meditation saw me talking to the Source about nothing in general when He slipped in the word "coadunation" again.

ME:     *Why are we speaking about coadunation again?*

SE:     Do you remember that I described returning to the Source as coadunation and not loss of individuality? I said that it is being one with the whole whilst remaining individual. I added that "returning souls/spirits/entities need not fear loss of individuality, for there is no loss." Well, the word *coadunation* is also a good word for describing what will happen when humankind gains a critical mass of people who are in contact with Spirit and themselves. This is a way of returning to Source while in the physical.

ME:     *What do you mean?*

315

SE:    People who are capable of being in touch with their real selves and Spirit through their core star will be able to contact all that there is in the universe. This means that they will be able to contact Me/us/, other incarnate/disincarnate beings, the spirits of the planets, the stars, the animals, and plant life of the planets at all dimensional and frequency levels.

ME:    *So it means communion?*

SE:    It is actually much better a descriptor than that; it also involves the rest of the "aware" universe in its entirety, a joining together in wholeness again.

ME:    *I have a different question. Just how expansive are you?*

SE:    Very. I am/We are so expansive that you can't possibility understand it in your current condition.

ME:    *O.K., try me.*

SE:    Very well. Imagine you are able to travel as far as you can in any direction in any time in any dimension; I will still be there.

I did this and found that when I projected myself in a specific direction the area around me remained bathed in a bright white light. I tried to go as far as I can by making my intention very well known. No matter how far I went, the brilliance of the Source Entity was there.

SE:    Now do you understand that you cannot perceive just how expansive I/We are in your current incarnate condition?

ME:    *Yes, I think so. Can you help me understand a bit more about your expansiveness?*

SE:    Yes.

ME:    *How can you possibly know what is going on at any one point in time, space, and dimension when you are literally all over the place.*

SE:    Imagine your current body. If you get an itch on your leg, for instance, you instantly re-focus your attention to the area of the itch and give it a scratch. The same is true if you hurt yourself; you instantly re-focus your attention to the area of pain.

ME:   *Yes, I do.*

SE:   All this is done even though your attention is mostly in your head.

I tried this and was suddenly surprised that my attention changed from my head or other things that I was doing to the point of the itch or discomfort when I pinched myself.

ME:   *Yes, I see.*

SE:   Well, imagine that I can do this an immeasurable number of times all at the same time. This allows Me to talk to you and others like all of you at the same time, even though you might be in different spaces, dimensions, or time frames.

ME:   *So that is how you extend your expansiveness.*

SE:   Yes, I do this by having communication sensors in every molecule in every dimension. This allows Me to pick up on the "itch" and talk to one of you from anywhere without a delay.

ME:   *So you really are expansive.*

SE:   Yes.

ME:   *That's funny. I feel that there is an end to your expansiveness.*

SE:   Very perceptive. There is, of course, an end but you knew this, deep down.

## Beyond the Expansiveness of the Source

I changed my mental focus to extend myself beyond the expansiveness of the Source. I saw that the Source was, in fact, very expansive, but what I saw surprised me. The area around me was in negative format with the Source below me displayed like a bubble with all the universes and dimensions and galaxies contained within the bubble. As I looked around myself, I saw that there were others like the Source, all with similar looking bubbles. I returned to my conversation with Source.

ME:  *There are more of You.*
SE:  Yes. We are all part of something bigger, and We are all experiencing Ourselves in different ways. My way was to split Myself in half and make the many immortal souls that you are and task you with going out into the universe to experience as many different things as you could. Others like Me have done this in different ways or not at all.
ME:  *All the universes you created look like black spheres inside a dirty white sphere, and they all have gaps in between them.*
SE:  Yes, that's correct.
ME:  *Why are they here?*
SE:  To allow My helpers to move between the universes without interaction with them. Consider them My back door.

## Active Engagement in the Evolutionary Process

I looked at the other spheres that looked like our Source Entity or God.

SE:  They/We are all part of a bigger entity, the Origin. What I have divided Myself into, all you smaller souls, is similar to what the Origin has done to create Us, discounting the smaller souls, of course. Everything is disseminated; everything is actively engaged in the evolutionary process of understanding self by experiencing new things in different environments in order to feed this back to the Whole to make the Whole (the Origin) appreciate what It is.
ME:  *So I am privileged to see this.*

SE: You are only seeing a very small part of it in your very limited physical incarnation, but yes, there are not many people that have seen this, let alone made some sort of sense of it in their current state.

# Chapter 23:
## *The Source Entity's Observations of Souls on Earth*

## Witnessing The Source Entity Dividing Itself into Myriad Parts

One morning saw me doing my usual morning meditation and hara line work. I had the intention of going into my mind to talk with aliens but was surprised to find myself in the presence of the Source Entity again. This I didn't expect although I knew I was in His presence as I saw Him/It from a very great distance as a nebula of white clouds in space.

SE: You are witnessing the great division when I divided Myself into Me and the smaller parts of Me.

I could see the cloud of light coalesce into smaller points of light that I knew were the new souls being born.

SE: Each smaller part of Me will have Its own independence and decision process to follow.

*ME: Why did You split Yourself into many pieces like this?*

SE: To see the difference/s between "what is" compared with the many different forms of "what could be."

*ME: What do you mean?*

SE: What I was I could understand, but I felt the need to experience what could be. If I had just divided into two, this would have taken a long time, so I decided to make half of Myself into many billions of souls. Each would experience different things at the same time and feed the information that they are experiencing to Me as they experienced it. The objective was to experience everything that I could by putting Myself in as many different environments, situations, positions, times, civilizations, dimensions, etc., etc., as I could think of, all at the same time to make Myself grow through experience. The Earth is a very interesting case and is providing a lot of evolutionary material.

## The Incarnate Soul's Lack of Contact with Source

ME:   *What makes Earth interesting?*

SE:   The Earth is interesting because I didn't envisage Earth and its incarnate souls falling down the frequencies as occurred. This I found most interesting because on all other planets with all the different types of incarnate beings, the beings are all still in contact with Me in some way, shape, or form. When a soul incarnates at the Earth level at its current frequency, the part of the soul that incarnates is totally unaware of My presence—so much so that it needs to have a team of souls helping it during the incarnation process. A soul is truly on its own and is free to make its own decisions without knowing whether it will be a good or bad decision when, in fact, there is no good or bad decision, only choices.

ME:   *So we truly are deaf, dumb, and blind.*

## Souls on the Cusp of Recovery and Acceleration

SE:   Yes. What is even more interesting is that although over the millennia, you have all risen and fallen many times in terms of civilization, spirituality, and technology, but you have never been this low in frequencies. Of greater interest is that you are now on the cusp of recovery and are destined to rise again through the frequencies to even better than before. This was totally unexpected.

ME:   *How can this be unexpected for the One Who is all seeing?*

SE:   Of course, I expected it, but expectation and experience is a different kettle of fish, which is the whole reason for My dividing Myself in the first place.

ME:   *I see.*

SE:   Yes, I think you do. IF this works out with Earth, I will allow this process with other planets and civilizations that are less in control of their own future from an individual entity's point of view.

ME:   *So Earth is an experiment.*

SE:   Yes, but everything is an experiment; everything is an experiential experiment. Experience is everything. Without experience you only have theory.

ME:   *Why is that?*

I knew the answer to this question before the Source even answered, or did I?

SE:   Because in the first instance, it involves the interaction of the individual without the prior knowledge of what to do, so he/she has to make decisions based upon his/her circumstances and react accordingly. If he/she gets it right, he/she learns; if he/she gets it wrong, he/she also learns. It's a win-win situation, filled with opportunities to learn or experience something.

When the individual has more knowledge or experience of an issue or problem, it makes finding the solution to the problem more efficient.

## The Fastest Way to Evolve

Experiencing things by having put yourself in a situation where you have to work it all out for yourself is by far the fastest way of evolving. It is wonderful.

ME: *I don't think that is so because you may go down the wrong path in your solution because you have based your assumptions on data from a different situation.*

SE: Good, you are thinking but accept the fact that the understanding/recognition of going down the wrong route is faster than it would have been without prior knowledge. It's true. Consider the lab rat in a maze. Once he has sorted out the way to the center and back again in one maze, the time it takes him to solve the puzzle when he is put into a different maze, is faster than it was in the first maze. The third time will be even faster.

## Author Questions Speech as a Form of Communication

The next day saw me once again zooming into the mass of light that was the Source Entity. As I closed in on Him/It, I saw all the souls who had decided to return to the Source as a nest of stars moving gradually ever closer to Source. I dived in and immediately saw Him as a wizened old man in a brilliant white robe.

ME: *Why do we speak or appear to speak to each other? Why not use another method of communication? Like images?*

SE: Because this is what your focus is on. You communicate better this way whilst you are an incarnate being.

ME: *Could we not communicate in the way that we do when we are disincarnate?*

SE: We can't do that because your focus is currently on this method of communication. If we used the other seventeen senses that you have when we communicate properly, your conscious self would not be able to cope with the massive and sudden influx of new data. You would just pass out.

ME:    *What are these other senses?*

SE:    Some of them are too difficult for you to understand at the moment but suffice it to say that when we communicate properly, you receive not only the spoken word (which is really very limiting, sort of like trying to type with one finger!) but also you receive twenty-two channels of input, including images, feelings, emotions, smells, perceptions, tactile impressions, and other senses that you wouldn't even know you had or could use.

ME:    *Wow! So for the moment the spoken word really is the best way.*

SE:    Yes, at the moment.

## Animals in the Ionosphere

As I then started my core star meditation, my attention focused on the Earth, the animals, trees, birds, and fish. As I logged into each of these animals, I was suddenly one with them, flying in the air, hunting for small mammals, swimming in the sea. My thoughts then went to the Earth, and I wandered into the ionosphere.

ME:    *I suddenly got the impression that there are animals in the ionosphere as well!*

SE:    Yes, there are; they are gas animals. You haven't detected them yet because you don't have the equipment to do so. There are many, many animals that live on or around the Earth that you don't know about.

ME:    *Can I ask about their purpose on Earth later?*

SE:    Please do.

# Chapter 24:
## *A Bit about the Author's Past Lives*


A follow-up meditation days later saw me contacting the Source rather quickly. I was starting to just "go there" rather than needing to go through a series of steps. When I arrived, I wanted to talk to Source about the other lives I had on Earth.

*ME:*   *What have I been in my other lives on Earth?*
SE:    Many things. You have been kings, lords, paupers, and common folk, but in all of your incarnations, you have been yourself.

*ME:*   *What do you mean? I have been myself?*
SE:    By this, I mean that you have been YOURSELF in its entirety. This means that you were not trying to be something that you were not, and you were also in contact with all of your "self," which would include what you call your higher self.

*ME:*   *What else have I been?*
SE:    Many of your lives have been assisting people to remember or not forget the reality of the universe and who they are. This included the use of and sensing of energies. You did this by teaching them how to feel the energies and then how to see them.

*ME:*   *Why did I do this?*
SE:    To assist in the great remembering that is going to happen. There needed to be and still needs be a critical mass of incarnate beings that have remembered enough to allow the knowledge to be passed on through the centuries and not forgotten forever in the physical world. It is this that you will be doing in this world but with the knowledge that you will gain later. You will know that the remembering is to be soon.

*ME:    How will I get this knowledge?*

## How to Have Consistent Contact with Spirit

SE:    By making your contact with Spirit/Me consistent.

*ME:    How will I know when I have gotten there?*

SE:    You will know. For instance, when you can meditate without any stray thoughts for ten minutes, you will be in a position to make the link because you will be able to do it for longer, much longer. When you can live your life to the point where you are not worried about what other people think of what you say or do, you will understand this to be the human condition, and you will not live in fear. At this point when these two things are present, you will be in contact with Spirit on a permanent basis. You will be at one with yourself and the universe/Me and be able to exist in peace. You will then have the peace of someone who understands the truth and does not need to prove anything to anyone nor himself. You can, therefore, assist Spirit to the best of your ability. Without ego, you will be able to handle the power of energy without corruption. You will be able to do anything; you will be able to perform miracles.

## Significance of Sun and Moon Energies

We had discussed a lot about the sun and moon energies in my healing courses, so much so that I wanted the Origin's view on this subject.

*ME:    What is the significance of sun and moon energy?*

O:    This is relative to the level of work the individual is doing. In the past this was relative to what work the individual was doing for the general population.

*ME:    Such as?*

O:    Sun energy is power energy and sun energy priests (experts) used the power generated by the sun to manipulate large objects, trans-mutate objects, or

328

merely as a power source for things, such as lights or flying machines. It was really the "working" energy by which everything was powered. There were, of course, different levels of power that were relative to different types of tasks/work, and different individuals would specialize in these levels. Some priests, however, could use all the powers and levels that were available and so were highly revered.

ME: *So what were the moon energies for?*

O: These are basically healing or repairing energies. These sorts of energies are only really manifested in the physical realms. They are used to repair the physical vehicle if the task of the soul is not yet complete and that vehicle is still required to complete that task.

ME: *So what is the difference between healing and repairing energies?*

O: You know the basic answer to this, as it is self-explanatory. Repairing is the healing of inanimate or soulless objects or entities that are manifested in the physical realm, whereas healing is repairing of animate and inanimate objects that possess a soul or group soul.

ME: *Inanimate objects have a soul?*

O: Yes, all minerals are inanimate but have a soul. Animate objects are higher level objects that are used for the evolution of higher souls/entities and, therefore, need to be more independent than those bodies offered by vehicles, such as planets, etc.

ME: *And the moon priests were experts in healing them?*

O: Yes. They knew all the energies of this type that were available and what healing they could be used on. As with the power priests, they also had people who were experts in some methods and others or "high" priests that were capable of all levels of healing.

329

## Lives in Egypt and Atlantis Changing the Atomic Composition of Materials

I then got a flash of one of my past lives. I had the impression that I was well in tune with the ways of manipulating energies over a number of incarnations. In some I was a priest and in another I was both a priest and a king at the same time. The images I received showed me on the top of a number of pyramid type structures. At first I thought this was Egypt, but I was told by the Origin that this was both Egypt and Atlantis.

O:      In those days you were able to change the very atomic composition of any material.

*ME:    How did I do this?*

O:      You were able to look into the material at the atomic level and add or remove protons, neutrons, and electrons to change the base material you had into anything you wanted it to be. You could make materials very light in this way by moving the atoms you needed to remove to change the composition of the material into another frequency whilst you moved the base mass of the material to another location. Once the new location was established, you returned the missing electrons/atoms to the material, and it regained its original form, structure, and density.

*ME:    That sounds very complicated.*

O:      Yes, but you also had other ways of doing this. You also placed all but every $3^{rd}$ or $4^{th}$ molecule into the nearest dimension or frequency, leaving behind in this dimension the bare skeleton of the object and its material so that it could literally be man-handled into place by a small number of people or, in some cases, only one person—one that could perform low grade telekinesis, provided that the mass of the object was not too great.

*ME:    I can't believe that I could do this.*

330

O:    Any entity that is not in this plane of existence can perform these tasks, as every entity is part of Me and has the ability to do anything it desires.

## Chapter 25:
# *Stars, Incarnating Souls, and Root Races*

## The Origin on the Creation of the Stars
On another meditation I was pondering over the work of the stars. The Origin offered to comment.

O:      The stars were made by the Source Entity.

*ME:    How did It do that?*

O:      By commanding the workers of the galaxies to gather together and coalesce the denser matter that was manifested in the physical level of the universes.

*ME:    When did Source Entity do that? At the start of the evolution program?*

O:      Yes, the objective was to provide an energy source close to each area where a collection of beings were going to stay to work through their evolution/learning plans. The stars provide energy for all the entities and the masses (planets) that they gather around on all dimensions and all frequencies.

## The Necessity of Working with the Nature Spirits on Earth
*ME:    So how do we affect the energy that the Earth takes from the sun?*

O:      Those of you who are aware can act as a conduit for the energy and give the Earth a sort of supercharged method of gaining energy that allows it (and yourselves) to move up the frequencies. This is why it is essential that you work with the Earth and its nature spirits (caretakers). Then all of you will benefit energetically which will allow you to move up the frequencies, gain more of your memory back, achieve more, and be more in contact with your true higher selves.

It's also true that you are so close to making this first transition—so close that even those who are negative and angry are not able to affect the change. This is wonderful news and such a forward step for the human experiment!

I was expecting to do just a "just being" meditation after completing my morning hara line meditation when I caught a glimpse of thousands of stars close together in my mind's eye. I asked the Source Entity what they were as it wasn't clear.

## The Variety of Souls Waiting to Incarnate

*ME:* *What are these stars? They look like a close-up of a nebula?*

SE: They are the souls that are waiting to incarnate on Earth. They can't wait to incarnate and surround the Earth in anticipation.

*ME:* *I also get the impression that there are other souls there as well.*

SE: Yes, there are. These are the souls of people who are more earth bound. They have become addicted to incarnate life and, therefore, can't break away from the Earth plane properly. They wait for the opportunity to sneak into the body of a person who is very drunk, as the aura is forced open by the high alcohol intake and allows another soul to invade it and, therefore, experience incarnate life again, albeit for a short moment.

When I told my wife about this, she immediately said that there were also the root six and seven souls who were waiting to incarnate and continue the next stage of human evolution. These souls, when incarnate, will retain all memory of who and

334

what they are and will help in the environmental events that will happen as a result of the raising of the Earth's frequencies.

I meditated on this subject again the next day.

## The Differences in the Root 5, 6, and 7 Races

ME:     *So what is the difference in the root 5, 6 & 7 races?*

SE:     The root 5 race has to go through a lengthy process to get into a position where its members are in contact with their higher selves and start to access their true abilities. This is quite difficult to do and requires the individual to re-learn how to access these abilities from the physical plane. The individual also needs to cleanse himself/herself and remove all the blockages accrued over lifetimes to date.

ME:     *So what about the 6$^{th}$ root race?*

SE:     It is their job to pave the way for the root 7 race. They will be more aware of their abilities and spiritual issues from birth and will take on the task of preparing the rest of the human race for the progression up the frequencies. They will make them more aware of spiritual matters so that they can start to realize that there really is more to life than just considering their one shot here on Earth. This will start to make them think from a spiritual perspective on a longer term.

ME:     *So what will the 7$^{th}$ root race be?*

SE:     They are those masters who wish to re-incarnate. They will be fully aware of their true selves and their abilities from birth and will actively and openly teach and affect the changes necessary to raise the frequencies of the Earth and its inhabitants to the levels required to project it up to the next level, so that it may continue its rise up the frequencies back to where it belongs. At this point heaven on Earth will be a reality.

# Chapter 26:
## *No Such Thing as Psychic Powers*

ME:   *I want to know about our psychic powers. Do we have any, what they are, and if we do, why can't we use them now?*

SE:   This is quite a low level question for you.

ME:   *Thanks, but it is something that I guess many people would like to know the answer to.*

SE:   O.K. First, there are no such things as psychic powers. There just are the faculties that you are able to use whilst in this current projection into the physical. These may or may not include some of your normal functions when in the energetic state.

ME:   *What may these be?*

## The Alienation and Limitations of Special Powers

SE:   Anything that is relevant to the needs of this incarnation. Most individuals who incarnate have no need whatsoever for any of their normal faculties whilst in the physical. Indeed to have them would invalidate the reason for being in this limited space in the first place since the whole point is evolving and understanding self. Having what most of the world would classify as special powers would simply alienate you from the rest of society and limit you in terms of your life's direction. Your focus would be almost totally on this power rather than working with what you have, which is what everyone else has, basic limited functionality. You can see this if you look at "so called" psychics. Their lives are limited to working with the one function that can be attributed to the higher self. They focus specifically on this to the detriment of working with the other challenges of life in the physical, such as working with people. The other thing to note is that you choose not to have access to your higher/normal self when you incarnate and, as a result, limit yourself freely. Finally, it should be noted that the current level of the frequencies in this dimension does not readily support higher self functionality due to its low levels and restricted communication lines between the projected self and the energetic self.

To answer your question about what your psychic powers are, I will answer it with a question to you: "What do you think they are?"

ME: *I would expect them to be everything that I can think of.*

SE: Good answer. In fact when you are fully back in the energetic state, your abilities are only limited by your ability to think of them. In reality, your abilities are limitless, hence, why they don't come with you into the physical. If you brought them all with you and used them in the physical environment, you would not only be classified as a god but could wreak some real damage.

ME: *Has humankind ever had some of his abilities available to him in the past?*

## First Experiments of Energetic Man Having a Fully Retained Memory of Abilities

SE: As I have explained before in previous dialogue, the first experiments made by energetic man into the physical included fully retained memory and the ability to communicate with others both in the energetic state and in the physical. These were the main faculties that were maintained during incarnation. The issue with that is that knowledge of what you could and couldn't do whilst in the physical actually caused distress in a high number of those who chose to incarnate. You can liken the response to an attack of claustrophobia. It was

338

because of this that it was decided by the creators of physical man to cut off all links with the remaining energetic self whilst the entity was incarnate. Imagine what it would be like to know what you are and what you can do but not be able to do it; the frustration would be immense. However, there are and have been in the past certain individuals who elected to leave certain faculties turned on whilst in the physical in order to use them for the good of others. Others have had them turned on to allow them to experience the isolation they create. Knowing that you can do something that appears to be rather incredible and that others can't do does in fact create a certain level of isolation within the psyche. The other reason for these not being available to all is that at this point in time, they would be misused and not used for the common good. Instead, they would be used for the betterment of the individual in the physical. When humankind was a younger race and, indeed, of a higher frequency, certain functions were allowed. These were basic functions of telepathy, telekinesis, and healing. Healing is the more benign of the three and is the first one to re-appear as a race starts to reverse its decent into the lower frequency levels, which it is currently doing, hence the re-appearance of this function.

## Requirements to Use Energetic Functions

The main requirement of the ability to use some of the normal everyday energetic functions in the physical is, of course, purity of heart and a total lack of aggression and personal ambition. The latter two (aggression and personal ambition) together are a dangerous combination when combined with the power to influence the environment of others because they create tyranny, and that could not be allowed. In fact, it is that very combination that has been a component that led the human race to descend into the lower frequencies where it is now struggling to pull itself away from.

ME: *You mentioned three faculties of telepathy, telekinesis, and healing. What would the others be?*

SE: As you said yourself just a few minutes ago, you can do anything you want in the energetic state; all you have to do is do it—teleportation, time travel, dimension travel, creation, anything! All you have to do is want to do it, and it is done. The most important faculty that all humans still have though is the one that is most ignored—the ability to tune into reality and communicate with themselves, Me, and the universe around them. This is the way to enlightenment and is part of the reason why all of you incarnate into the physical human form: to experience, evolve, and return to Source, Me.

## The Physics of Telekinesis

ME: *I have a question on the physics of telekinesis. I thought that this worked by giving energy to an object so that it lost some of its density and, therefore, became lighter, light enough to be moved by the etheric.*

O: Close, but the real way is to make the area around the object denser than the object itself, therefore, allowing the object to float rather like a ball floating to the surface of water. You then make it move by making the local level of density less dense, literally making it "fall" in a certain direction.

ME: *So how do you do that without creating a physical object, such as ice?*

O: By changing the energy field characteristics of the surrounding material. That's how magnetism works.

ME: *But magnetism relies on two objects being magnetic in some way.*

O:      Of course, the reference to magnetism was just a reference to help you understand. The energy field surrounding an object can be made more dense by simply making it stronger and allowing it to push less strong fields out of the way. If the field is underneath the object, it is lifted; if it is weakened, the object falls back to Earth. This can be done in a cradle effect so that lateral movement can also be achieved.

## The Great Illusion

In another meditation the Origin showed a brief description of life on Earth as an illusion.

O:      An illusion is at its best when it is able to distract the observer to the point where he/she is totally convinced that what he/she is experiencing with his/her limited ability/senses is reality.

ME:     *So we are living in a particularly convincing illusion.*

## Trusting One's Intuition

O:      No, you are not, but you are all easily convinced that physical life is all there is, and this is because you are not able to trust your higher senses. This is because you rely too much on your human senses rather than accept that your higher senses are there and are accurate. You need to trust your intuition.

ME:     *So the more I trust my intuition, the more I will use my higher senses, and the more I will see that this life is mere illusion, one for the benefit of my evolution.*

O:      Yes, now you are getting it. This is fun.

ME:     *Why?*

## Evolution's Fast Track

O:      Because all of you feel that you are suffering for such a long time, but in reality, that is REALITY, you are here for a fraction of the blink of an eye in relation to the

341

length of time that you have all been in existence. Earth is an evolutionary fast track of astounding potential. You can evolve in years here what it might take thousands of years or even eons to accomplish in the pure energetic. Yet when you are incarnate, it feels like such a long time. Rejoice in the fact that this reality is so short.

# Part Three

# Communication with Aliens

# Chapter 27:
## *Hum on Other Entities Commonly Called Aliens*

I considered what Byron had said earlier about communicating with aliens and decided that I would dedicate some meditation time purely for this cause. Hum was to help me here.

*ME:*     *Hello, Hum. Can you help me a bit on the subject of aliens. I have received a smattering of information on this subject during one of my meditations and now would like to commit some time for dialogue on the subject.*

HUM: First, there is no such thing as aliens. That is just a description that people on Earth use to describe people or beings that don't come from Earth. Based upon this, there are only other entities, not aliens that live on planets in this and other galaxies, universes, dimensions or frequency levels. They are really our brothers and sisters as we are all from the same Source energy and are all working to expand our evolution and progress towards being re-united with the Source Entity again.

Life in other universes and dimensions is as diverse as the number of insects and mammal life here on Earth. There are beings of pure energy, which our souls/spirits are really, and beings that are based upon physical components. Some of the body types are close to the sizes and shapes of human bodies, whereas others may appear to look like squids or birds or lizards or fish, some even being a mixture of two or three mediums. Some beings are able to change the shape and size of their physical appearance at will, as they have control of their higher mental and spiritual capabilities. Beings that exist in the higher frequencies have physical components that are as solid to them as your bodies are to you. If you could perceive them and touch them, it would be like trying to touch the wind or a very rare gas.

*ME:*     *Do aliens visit Earth?*

## The Consistent Presence of Visiting Entities

HUM: Yes, other beings do visit your planet on a regular basis, and there are many different types of beings that do so. They are here to help you evolve and make the leap to the next spiritual level. They help raise the frequency of the Earth which will allow you to start to remember more about who you are and what your job here on Earth is. Their primary task is to help prepare and assist you for the coming changes at this turning point in your evolution. Once you have achieved the raising of the frequencies, the beings will make themselves known to all of you here on Earth. At that point they will feel safe in the knowledge that you will be more tolerant of different body types and will not shoot them on sight as many of the 1950's B movies predicted. Instead, you will accept them for what they are: your friends and brothers in evolution.

As previously mentioned, the Earth is at a very important juncture in the experiment of free will, with ultimate choice being the responsibility of the individual. Success of this experiment will allow you to increase this power of individual free choice to other races within the universe/universes and will increase the speed of evolution of individual beings and whole races of beings, including human spirits, further increasing the frequency of the Earth and its inhabitants. Once the Earth's frequency is raised, its purpose will be known, and it will be able to function properly. Like an important circuit in a computer that is broken, once repaired it will allow the whole universe to function as it was designed to function, as a living being in its own right. This is what your brothers and sisters from other planets are here to help you achieve.

## Methods for Traveling Among the Stars

The subject of traveling vast distances in an efficient manner has always been a dream of science fiction writers. I decided to ask Hum about this subject to see if it was consistent with my existing level of understanding.

HUM: What you call "alien space craft" travel the vast distances between the stars by translating themselves into a higher frequency or dimension. Within this dimension the beings on-board can literally use mental power to project themselves to another star system or planet. This is achievable because the different frequencies or dimensions of all the universes are literally overlaid on each other. Since they exist at the same time, the physics of higher frequencies results in the molecules for a lower frequency individual to travel in a higher frequency realm even though they are essentially further apart.

There is an infinitesimal reduction in resistance that allows traveling from star to star to happen much faster, in fact at the speed of thought. This is so fast that to the observer in the lower frequency, traveling from A to B appears to be at the blink of the eye, like teleportation.

There are also a different set of physical rules with higher frequencies that allow the individual to have access to information and mental abilities/powers in higher frequencies that they would not normally have in their own home frequency. Hence, they have the ability to mentally project themselves as they suddenly remember how to do this. Once the space ship reaches its destination in the higher frequency, it is then converted back into its original frequency and appears at the point of destination. The down side of this is the rapid forgetting of mental ability as the craft and its inhabitants convert to the lower frequencies. This is not the only way to travel great distances though.

ME:     *It isn't? What are the other ways then?*

HUM:  There are many ways to perform interstellar travel, both easy and hard. In general though, four main methods are used. The first is to use conventional travel as you know and understand it, which, of course, takes too long and would require a space ark even at 90% light speeds. The second uses inter-dimensional jumps to cross the bridge between two points in space. The third uses pure thought to drive a space ship or mental construction to protect the entities from the decrease in frequency that results in dropping into lower frequencies. The fourth requires travel in the higher dimensions only and is done purely on a mental basis and requires no protective mental constructs whatsoever.  The entities who perform this sort of travel don't generally venture this far down the frequency ladder and find these lower frequencies very uncomfortable, just as you do when you have some of your senses and abilities reduced when scuba diving. They merely think or focus on a galactic, planetary, or system location, and they are there. Again this is possible because an entity is really in all places at the same time and is able to focus its attention to one particular special or temporal point at will and coalesce there.

## A Most Interesting Method of Transportation

The third method is the most interesting, however, as the ship or mental construct has other functions other than protecting the entities from the lower frequencies and allowing them to travel from point to point. Due to their make-up, these entities lose their higher abilities as they come down the frequencies just as you have lost your ability to remember who and what you are when you incarnate into the physical. They start to forget what they knew and what they could do.

To combat this, the ship or mental construct can perform one of two techniques. By using a number of different ways, the ship can memorize the higher individual frequency knowledge of all the entities protected within its environment as they forget and come down the frequencies into your dimension. Doing this will allow all their knowledge and abilities (through an amplifier) to still be available. The second function the ship or mental construct can perform is to maintain a dimension within a dimension (or frequency within a frequency). The ship is able to exist in the lower frequencies whilst maintaining an internal frequency consistent with that of the entities within.

As a result $12^{th}$ level frequency entities can travel in the $3^{rd}$ dimension within a ship or construct that is maintaining a higher frequency bubble inside the shell of its construct, thereby allowing these entities to maintain their personal higher mental and energetic functions whilst performing whatever jobs they have to do on the Earth plane. To draw a parallel with something you do in the physical world, the higher frequency or dimension within the ship could be considered as a similar concept to submariners traveling at 60 meters, 7 bar pressure, underwater in a submarine or bathysphere but only having 1 bar pressure, or ambient pressure, inside the submarine.

# Chapter 28

# *Hum on the Om*

On a particular short meditation I found myself logging into Hum, who furnished me with a very short explanation of what the Om are and how they interact with Earth.

ME: *Hello, Hum. It is good to speak to you this morning.*
HUM: It is good to speak to you as well, for you will no longer need Me soon.
ME: *Why is this?*
HUM: You will be able to communicate with any being/entity you wish without guidance or backup.
ME: *Oh. O.K. I have a question for you. What are the Om and how have they manifested on the Earth?*
HUM: This will be a very short answer for it is steeped in your folklore and legend.

The Om are an old race that can only be described as light beings that live in the heaven levels (very close to the Source Entity). There were many Om beings incarnating in the Atlantis days, and this is why there are many old Atlanteans here on Earth today to help the Earth recover from her position of -9 on the frequency levels since Earth has fallen nine frequency levels from where she originated. The Om did not need to incarnate on the Earth plane, but they felt the need to help the planet as they understood the impact that the Earth could have on the universe, in terms of evolution for all beings. Although we incarnated in the Atlantean days, any help would have been limited as the Atlanteans were quite an insular civilization whereas the help needed to be more global.

## Old Atlanteans Who Are Really of the Om

This is why there are many old Atlanteans incarnating today, but they are not really old

Atlanteans. Instead, they are really Om. The Om understand that with the Earth now having a more global civilization, the opportunity for progression is vastly improved so they are, therefore, getting more involved at a "coal face" level—the most basic level. This is your reason for being here, for you are of the Om.

Know this, the Om aren't beings. They just are! As for our help, as you increase your movement up the vibrational levels, more and more people will be able to get in contact with their higher selves. Many others will be born knowing who they are from the start. Most of those who will start to remember, however, will be old Atlanteans or will be of the Om.

# Chapter 29:
## *Aliens/Other Entities and Intention*

During a morning meditation in December 2003, I was wondering where or what subject Hum and I were going to address next. I was trying desperately to not pre-conceive what this would be when I suddenly saw myself traveling around the galaxy at a speed that was inconceivably fast. I was very surprised when I arrived back on Earth, for the alien/other entity that I had spoken to on my earlier visit was there to greet me; Hum was also by my side.

## The Ripple Caused by Intention

*ME:*    *How did you know that I was coming over here to see you?*

A:    We/I received your intention to be here and so had time to prepare.

*ME:*    *How can that be? I just had the impression that I have been three times around the galaxy. I was as far away from the Earth as I could be.*

A:    Yes, but we received your intention to be here.

*ME:*    *How do you mean you received my intention? How do you receive my intention?*

A:    Your intention to be here arrives before you do. The intention travels toward us and causes a ripple. It is these ripples that we pick-up/receive and act upon.

*ME:*    *How did you know it was me?*

A:    By the signature of the ripple we felt it coming in, and when we established whose signature it was, we prepared ourselves to receive you.

*ME:*    *Can you please explain? I would have thought that if my intention caused a ripple, then it would be much slower that my actually traveling here. I was traveling fast enough to go three times around the galaxy before I got here.*

A: Yes, but the intention that is transmitted is in on a different dimensional plane. This plane is specific to communication and intended actions/thoughts and, hence, is not interfered by nor interferes with the dimensional plane or frequencies of the individual entity.

ME: *O.K., but a ripple indicates some sort of resistance or other and, therefore, suggests that it is slowed down in some way.*

A: This is not so in the dimension that your intention operates within. The best way to describe it is as a bow wave. When a ship is on the water, the bow wave goes before the boat because the boat is pushing/displacing the water out of the way to make way for the hull of the boat. This can be picked up at various stationary points in front of the boat and measured; based upon this information, the size and tonnage of the boat can be extrapolated. This is its signature. Your intention is similar but in a different dimension. The distance in relative terms between the bow wave of the intention to travel to a point in the universe or dimension and the action of the individual entity that follows can be infinite, but it is nevertheless discernable by the receiving entity and measurable by ascertaining the amplitude of the intended action, therefore, allowing time to prepare for such a visit.

ME: *So this is how you are always ready for me.*

A: Correct.

HUM: This is exactly how we perceive your intention to communicate with us as well.

ME: *What happens if two sets of intention collide with each other?*

# The Impossibility of Two Sets of Intention Colliding

A:     They don't.

*ME:    Why not? Surely it would be like the bow wave of two boats interfering with each other. They would slow each other down and interfere and distort each other's signals.*

A:     No, they don't.

*ME:    Why?*

A:     Because each entity has its own signature, as previously stated. Liken the signature to the frequency of a radio station. Each signature can be one second (and this can be minute fractions of a second) of phase on a radio signal that has infinitely variable amplitude, frequency, dimensional basis, and density.

*ME:    So the chances of two entities having the same signature are small?*

A:     No. They are not possible because you also have to take account of the direction and end destination of the intent which also adds to the uniqueness of the intent signature and the resultant "bow wave."

*ME:    So two bow waves would never interfere with each other.*

A:     No. Never.

*ME:    Thank you. That explains it.*

# Chapter 30:
## *Aliens/Other Entities on Universes, Null Space, Hyperspace, Collective Beings, and Hillside Space Bases*

I continued the conversation the next day. This time I was on my own. I felt that Hum had done his job here in being part of my earlier dialogues with the aliens. He had been there to "hold my hand," so to speak.

ME: *It's good to be here again and to log into you.*

A: Yes, it is also an honor for us to talk to you. To be able to extend some of our knowledge to your race is a great opportunity for both of us.

## The Multifaceted Universes

ME: *Thank you. I have been picking up strands of things about the universe for the past two days, stuff about the multiplicity of it. I have also been receiving images to explain it.*

A: Yes, we have been sending you images to grab your attention. The universes are truly multifaceted. They overlap many times in many places, all at the same time. The space is not relative to the human convention of space or time, for it can be frequency or dimensionally based. The image we sent you showed the universes are a series of spheres all interlaced upon each other with the spatial position varying slightly or greatly one from the other.

ME: *That's right. That's exactly how I saw it.*

A: That's exactly how it is. We use/exploit the closeness of the different universal spheres to translate ourselves

357

between them. We can use this opportunity to move great spatial distances by moving along the adjoining spherical edge, the area closest to the two spheres, but not actually entering either of the two universal environments. This area is or can be classified as a null area.

ME:   *Hyperspace?*

## A Description of Null Space

A:    No, not quite. Hyperspace, as you call it, is still space, space that is constrained by a law particular to the universe it is associated with. This null space has no association and, therefore, is open to manipulation by those who know how to manipulate the energies there, which of course, we do.

ME:   *I just got this picture of an energy that keeps the universes apart and learned that this is an environment that supports energetic life in itself. It sort of repulses the universes away from each other while it nullifies their natural attractivity to each other. It's just like an aura.*

A:    Well done. This is exactly what it is and as you quite rightly observed, it is a force that acts as a repulsive agent between any of the universes in question.  This area is, if you like, the back corridor that allows those entities who work for the maintenance of the greater universal environment safe and fast passage between the areas, universes, and worlds they are responsible for.

ME:   *Why safe? Do you mean they can get attacked or something?*

A:    No, but they can get waylaid by other entities in the universes they work with who ask them for help, which delays them from getting on with the work they had planned to do. Traveling in null space allows them to move from location to location in peace, for these others do not know they are there or are not allowed by local law to translate to null space.

## Here Right Under Your Nose

Just to give you an example, you cannot see the base, the environment we have created for ourselves here where you currently are, but you know we are there because you are in tune with the wider environment. To you, we are to all intents invisible; we do not exist. Nevertheless we do exist, and we are here, right under your nose. However, we do have to say that we are not in null space but just a couple of frequencies above you, enough to maintain ourselves and low enough to communicate with you.

ME:     *So how do you translate yourselves into null space?*

## Translating Themselves into Null Space

A:     Wouldn't you like to know?! Sorry, a little joke. Well, it's all about changing the frequency and dimensional relationship of the craft (construct) we are in and ourselves on a random and regular/irregular basis to the point where we are no longer associated with our home universal dimension or *any* other dimensions or frequencies. This needs to be done at a speed so that we are no longer recognized by a particular universe as part of its content and, therefore, not bound by its attractivity and subsequent laws of operation. Simply put, we mess with frequencies and dimensionalities enough to belong nowhere else but in null space.

## Defining Hyperspace

ME:     *So if null space is in between universes and is not relative to a particular universe, how would you describe hyperspace? This is what science fiction*

359

*writers and, to some extent, current physics is suggesting.*

A: As we previously stated, hyperspace is relative to a particular universe. If there are twenty universes, there will be twenty versions of hyperspace: one for each universe and each bound by the attractiveness and laws of the universe with which it is associated. The laws are of functionality, for each universe has its own role to play and, therefore, its own operating regime. What you call hyperspace is simply a moment of frequential and dimensional phase that is different to the normal graduations of phase. It does not allow faster than light travel, for this is a physical metric that is related to speed in the physical, nor does it allow instantaneous travel from one position in physicality to another. It is not a physical short cut, as it does not warp physical space or time. What it does is allow movement between dimensional and frequential environments, for its phase is not static.

ME: *So it is the local universal equivalent of null space.*

A: If you wish to consider it as such, then that is up to you, but it is clearly not the same.

ME: *So is it useful for traveling great physical distances? Does it have any advantage in this area?*

## Moving to a Different Locale Using One's Will

A: No, only as a medium for travel between frequential and dimensional environments, but there is a way to use the travel between these environments by jumping from one environment to another and choosing your re-entry point. However, this takes time and calculation to understand and waiting for the correct event or opportunity to use as an entry point. The dimensional and frequential relationships are not static, and this can be used in your favor, but it is not an efficient way to reduce physical distance or journey time. The best way to do that is in the energetic state using your "Origin-given" right to use the powers of the total universe to move your "will" to a different focal point. This does not need physical means, no matter which dimensional or frequential environment you are currently linked to. It needs your "full" awareness.

ME: *While we were on a tour in our car, I had the image of a large space ship located up in the mountains, not landed, but hovering.*

A: This was not a space ship as you were expecting but a construct to allow us to work in your frequency. What you were seeing in your mind's eye was your mind's representation of what you perceived. It overlaid what it had seen with something it knows you would be both familiar with and comfortable with. The shape of the construct is nothing you would recognize nor relate to, as it is energy not physicality. Although everything physical is energy, not everything energetic is or needs to be physical, and physicality is not specifically or normally as dense as your physicality. The construct we use is merely an interface between the environments we both exist within, which allows us to move around and experience what you are experiencing from an evolutionary point of view and see how you are applying what you have learned for the benefit of all.

## Humanity Working Individually Rather Than Collectively

We are most interested in the differing of opinions you have individually on this, as this is something alien to us and is a result of your gifts of individual choice. This is a very rare level of functionality, for most physical beings operate in a collective basis. In this mode of operation what one does, one does for the benefit of the whole and on behalf of the whole, not for the benefit of the self or on behalf of the self. Being of service to the whole is the way of the universe as a whole, including all the dimensional and frequential states and universes that are part of the Source Entity. It is by way of individuality that the individual entity eventually realizes this, for selfishness is counterproductive to the evolution of the collective and the individual.

ME: *Rather like ants or other insects.*

A: In terms of the individual working for the collective, yes, it is similar but dissimilar since in the case of the ant, it does what it does without thought or reason. It is merely an arm or a function, (a better description would be a cell in a brain) of what is a collective mind. Everything the ant does is responsive to the requirements of the whole as a whole, not a singular action made in the knowledge that it will benefit the whole "for the benefit of the whole," In our instance we are conscious of the effect that our actions and thoughts have on the rest of our community, no matter where they are individually or in collections in the universe. This is why we work together the way we do. We know how to progress the evolution of the race because we can see the fruits of our efforts in a collective way. In this way we strive individually to benefit the whole, and in doing so we fulfil the universal desire to be of service. This is the highest form of work any entity can undertake. The main difference between our rules of existence and those of the human race is that you have total free will to do any action, no matter how it affects the whole. The most interesting thing is that all of you have the ability to know how you affect the whole, but you choose not to use this facility. This is a most interesting denial of self, for in denying the self, you deny the whole, which in turn denies the self of its opportunity for evolution through the actions available to help the whole progress towards perfection. The efforts spent by the individual to help only the individual are wasted, for they are a finite benefit, which in most cases disenfranchises those closest to the individual, rather than helping them.

Everything we do is for the benefit of the whole. Just as the ant works to benefit the whole in its selfless fashion, so do we in a selfless fashion. We also realize that in observing your race and helping your race, we are opening the door for other physical races, including our own, to achieve individuality within co-dependence. Once the downward spiral resulting from independent and individual choice resulting in the selfish application of power is broken and self-realization is achieved, the opportunity for real growth is available, both on an individual and on a holistic basis. This is only possible because the individual, knowing that one particular action will benefit itself, will willingly choose another action to help others of its own kind if the opportunity is available.

ME: *Forgive me for saying this, but you sound just like the Source Entity.*

A: This should not to be a surprise to you as we are all part of the Source. The fact that you are in communion with the Source yourself and that you think we talk to you in the same way is an honor, for we strive to be one with the Source at the earliest opportunity. Our dialogue with you is designed to be in a method you will understand and be able to convey easily without the need for interpretation and subsequent loss of correct information. This would portray the wrong image and cause rejection amongst those who would benefit from our communications. For this we thank you for recognizing us and our word. We leave you now until the next time.

363

## The Bases Perched on Hillsides in Crete

During a core star meditation on the roof of our cottage in Crete, I concentrated on the hill at the back of our garden because my wife had previously stated that she had felt a lot of energy there. During the meditation I received the impression that there was an alien base perched on the hillside with a craft also perched on a landing pad. I then sensed Hum's presence and with him keeping a fatherly eye on me, I extended my consciousness up towards the hillside until I perceived a thin metal fence and was instantly greeted by an entity.

*ME:*   *Why do you have a base here?*
A:      We have a base here because the energies are pure, and the local inhabitants have not yet ruined the energy flow.

My mind went back to a previous meditation where I mentally saw rivers of energy flowing around the hills and mountains in the area.

A:      They, the old ones at least, still respect and use the land working together with the nature spirits although they aren't fully aware of it.

## The Shape of the Spaceship

I asked the being about the shape of the ship.

A:      Our ships are always the shape that offers the least resistance when traveling inter-dimensionally, which is spherical.
*ME:*   *So why do I get the impression that the craft I perceived is a flat shape like the shapes reported in UFO sightings.*
A:      That is because our craft join together to make a sphere with each craft a larger or smaller slice of the sphere.

364

# The Temple of Zeus

*ME:*  *O.K., thanks. Some spiritualists believe that there is a
structure called The Temple of Zeus. Does it exist or is
it just misinterpretation? For example, is this "temple"
a real place?*

A:  Yes, it was and still is. The structure was called a
temple because of the limited ability of the humans at
that time to understand what it was. It is, in fact, a very
large craft that can be classed as a floating city in
today's terms. The local inhabitants that could be
trusted were translated into the dimension that the craft
was in and were flown up to it by telekinesis. The effect
of levitating them to the craft in this dimension and the
fact that they were "there" but couldn't be "seen" made
the locals think that the craft's inhabitants were gods.
The craft was so big to them (as big as a floating city
which also had balconies) that they thought the craft
was a temple. Zeus was the name of one of the aliens at
that time, and this stuck in their minds.

*ME:*  *Is the craft still here?*

A:  Yes, and you just managed to perceive its existence
when you were at the village you stay in. You sensed it
rather than saw it.

*ME:*  *Are there many bases here in Crete?*

A:  Yes, they are all over the hills; we are using them to
monitor all of you. The energy here is pure so we stay
here rather than anywhere else. The locals are in tune
with the energy of nature here.

I shifted my attention in my mind's eye to the surrounding hill
sides and saw lots of platforms dotting the country side.

*ME:*  *Why can't we see you?*

A:  Because we are in a different frequency or dimension
than you. YOU can't see the higher frequencies but a

person in a higher frequency can see things in a lower frequency. For example, you can see this effect when you look at the different frequencies and states (or vibration levels of molecules) that water adopts at different temperatures. You can just perceive a gas when it is at the slightly lower vibration of steam but any higher, and it goes out of your visual range literally into another dimension (frequency). Of course, you see it when it is lowered even further down the frequencies and becomes ice.

ME: *So it is better to be in a higher dimension or frequency.*

A: Yes, you can see and do more. It is better being a gas being as you can perceive everything on the gas vibration level and on the lower frequencies of the physical as well.

# Chapter 31:
## *Extended Dialogues with the Aliens/Other Entities*

## On the Aliens' Balcony

One wet weekend morning I was meditating on the back porch of our house with the back door open. Some of the rain was hitting me in the face and was making it difficult to concentrate. I thought about raising my frequencies and found myself on the aliens' balcony.

*ME:*   *I am surprised to be here.*
A:     Don't be. This is where you wanted to come.
*ME:*   *I want to ask some questions.*
A:     Go ahead.
*ME:*   *Are you the Om?*
A:     No, but we do work with the Om.

## From Beyond the Pleiades and Orion's Belt

*ME:*   *Where do you come from?*

The words Pleiades and Orion's belt came into my mind momentarily. I asked if this was correct.

A:     No, it's in that direction, but your conscious mind inserted a name you know (Pleiades and Orion's belt) as you wouldn't know the name of our origin.
*ME:*   *It seems that with all these bases here, it is a bit of a prison camp.*
A:     It is not intended to give that impression. Our bases and the ship are positioned in this area because of the unique energy properties that are in this locale. The

energies are such that it makes translation from our dimension to yours easier than normal.

There are many others also positioned in similar areas.

ME: *How much power is required to keep this huge ship?*

A: Not much, it's . . .

The dialogue dropped suddenly, and I got the image in my head of a car engine and the units "kilowatts," so I had the impression that the power a car engine produces is what is necessary.

ME: *This is not a lot.*

# Movement by Affecting the Quantum Level of the Material

A: No, you only need to affect the quantum level of the material so that the quantum force is aligned in an opposing manner to the ambient quantum force. This can be manipulated to allow movement in different directions.

I then received the image in my mind of a bed of ball bearings (which represented the molecules of a material bunched up together) moving independently to effect changes in the quantum force that would allow the anti-gravity effect and movement in all three axes.

ME: *Isn't this the same as magnetic repulsion?*

A: No, magnetic repulsion is created by aligning the molecules in a metal in one direction by using electricity flowing in a known direction, so that the attraction of the molecules is all one way. A push or pull force is experienced at what you call the poles of the magnet and is relative to the direction that the molecules are orientated. Simply put, materials with the molecules arranged in the same direction but positioned opposing each other create opposition. This is only true for metals or materials where the molecules can be organized by exposing them to a circular electric current. The quantum changes necessary to effect antigravity are applicable to ALL materials, as it affects them at the smallest level rather than just affecting the electrons and protons that make up the material, and are, therefore, at a higher quantum level. Consider the difference being in manipulating the molecules in the grains of sand that make up a house brick in comparison to manipulating the building that is made of the bricks. There is a key to doing this level of manipulation; atomic fusion is a step in the right direction to finding this key.

ME: *O.K., thanks for this, I have to go now.*

As I type this up, it starts to make my head hurt as I try to get to grips with it. But the information received did seem reasonable.

## One Thing at a Time
The next day saw me back at the alien base and talking to the alien again.

ME: *What level are you from?*
A:  The 50th.
ME: *Wow, that's high.*
A:  We don't see it that way.
ME: *What are you doing here on Earth?*
A:  We are here to help the evolution of the Earth and its inhabitants. You are part of this task, that's why you were attuned in Sweden. It is this attunement that has enabled you to increase your awareness to the level you have in this short time. It is also the reason you have been able to contact and perceive us so easily.

369

*ME:* *What do I need to do to evolve?*

A: You need to concentrate on removing the chatter from your mind so that you can hear the real you. To do this, you need to slow down and become more linear in the jobs that you are doing, doing only one thing at a time and thinking of only one thing at a time. This is only one way of creating focus. You are used to working on many things in many dimensions all at the same time. Your subconscious remembers this, and, as a result, you try to do the same thing on the physical plane. This is difficult and you are doing it well, but it doesn't allow you to focus on expanding your awareness to your higher and real self.

## On a Spaceship in the Dimension Above Earth

The next morning I was in a hurry and didn't expect too much from the short meditation I performed before going to work; however, I found myself on what I can only describe as the observation lounge or room of a space craft in orbit far above the Earth. The alien I had talked to was also with me. In front of me was an amazing sight. All around the Earth were myriad ships and stations of different designs. In the background was a wonderfully colorful vista of nebulae and other planets close by.

*ME:* *Wow, this is incredibility beautiful.*

A: Yes, the universe is beautiful and so are we, as we are also part of the universe.

*ME:* *What are all these planets and nebulae doing here? I thought that the solar system was spread apart with just a few planets (nine, eight if you discount Pluto), just as we are told by our astronomers.*

A: Yes, it is, but we are in the next dimension up from the Earth plane, so you can see that there are many other planets that exist in the vicinity of the Earth that are not visible or detectable from your dimension but are nevertheless there. You are truly limited by your physical perceptions.

ME: *What are all these space ships and stations doing here?*

A: These are the orbital bases and transportation for all the races that are helping to raise the evolution of humankind to a level where the frequency of the Earth is back where it should be. When this happens, we will make ourselves known to humankind as you will be able to accept the differences in us by then.

ME: *Why are you in this dimension?*

A: Because it's the closest we can get to the Earth plane without being detected. It also makes translation to and from your frequency easier.

## Natural Portals

ME: *I thought that you used certain portals for this.*

A: Yes, that is true. It is even easier to translate in the vicinity of these natural portals because they are areas of instability.

ME: *Hang on! I thought they were pure in energy, and that is why you used them.*

I was getting confused here as my mind received about three answers at the same time.

A: That is right. These natural portals are unstable in the physical sense because they are so pure in energy. They have not yet been contaminated by man, and he has not yet brought the frequency of the area down.

ME: *Can you explain further?*

A: The frequency properties of the materials that make up the mountains and the trees in the area are at a higher frequency than other areas in the world, so by definition, they are closer to the frequency levels that we operate in. They, therefore, become a portal between dimensions, a crack in the door, so to speak.

371

To explain further, as the frequency of an object is increased, the closer it gets to translating into the next (higher) dimensional level; thus, from the point of view of the physical dimension, it becomes unstable physically as it loses its density.

ME: *Now I understand. Thank you. I am in communication with another being (Byron). I was told that you translate to a higher dimension to help travel long distances faster.*

A: Yes, this is correct. Because of the frequency of the higher dimension, the resistance is reduced and allows less friction when we travel—hence, the ability to travel faster in the higher dimension. The reduction in travel time is very significant.

## Translating to a Higher Dimension

ME: *So how do you translate to the higher dimension? I would have thought that if you would increase the frequency of an object, you would lose the ability of the molecules that make up that object to maintain their cohesion or form.*

A: Yes, it's an interesting conundrum. However, the molecules of the object are raised to the next dimensional level by raising their frequency through a process of acceleration whilst maintaining positional integrity. It is a difficult concept for you to understand, but it is possible to make an object move without it actually moving. In actual fact, the acceleration is a back and forth or rotational movement. There is some positional movement, but this is measured at a quantum level and is therefore insignificant in terms of maintaining the form that the molecules make up. The form or shape, functionality, and physical properties of the object are, therefore, not compromised and are, therefore, not affected in any way. It remains to all intents and purposes unaffected with the exception that it is now in another dimension.

ME: *So how do you translate an object or person into the higher dimensions?*

A: As I said, we accelerate the object at the quantum level.

ME: *Yes, but how do you do it? Do you use magnets or what?*

A: It's not as simple as that. What we do is affect every molecule in the object with a field of energy which affects the quantum level of the object being translated. The field is then manipulated so that the level of acceleration and direction of acceleration affects the object's molecules at the quantum level. The level and direction is known and controlled so that we know where in the dimensional state the object is. The whole object and field, including the field generating hardware, are also translated.

ME: *If you are working at the quantum level, you must need a massive amount of computer power to map the molecules and quanta of the object and note the position of each quanta at any one point in the acceleration throughout the translation process so that the object doesn't fall apart.*

A: Yes, you would need a massive amount of computational power to achieve this, but in actual affect, you don't need to do this. This was our initial thought when we first experimented with translating to the next higher dimension for space travel.

ME: *So how do you do it then?*

A: We just accelerate everything within the field applying the acceleration level and direction equally throughout the field. Because the acceleration is equal throughout the field the position of the molecules of the object are not compromised and therefore the object maintains its shape and function. This makes it much easier and requires significantly less computational power.

ME: *So how do you handle translating more than one object at the same time?*

A: Multiple objects are not affected collectively but separately and, therefore, do not affect each other when more than one object is to be translated at the same time.

ME: *So objects do not merge together?*

A: No. This can only happen if you try to do this outside of an acceleration field.

ME: *So how do you translate a space craft?*

A: The craft has the field generating hardware positioned around the periphery of the craft; everything inside the field is then accelerated up to the next dimension.

ME: *So once you have translated, don't you tend to leave the acceleration field generating hardware behind in the lower dimension?*

A: No, because the field leaks beyond the generating hardware. This has the effect of allowing the hardware to be translated at the same time without being left behind in the lower dimensional frequency. Sometimes it is better to be imperfect!

## Moving from Point A to Point B via a Shunt

ME: *O.K., so once you have gotten to this next level, how do you move from point A to B?*

A: We use the same method to create a shunt.

ME: *A what?*

A: A shunt. We use the field to shunt the molecules of the ship and its occupants in a known direction; the action is rather like a solenoid. Once the ship is moving, the shunt is used more and more, faster and faster, resulting in the ship being pushed up to a higher velocity each time the shunt is activated. The process continues until the ship is traveling at the desired velocity. The 0 to 60 speed is quite phenomenal.

ME: *Is there not a limit to the speed that can be achieved with this shunt?*

A: Yes, but at the moment the limit is too high for us to worry about it. The limit of the shunt is increased each time you go up to the next dimension so you are always increasing the potential max speed of the ship. The potential max speed is never actually achieved, as the limit necessary to affect translation is lower than the max, therefore, eliminating the max as a virtual ceiling.

ME: *So how do you slow down?*

A: Deceleration is the reverse of acceleration in so much as the same process is used but in the diametrically opposite direction.

ME: *This sounds all too hard to control and monitor.*

A: It is, with your current understanding, but don't forget that the computer controlling this is many millions of times more powerful than yours. And it is able to sense and take account of the changes necessary to allow the process to be controlled to a fashion where it is useful.

## Continued Dialogue on Multiple Topics

## Morality Issues Within Alien Worlds

I continued this dialogue in another meditation and started the discussion by asking a question about morality issues within the alien's worlds.

ME: *Do you have any issues with morality within your race?*

A: No, we all work together for the good of the whole race. There are races that don't take this opinion, and humans are one of these. Most don't even need to take the moral high ground because they don't put themselves or find themselves in situations which compromise them in relation to the good of the whole. The mental and physical health of the whole is the responsibility of the whole, and the individuals that make up the whole. It benefits us all, so we don't upset the balance.

## Maintaining Health

ME: *You talked about physical health as well. How do you keep your selves healthy?*

A: Our bodies need to live for a long time, so we don't consume any substance that compromises the health or frequency levels that the body needs to achieve to do its job of work. For instance, we wouldn't dream of contaminating our bodies with alcohol, tea, coffee, or cigarettes.

ME: *You know of cigarettes?*

A: I took it from your mind, but our race knows of this problem you have.

ME: *So do you eat?*

A: Some races need to take energy from the produce of plants and animals, but they prefer plants as the vibrations in animal products are low and can reduce vibratory levels. Most others, ourselves included, take energy from the universal energy directly. We are able to metabolize it by using specialized organs within our bodies, the receptors of which are integrated into what you would call the pores of our skin. Others take energy from the gases that make up the atmosphere of their home planet and use a lung like system of filters to extract the energy from the gases. Others use organs in their skin to do the same thing.

## Metabolizing Pure Energy

ME: *So how do the aliens that metabolize pure energy metabolize it?*

A: It is done at a quantum level. The energy centers or chakras, as you call them, take in energy at different frequencies. This energy is then distributed via the energy meridians (call them energy veins), which are positioned throughout the body. At the quantum level the cells pick up the energy and become energized and, therefore, go about their daily jobs as your cells do in your body. This is rather like the inductive charging of a battery. The body is simpler as it does not have to create energy from physical matter. It is also longer lasting for the same reason and is significantly more resistant to disease since it is not introduced to foreign matter on a continuous basis.

ME: *So the main difference with us is that our bodies have to breakdown physical matter into energy whereas the energy metabolizing aliens doesn't need to.*

A: Yes, however, the aliens that metabolize energy from the atmospheres of their home planets do a simpler version of what your human bodies do, and are, therefore, also more robust.

## Aliens/Other Entities on Emotions

The next day we touched the subject of emotions.

ME: *Are you happy with the job you do?*

A: I cannot say that I am happy because we do not have the same range of emotions that you have. All I can say is that I am satisfied with my performance, and my supervisors are satisfied. The work that I do is adequate to the work load and the output expected of me.

ME: *So you do not feel depression or elation or sadness or joy.*

A: Not in the sense that you do. We feel content with the level of our performance. We do not feel elation if we make a big discovery. We merely feel content at the fact that the work we have done has borne the fruit it was intended to.

ME: *Do you feel jealous that you do not feel these emotions?*

A: No. But we do find it interesting, and that is one of the reasons we are here. The Latin-based countries are very good at expressing their emotions. They are not inhibited by what people around them will think when they display the full range of emotions, and so we find the interplay of personal emotions vs. response of the people around them interesting. We don't get the same spectrum of responses from the English or German people, so we are not so interested in them. However, you are also interesting because you suppress your emotions. We have a lot of work to do on this subject here on Earth.

ME: *So it seems.*

A: Yes, it is also linked in with the free will experiment and is bearing interesting results as the emotional content affects the ability to make rational decisions and can result in incorrect decisions based upon emotional content rather than the logical content.

## Life Spans, Stress, Professions, and Genetic Modification

The next day I talked to the alien about age.

ME: *How old do you live to be?*

A: The physical part of us lives from 2,000 to 3,000 of your years.

ME: *That's a long time to live; you must get bored.*

A: No we don't. Don't forget that in the great scheme of things, the life span of a physical human is pitifully small and gives you absolutely no time to accomplish anything. The fact that you accomplish so much is a credit to you.

ME: *You think our lives are very short then?*

A: Yes, but you pack a lot in. Your lives are very stressful as a result. We don't get bored because our contribution to our society is based upon a longer term vision. We have jobs or projects that have a longer time scale within which to work and get our results.

*ME:* *How do you mean?*

A: We are working on a planetary and evolutionary level so things take longer to give results. In this respect we can do many things at the same time and plan them so that we get the results back in a staggered fashion that keeps us interested.

*ME:* *So how would you describe your lives in terms of length of life?*

A: We would also describe them as being short as they are packed with things to do.

*ME:* *What do you do for jobs? What are your responsibilities?*

A: We have many professions, just like you. We have doctors, engineers, artists, analysts, computer programmers, energy specialists, psychologists, etc.

*ME:* *What do you do with your time here?*

A: We assist with and observe your evolution.

*ME:* *How do you assist?*

A: We assist by giving health care to those key people who are destined to help the Earth and its inhabitants evolve in some way. We make telepathic suggestions to people to help them with their decision process so that they experience the right things so they evolve faster. We also make other suggestions to help with the progress of technology.

## Genetic Modifications and "On the Rebound" Incarnations

*ME:* *Do you do anything else?*

A: Yes, we also still make some genetic modifications to make your physical vehicle live longer so that your ability to experience more things is enhanced, therefore, assisting in your ability to evolve faster. Your lives here are so short that there is a backlog of souls

379

waiting to incarnate. It is quickly becoming the case that only those souls who are going to make a difference to the evolution of humankind will be allowed to make rapid "on-the rebound" incarnations.

ME:    *What does "on the rebound" mean?*

A:    It means those souls who need to incarnate straight away so that they can continue with their work. Extending the life span of your race will allow a soul to live two or three life spans in one body.

## Observing and Recording Energy Changes on, in, and Around Earth

ME:    *What else do you do?*

A:    We also observe and record the changes in the energies on, in, and around the Earth.

ME:    *Why do you do that?*

A:    Because both humans and Earth are special. They have energy bodies and physical bodies that both operate and depend on each other. This is rare, as most other beings and planets are either physical or energetic, not a mixture of both.

ME:    *So why the interest?*

A:    With the Earth there are areas where the two bodies join. At that juncture point there is a movement of energies between the physical and energy worlds, a vortex. This causes a gateway between the worlds which we take advantage of, but the interchange in the energies is very interesting to observe and experiment with. You have limitless energy available from this interplay between the two bodies; all you have to do is tap into it with your minds or even a special machine. If you had this, you wouldn't need to use coal or nuclear power to generate electricity.

ME:    *So we could have limitless free energy.*

A:    Yes, and this is one of the things (the machines to tap into this energy) we are helping you to develop.

# Life on an Alien's Planet

In January 2004, (my first day back to work after a long Christmas break) I started my meditation with the intent of speaking to the alien. When I focused my attention there, I asked about what life was like on his planet.

A:     Pretty much as it is on Earth.
*ME:   How do you mean?*
A:     We also have animals that are indigenous to the planet the same as you do.
*ME:   What do they look like?*

# Indigenous Animals, Fish, Insects

A:     They come in many shapes and sizes. Where do I start?
*ME:   Just try with a general outline, such as the number of legs, whether they fly or swim.*
A:     Some come with two legs the same as you and me. They even look humanoid but they aren't whilst others have up to twelve legs and are the size of one of your cows. Most of them eat vegetation, but there is the odd one or two that hunt or even assimilate the energy in the atmosphere.
*ME:   What are those like?*
A:     They are those that fly in the stratosphere of our planet and have, therefore, evolved to live off the more universal energies.
*ME:   What do they look like?*
A:     They are a bit like the cuttlefish you have on Earth, only they have a gaseous internal structure that allows them to rise and fall in the atmosphere by mixing gases internally. They do this by sucking in the atmosphere and separating out the component gases. Some gases they exist on whilst others are discarded. The rest are stored separately in different internal chambers and mixed together when a different gas is required.

ME:     *What about fish? Do you also have them on your planet?*

A:      Yes, we do have fish and other sea dwelling creatures. They are also as different in their size and shape as your creatures.

ME:     *Do you hunt or kill your animals for food?*

A:      No, because we don't need to eat solid food. We primarily evolved to eat vegetation and later evolved to use the universal energies.

ME:     *Do you also have insects like on Earth?*

A:      Yes, but only one or two species. In general, we don't have the same level of diversification of species, planet-wide, as you do.

ME:     *But you do have gaseous animals?*

A:      Yes, but you also have animals that are on different energy or dimensional levels on the Earth as well.

ME:     *We do?*

## Earth Entities in the Space Between Dimensions

A:      Yes. The Earth really is a special place. It has a much greater level of diversity of entities in one place than any other planet in this dimension or universe. This is another reason we come here—to see how you interact with all these beings. There are, of course, many more on the Earth that you have not yet discovered. They are in the depths of the oceans, in the Arctic, and in the space between dimensions.

ME:     *The space between dimensions?*

A:      Yes, they occupy the space between this dimension and the next one up.

ME:     *Will we ever see these animals?*

A:      Yes, some of you already have. They have been seen by those people who take drugs and are, therefore, able to see this space with their spiritual eyes forced open.

ME:     *I see. Are they similar to those on Earth?*

A:     No, they are different and cause people to panic as they do not expect to see such wonderful creatures.

## Star Burst Energy

My next encounter of any significance with the aliens was not until September 2005 when I was in Crete for a week on my own in order to meditate and do the odd jobs before my wife came over, so we could enjoy a real holiday.

ME:    *So what is the lesson for today?*
A:     First of all, let us say that we are so pleased that you are here with us. We enjoy your interaction. Star Burst energy is the lesson for today.
ME:    *What is Star Burst energy?*
A:     It is the energy that comes from the coalescence of matter in its physical form and its ability to be used by an entity to create.
ME:    *You mean it can be used.*
A:     Yes, that is the main reason for a star's presence in the physical universe—to provide energy for use in creation. This energy is used by all sorts of entities for all sorts of things from creating new planets for corporeal life to exist upon to creating works of art by using the energy to create gas clouds of differing shapes, sizes, and colors, including how they appear in the other dimensions.
ME:    *Can I use this?*
A:     Of course, and you do on a regular basis. We are here to teach you to do it again and enhance your abilities. This will be done whilst you are in meditation.
ME:    *Will I remember how to do this stuff then?*
A:     Not yet, as it will need to be absorbed by you first, and then you have to get yourself into the mental frame of mind to be able to wield such power in a safe and sensible way. This means that you will have to be able

to forgive people for anything that they do, or you will be frying them on the spot.

## How Aliens Generate Energy

I then asked the Alien how aliens generated their own energy.

A: We use the energy generated by the friction created between the dimensions.

*ME: The dimensions have friction between them?*

A: Yes, but not the sort of friction that you know that is created by two surfaces being placed together and then moved on opposing planes creating heat. It is more like the energy generated by attracting forces being close enough to affect each other but not close enough to interfere with each other's operation.

I then saw a picture of the distortion in vision one sees when heat is rising.

A: That's right. That is a good rendition of what it "looks like." We harvest this energy, or we just simply tap into it. It's free and easy to acquire provided you have the right level of technology and/or energetic abilities.

## Going with the Flow

*ME: What about going with the flow?*

A: Ah yes. This is a very important and misunderstood concept. You understand that everything that has happened, that will happen, and that is happening is occurring simultaneously?

*ME: Yes.*

A: Then trying to change this is futile and only causes resistance and unrest. Once you acknowledge this on the most fundamental level and truly feel it, then you will know that things happen for a reason. That reason is that this is how it is supposed to be, and anything else is going against the inevitable. Acceptance that what will be, will be and trusting in the universe is a truly profound realization that will relieve the burden of stress.

I had experienced this in a couple of ways at work and decided that it makes life so much easier and simpler. It did feel like a huge burden was lifted off me. By the time I had reached my last day on the vacation, I actually felt at one with the universe and that what will be, will be.

## The Alien Mind

A meditation early 2004 enthralled me. I was seeing lots of different colored fireflies in my mind's eye.

SE:     The universe is a many colored wondrous thing.

My mind went to the aliens. I then found myself asking about their independence.

*ME:*   *Do they have free will the same as us?*
SE:     No, they don't. You are unique in so much as you are cut off from your higher self and Me, so you are totally alone and able to make your own decisions and judgements in life.
*ME:*   *How does the alien mind work then?*
SE:     They are constantly linked into each other. Every one of them knows (if they want to) what the other is thinking or is capable of.
*ME:*   *So what would happen if one of them wanted to, or was about to, do something bad?*
SE:     They wouldn't be able to because the whole alien mind, that is every one of them, would sense it and would be able to collect together and stop the act from happening. This is a form of self-policing and leads to

385

the individual only doing what is right for the whole and, therefore, right.

*ME:* *So what is right for them?*

SE: Anything that accelerates the evolution race.

*ME:* *Evolution is a race?*

SE: No, but only in so much as the individual's purpose is to get to a level of evolution that allows them to return to Me.

# Chapter 32:
# *The Source Entity and the Council of Twelve*

## The Planets Zion and Zorpeton

I then thought about the question that a Bulgarian friend had asked me about the word Zion and asked Earth's Source Entity for an answer on this matter.

SE:    Zion is a moon that rotates around the planet Zorpeton.

*ME:*    *I thought this, too, but looking back at my notes, I found that Zorpeton is a moonless world.*

SE:    It is. Zion is really a small planet, but you might call it a moon as it is so small. Zion and Zorpeton rotate around each other.

*ME:*    *Wow, a pair of planets that rotate around each other and rotate around a pair of suns that also rotate around each other* [taken from my notes on a previous meditation on Zorpeton]. *That must be rare.*

SE:    Not as rare as you might think.

## Zion, the Residence of the Council of Twelve

*ME:*    *So what is the significance of it?*

SE:    It is where the council of twelve reside. Zion really is a beautiful planet. It is a garden planet and it is a real pleasure to be there.

*ME:*    *Are the Council physical beings?*

SE:    No, of course not, but they can manifest themselves physically to take advantage of and enjoy what Zion has to offer them.

## Roles of the Council of Twelve

*ME:*    *Why are there twelve on the Council?*

SE:     There are twelve because each member represents one of the twelve dimensional levels. They are the guardians or overseers of the level that they represent.

ME:     *So who do they work for?*

SE:     Me. They ensure that everything is running smoothly, and every opportunity for evolution is taken and not missed. They have been on Earth, too, but only in their energetic state.

ME:     *What did the council of twelve do on Earth?*

SE:     They were involved with the first civilization.

## The Council's Blunder with Atlantis

ME:     *Which was the first civilization?*

SE:     Atlantis, of course. The representatives of the twelve, including some of the twelve themselves, visited Earth on a regular basis to establish a civilization based upon the integration of the physical and the spiritual, a fusion of mind, body, and soul.

ME:     *So what happened?*

SE:     The twelve made a mistake. They thought that the spirits who incarnated as the Atlanteans could be left to their own devices, but this was not the case. They became too engrossed in the physical experience and lost the connection with their higher selves and with Me.

## The Greek, Roman, and Egyptian Connections with Atlantis

ME:     *So what is the connection with the Greeks* (Minoans) *and the Egyptians and the Romans* (the Romans have the similar architecture as the Greeks)?

SE:    The Greeks and the Minoans are one and the same, but their isolation from each other made their history different. Essentially they are the isolated remnants of the Atlantean civilization, but this is well-documented in esoteric and channeled texts.

*ME:    What about the Egyptians?*

SE:    They come under the same heading as the Greeks and Minoans. Their civilization is based upon the surviving remnants of the Atlantean civilization, complete with its astrological content.

*ME:    O.K., so how do the Romans figure in this equation?*

SE:    They were jealous of the perceived intelligence and intellect of the Greeks, so copied their architecture with the hope that other countries would hold them in high esteem through intellectual association of the architecture. They believed that the architecture of their buildings and temples spelled out to the other nations of their time that they were able to think above the level of their competitor nations, and that this provided them some sort of protection from invasion—i.e., our buildings are divine and the gifts of the gods, so you had better not attack us as we are in favor and are, therefore, invincible.

## Greek and Roman Gods as Remembrances, Not Legends

*ME:    We have heard a lot of legends of the gods, especially the Greek and Roman gods. Where did this come from?*

SE:    These are not legends but actual remembrances. They are the racial memories of the people of Earth at that time of the visitations of the members of the council of twelve and of their representative's appearances and communications with the people of Atlantis and Greek/Roman trusted representatives. Essentially they could not perceive them in other ways because they

389

were too engrossed in the physical by then and had forgotten who they really where, part of Me.

ME: *So they perceived them as gods because of what they could achieve with their knowledge.*

SE: Yes.

## More About the Work of the Council of Twelve

ME: *I would like to speak a bit more about the council of twelve and their work for You.*

SE: Their job is to help the other spirits and physically incarnating entities to work together and to attain awareness. With increased awareness, all of our (My/your/our) collective experiences increase.

ME: *How can that be? I thought the idea was that we experience more by being alone and not having access to our higher selves since awareness would give us more of an advantage due to having insight of the bigger reality.*

SE: This is correct, but the objective of the twelve is to achieve coadunation with Me when incarnate.

ME: *I don't understand. I thought that the objective of our incarnating with the forgetting was that we were allowed total freewill without prior knowledge of what could happen. Surely having awareness spoils this.*

SE: No, not necessarily, as you yourself know you can have freewill that is within certain parameters.

ME: *What do you mean?*

SE: You have freewill to make decisions, but you have a compulsion to do a certain thing in life. You have freewill within certain limits as long as you achieve your end goal. Most of the time this happens and would, in effect, be no different to having awareness of the real reality. You have total freewill, which is rare, and so with this comes even bigger responsibility for yourself and your actions. You have to find your way home without sign posts or GPS navigation, so to speak.

*ME:* *So how will the twelve help me?*

SE: By making your successful choices apparent to you after you have made them. By helping you to realize that they were the correct decisions. This help will not be apparent but will feel right when you look back upon what you have done and the roads you have taken. You are on such a road now, a junction; both sides of the road are enticing, but one will be the best one to take.

*ME:* *Will I know when I have taken the correct road?*

SE: No, but as a word of advice, you know in your heart of hearts what to do to be ultimately successful. Go now and know what you must do.

# Part 4:

# The Less Than Mechanical Side

As I moved through the details that were being given to me, I noticed that I was moving away from the mechanical angle of the universe and how humankind was developed into learning how to live in such an environment to the best of my ability by taking all of the opportunities that are given to evolve while not being dragged down by the lower frequencies that we are attracted to whilst being incarnate. I do note, however, that some of you may have noticed this transition earlier in the book while others might not, so it is at this point that I have decided to take the opportunity to point out to the reader that this transition has been fully made. And the content that is being read is truly to do with how to live life in the physical in the most efficient way possible. In addition, a few age old questions have been answered. This is, therefore, the next part of the book!

# Chapter 33:
## *Nature Spirits in My Garden*

### Appearance of the Nature Spirits

During a morning's meditation before I went to work, I decided to link into the nature spirits that are in and around my garden. As I turned my perceptual focus to the same energetic level as these nature-based entities, they instantly appeared in my mind's eye to surround me. They were delighted that I saw them since this is not always the case with human contact. As an act of friendship, they clung to me and climbed all over me, each one showing me that it was there. I then decided to ask a few questions.

*ME:* *How come I see you as smaller versions of human beings?*

Nature Spirits together (NS): We take the form of humans for two reasons. The first reason is that we appear in a way that is expected of us. That means that humans expect nature spirits to be smaller versions of humans with butterfly wings, so that is what we look like to those who see us. Second, we like the appearance that you give us.

*ME:* *So what do you really look like?*

NS: We will show you.

At this point I got the image of a ball of light slowly moving through the garden. Each time the ball of light was called to do some maintenance with a tree or a bush, an energy tendril grew from the ball and linked into the aura and energy system of the plant being maintained. This could happen to two or three plants at the same time. It was wonderful to see the fluid movement of this ball just slowly moving through the garden reaching out and touching plants as necessary.

ME: *So why don't you appear to people who see you as you really are?*

NS: Because they would not understand what they see as being nature spirits. To them we are fairies (small human-like spirits, the little people, and leprechauns). They are not yet ready to see the real world of spirit/energy beings. When they do inadvertently tune into our world/dimension, they use the image that they can cope with, the one of fairy tales.

ME: *I prefer to see you as you are, energy beings.*

NS: That is good. We like working with you.

## Nature Spirits and the Energy Vortices

ME: *Do you use the energy vortices here much?*

I had noticed that there were energy lines, small ley lines, in our garden and that these came to the surface as vortices.

NS: All of the time but they are best used by humans who can tap into the Earth energies. Those people can really do some good work with the Earth and raise the Earth's vibrations.

ME: *How do they do that?*

NS: By being antennas for the universal energies and directing them to the Earth for use by the Earth and the other entities that work with the Earth.

ME: *So there are other entities that work with the Earth other than nature spirits?*

NS: Yes, and we will show you who they are when you next log into us.

## The Origin on the Purpose of Animals on Earth

ME: *What purpose do the animals on the Earth play?*

396

O:     They are there to keep you company and bring you joy.

*ME:    Bring us joy?*

O:     Yes, do they not?

*ME:    Yes, I enjoy listening to the birds, and I enjoy the fact that my cats love me without reservation and are always pleased to see me when I come home.*

O:     Then they are doing their job. It would be a lonely place on the Earth without the animals. They also do Me a service as well.

*ME:    What is that?*

O:     They experience life without complication, without striving, without greed, without needing anything other than to be what they are. They have no fear of death and disease and, therefore, accomplish quite a lot by experiencing things in a most un-filtered way. They are, therefore, a useful datum line for Me to have when comparing the evolutionary experiences that you have in human form, where you have all the freewill you want, to those who clearly do not have any free will.

## The Source Entity on the Purpose of Animals on Earth

SE:    Animals are an integral part of the spiritual biosphere of the Earth. They form a function of tending to the needs of the Earth in certain ways, rather like nature spirits. They work on the more physical levels of the Earth, those that the nature spirits have difficulty with due to their level of frequency.

*ME:    But they appear just as animals to us and don't appear to do anything special.*

SE:    That is because you cannot see beneath the level that you are experiencing. Without the animals doing their work for the Earth, the spiritual biosphere would be even more stagnant than it is now. They clean up and re-align the energies that are at the very bottom of the frequencies, making up for the lack of care that humanity is currently taking of the Earth.

ME: *So animals are essentially lightworkers?*

SE: Yes, they are, and humanity incarnate does not even recognize this. Everything that the animal kingdom does is for the benefit of the Earth and its senior inhabitants, humankind; you just don't recognize it. Consider the insect kingdom, for example. You recognize the work that they do on the small level that they have to work within, but you totally miss the work that the bigger animals do because they are so close to you in size and shape and makeup. What's more, the animals are also spirits in their own right.

ME: *You mean that they are like human spirits?*

SE: No, they are not at the same level. Remember in a dialogue we had right at the start of this relationship where I mentioned that when I separated Myself out to form all of you, I also created entities that were not quite the same. This was because the amount of energy was not consistently distributed when I created all of you. These are also sentient beings, but the sentience is of a different level. They can, of course, move up to the same level as you if they work with humanity over a period of time. Not many do this, but there are enough that are either on the cusp of moving up to the same level as the human energy level or are capable of doing so, purely as a result of their continued interaction with loved humans, or humans that love them and ask them to incarnate with them. Again on a different level, the plant and mineral spirits are also capable of moving up the frequencies to the next level, but that is a much bigger job for them to do, taking many, many millennia to achieve purely due to the level of interaction that they have with entities that are higher than themselves and the number of opportunities to be exposed to the environments that give them the contact with entities of higher frequencies. It is the regular or even constant interaction with entities of a higher frequency that helps them move onwards and upwards.

ME:     *So working with this is the Earth, an entity in its own right.*

SE:     Yes, of course.

The planets have other roles to play within the universe as well, for they exist in an environment that needs a lot of, shall we say, housekeeping, to keep it in good running order. They are good at mopping up all of the stray energy that has no clear association that exists in both physical and spiritual form and provides a location/association for it, giving it a direction, a purpose. All energy should have a purpose and what better way than to be part of a planet, a large entity that has a purpose, the maintenance of the equilibrium of the universe from a multi-dimensional point of view. The great opportunity you have is for humanity to work together with the animals, the plants, and the minerals to support the requirements of the planet that attracted you, for all entities are attracted to those with whom they feel they can work best to help them evolve.

Even though the animals are a simpler entity than the human entity they are in some respects closer to God, for they are pure in their actions and intentions when they are incarnate. You should consider the animals as your friends and helpers, for this is what they are. They exist in this environment purely to help you evolve and return to the Source. In doing this, they ask for nothing; they work only to be of service. When one of them is given the opportunity to progress to the human energy levels, it is a great honor for them, for it is not in their nature to work with humanity with the ulterior motive of being able to jump to the next level. They are too pure in this sense, as they have not been corrupted by the lower levels of frequency that humanity creates for itself by trying to better itself without any consideration on how that might affect the entities or environment around them. Animals do not affect the environment adversely; they work with it, even locusts do. As I have just stated, all animals have specific jobs to do and do them for the sake of the environment and not themselves. They do this because they are not capable of thinking this way. As a result, their thoughts and actions are pure of heart and are committed to being of the best service that they can with the physical tools they have at hand. They also have energetic tools as well that they use in complete harmony with the Earth and the universe and in a completely unknown and unrecognized way by humanity. If humanity incarnate was aware enough of how much important work animals do for them behind the scenes, they would be humbled to the point of change. They would no longer do the things that they do to animals and the world. The animal kingdom sacrifices itself on a regular basis for the good of humankind, and humankind does not even bat an eyelid. It's time they did.

## The Necessity of Working with Nature to Achieve Balance on All Levels

*ME:*   *I was pondering on what a wonderful life the old Greeks must have had working on the land and being in tune with the seasons that nature has given us.*

SE:    Listen, this is an important thought process and one that needs serious consideration in this day and age. The world balance would be maintained if man worked together with nature, such as when you worked in harmony with the forests in a sustainable way. If man could see this as a good way of working, then all of the damage caused by industry could be undone. A modern way of doing this would be for man to live either off world or underground. This would leave the Earth to return to its natural ways on the surface. If man could even tend the earth in the agricultural ways without using pollutants, it would maintain the balance.

Man is inseparably linked to nature. Everything he does has an effect on nature, and everything that happens in nature has an effect on man. The trees, the animals, the seas, the rock, the atmosphere, and the magnetic field/Earth's aura all have an effect on and are affected by man. Nature spirits aligned with trees and forests are disappointed with the human race for destroying most of the forests and their disregard for nature in general. If man could learn to live within the laws of nature by producing technologies that are complementary to nature, like sustainable energies, such as wind, sea, or solar energy, rather than fighting or polluting, humankind would evolve a lot faster. Technology is there to help you progress and find ways to relieve you of your daily burdens, but you need to ensure that it is not your undoing. It will, if used properly, allow you to work more within the rules of nature and progress spiritually.

Man is not only linked with nature here on Earth but also linked to nature on the universal level. Indeed, nature is part of the Source Entity (Me) or God and is, therefore, everywhere in all the galaxies in all the universes in all time. Thus, what we do here on Earth has an effect throughout the universe. No wonder other beings are worried about what you do to your planet. You are linked to all parts of nature throughout the different planets, solar systems, galaxies, and universes. Every part of you is interdependent upon the other, each having an effect on each other. Connecting with nature, therefore, allows you to connect with the universe and communicate with God (the Origin, the real Us).

ME:   *Who would be the best to learn from in this day and age?*

SE: Learn from the wizened ones (wizards) and witches. They are still around; they just don't wear pointed hats or ride on broomsticks. They are people who are knowledgeable in the use of nature. They know all of the herbs and plants that can be used for healing and to aid meditations. They also know how to see and use energy for healing, manipulation of matter and alchemy, including other higher functions. They can see and talk to the nature spirits and work together with them within nature's framework. Essentially they are masters of their environment as they have a total understanding of the universe and its workings. So-called "modern" humankind could learn a lot from them.

## The Essence of Trees

In this dialogue I communicate with the Source Entity on the subject of trees. I personally like trees and feel that they have a special association with us. Once I had focused my attention on the Source Entity, communication was instantaneous.

*ME:*   *I have a question on trees.*
SE:    Fire away.
*ME:*   *Can you please tell me the importance of trees and why New Age people revere them?*
SE:    You know that trees are energy fonts and that they grow on/follow the position of the ley lines.
*ME:*   *No. I didn't think of them in those terms.*
SE:    Well, they are. Let Me explain. Pictures of druids dancing or at prayer around a burning tree is generally an artist's impression of what the artist was told that a "sensitive" could see in terms of the energy flowing from a great tree, especially if the tree was at the end of an energy tap or divert. Also, as lower energetic beings, trees of the same type are all part of a dendro (tree)

gestalt mind. For instance, elms are all of the same elm mind, and oaks are all the same oak mind.

One of the interesting things about trees is that if there is only one tree of its species left in a forest and some of its seeds are planted, then as they grow, the tree's mind expands. The individual trees are not individual trees with individual spirits. They are all part of one group spirit. So a lone tree species in a wood is still in contact with the other trees of the same species on the Earth, but it is an outpost until saplings grow. This is unlike the human race which as they reproduce, they reproduce individual thinking beings.

As trees covered the entire planet, at one point the wizened ancients used them to communicate with other wise ones. To achieve this, they connected with the tree's spirit (i.e., a beech) and then sent a message to the tree spirit. A wise one in another location could then tap into the same tree spirit (i.e., a beech) and recover the information sent. A message could be sent any distance using this system. Of course, there are also trees on other planets. Although some trees are vastly different to those on Earth, there are some that are similar. As a result the tree spirits on different planets can communicate with each other. Similar tree types allow communication to become easier as their spirits are linked. This means that a person who links with a particular tree spirit can receive images/communication from other trees of similar types on other planets.

ME:    *That's beautiful.*

SE:    Isn't it? Let Me give you another example of how humanities disregard for trees affects energy. This part of the world is asleep (March 2003); the trees and plants are just starting to wake up from a long winter's slumber. The apple tree behind you needs to have a dead branch cut off. The trees don't mind this type of surgery as it keeps them in good condition. They used

403

to be looked after by humans in the past when humans were working together with the energy of nature and the nature spirits. Now human beings have largely abandoned them energetically. They go out of condition, and their energy flow is no longer efficient. The energy going to the dead branch, for example, is wasted and causes eddies and ripples in their energy flow.

# Ley Lines, Standing Stones, and Earth Energies

## The Partnership of Ley Lines and Trees

For two years running during our New Year's Eve and New Year's Day sabbatical from civilization, my wife and I visited areas where ley lines and great standing stones were positioned. In doing so, we both felt lots of energy in and around the areas. Intrigued and thirsty for more knowledge, I decided to contact the Source Entity on this subject to gain a better understanding of their role on the Earth.

ME:   *What can you tell me about the ley lines and standing stones that we have on the Earth?*

SE:   Ley lines and standing stones are the planet's energy veins and major energy junctions. A little known fact is that ley lines are usually marked by the presence of a "great" tree, such as an oak or an elm because they work well with the energies. They can be easily located as a result. Today ley lines are in poor condition as they are either not fully functioning or in disrepair as humanity no longer services the ley line grid.

ME:   *So how would we repair a ley line?*

SE:   To repair a ley line or a ley line junction (without a standing stone), a person or group of people can inject or channel energy into the earth and mark it by planting a great tree sapling. Ley lines have fallen into disrepair mostly because of man de-foresting the world, as the trees are part of the ley line energy circuit; therefore, this is the need to mark a new energy juncture by planting a great tree.

If you could see the energy of the ley lines with your naked eye, they would look a bit like stitches holding the segments of a leather case football together as they dip in and out of the ground.

## Using Ley Line Energy

ME:    *So how would we use the energy or separate it for use?*

SE:    The ley line energy could be separated from the main stream by placing a stone in the way of the energy flow. This changes the direction of the energy by splitting it into two. Subsequent stones can be used to put the flow back on its original course, and the "hived off" energy can be redirected with more stones to an energy collection point. This is usually signified by a ring of stones or stone circle where individuals who can manipulate energy could use it or "charge" items that run on Earth energy, for instance, lamps or healing stones.

Of some interest to navigators may be the knowledge that the lines of longitude and latitude correspond with ley lines and their junctions. A being can, therefore, use them to navigate, as they are magnetic. There is no coincidence that the ley lines and longitude and latitude are in the same position. How do you think pigeons navigate?

ME:    *So who used this energy?*

SE:    The wizened ones, wizards. A wizard's staff was used to channel and focus energy. It was made of wood (elm), a precious metal, and a crystal. Each material is used to tighten the focus and, therefore, intensify the energy channeled. Some wizards were able to tap into the ley line or Earth energies by tapping their staffs on the ground three times where a ley line was found. This is still used, although greatly misunderstood, by magicians when they do their illusions today.

## The Functions of Stones

*ME:*    *So tell me more about the stones and their function.*

SE:    Stone circles were used to trap and focus ley line or Earth energies. They have magnetic qualities and direct energies rather like the large electromagnets in the CERN particle accelerator. For instance, the stones you visited at Kilmartin (Argyle) were used to focus energy; they were also the point of a major ley line junction. The two lines would mix in a big ball of energy and send energy in directions at 90 degrees from their origin, forming a crossroads. A good example of a large ley line focal point is the stones at Avebury which are a channel and compressor of energy.

*ME:*    *So what else do stone circles do?*

## The Uses of Stone Circles

SE:    A stone circle had two uses. First, the wizened ones could lie on a table in the center of the circle, and the energies that were gathered from the junction would travel around all the stones before being projected onto the table in the center. This would give the person on the table enough energy to project himself/herself into the astral worlds. Second, the stones would be carved with cups and circles. These cups and circles represent (although this has been dismissed by your researchers) the star configurations seen when an individual is lying on the table at the center of the circle. They represent certain points in the year and are, therefore, the "seasons" as they knew them then. The "seasons" were split up into periods of less than a month then and indicated when certain activities should be started or finished, not as they are now: winter, spring, summer, and autumn. Most stones in Avebury and Kilmartin transmit energy today.

ME: *I have seen many stones in pairs, some with one fallen.*

SE: Stones that are no longer maintained are those that have fallen. Those that are in pairs—you see many stones together with one standing and one fallen—are used to guide and compress the energy. This lack of maintenance has resulted in the energy being diverted for use but not re-directed back to the original energy stream because the re-directing stone has fallen or been vandalized and is not doing its job. This is the major cause of dysfunction in the Earth's energy grid (etheric layer) or ley line system and is one of the reasons (along with deforestation) the Earth and its inhabitants fell down the frequencies. This reason for the Earth falling down the frequencies is, in fact, a result of humans using the Earth's energies for their own use and not maintaining the old "machinery" of energy-diverting stones.

## Earth Energies

### Injecting Energy Back into Earth

ME: *Tell me more about the Earth energies.*

SE: First, a bit more on how to inject energy back into the Earth, as this is an important job that humanity can do for the Earth as payback for pulling it down the frequencies with them. Let's start with posture whilst delivering energy since this affects delivery efficiency.

A good example of the posture to achieve is the Christian cross as it is a good illustration of how to receive/channel Earth energies. Although the best configuration involves planes in X, Y & Z, the illustrations below show how one or more people can

407

channel Earth energy. Those with the dots are the head of the channeler with the lines being the arms.

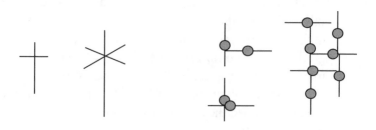

The Earth has seven auric layers. The ley lines exist on what would be the etheric level of the human aura and energy level. The grid lines on the human body at the etheric level, for instance, those linked to the major and minor chakras where 21, 7 and 4 energy lines meet (and which some healers see when tuned into this level) are similar to the ley lines that are a grid around the Earth. Hence, someone repairing the Earth's ley lines is repairing the Earth on the physical level. When all ley lines are repaired, the Earth will function correctly and rise again back to its correct frequency.

A being can sense the different auric layers by "tuning" into the energy level or frequency associated to it. On a basic learner level, this is done by opening and spinning the relevant chakra. For instance, if you want to sense or see the energies on the etheric level, you open the base chakra. If you want to see the emotional level energies, you open and rotate (in the correct direction) chakra No. 2. This works the same way for sensing or seeing the Earth's energies, for it also has auric layers. So to sense the Earth's ley lines, one must first tune into the energy level that is relative to that auric layer by opening and spinning the base chakra. The Earth's emotional level energies can be sensed or seen by tuning into that level by opening and spinning the second or emotional chakra. Again, this is a very basic and rudimentary way of achieving this.

## Earth's Auric Levels and Chakras

*ME:*    *So does the Earth also have auric layers?*

SE:    Yes, as stated above, the Earth has an aura system and a number of auric layers corresponding to the number of major chakras it has. The auric layers have been detected by man but not yet recognized for what they are although these rings have been described as some form of planetary phenomena relative to ozone, radiation, magnetism, etc. The major Earth chakras are positioned in each of the following places: North and South Poles, the center of the Earth, and along the equator in a north, south, east, and west configuration (as if looking down from the North Pole). Some chakra locations are marked by the location of old world major monuments, such as the pyramids in Egypt, Machu Picchu in Peru, the sunken temples (The Temple of the Sun) off the coast of Japan, and the temples of Angkor in Cambodia. These old world monuments were built there by the ancients to access the myriad Earth energies that were available at these energy junctions. They were used for healing, astral travel, matter manipulation, and for directing energy to other parts of the city or even other parts of the planet. All ley lines cross at these points and as with human chakras are the points where the most lines cross.

*ME:*    *How would cosmic energy, for instance, be used with Earth energies?*

SE:    The energy you call cosmic can be made into a tube to contain and direct the ley line energy; it can also be used to bend matter. To do this the cosmic energy is used to increase the frequency of the matter to be bent and the cosmic energy is woven into the shape required. This is done similar to a hoop being cast around an energy line with more and more loops being added with their position changed to change the direction of the energy line.

## Earth and the Universe

In past meditations I have noted that the Earth has a particular role to play in the advancement of the evolution of this universe. I have also noted a number of ways in which the universe works and how to traverse it when in the physical. I asked the Source Entity to clarify these subjects in order to help me understand the importance of our living on the Earth.

## Earth's Pivotal Role in the Progression of the Universe/s

ME:   *In a past dialogue, you briefly commented on the importance of the role of Earth in the universe. Can you explain a bit more on this, please?*

SE:   Of course. The Earth is pivotal in the progression of the universe because of the ability of its intelligent life, humankind, to have independent thought. Hence, raising Earth's vibrational levels is of the utmost importance. In support of this, many other intelligences are also helping to increase the vibration levels. I will clarify further. The Earth can be considered as a piece of important circuitry in a computer. Without its circuits being complete (ley lines), it does not work properly and doesn't allow the rest of the circuit (the ley lines or wormholes to the other stars and planets) to function. Hence, the rest of the universe cannot move up the vibration levels until the Earth's ley lines are repaired, and the Earth starts to function properly, which will then allow it to increase in vibration level. This will also have a positive effect on the function of

410

the multiverse as this universe is a component of the greater multiverse.

ME:     *What will this mean to the universe/multiverse?*

SE:     The big picture is that if the experiment in individual thought is successful and the Earth manages to survive as a result, then individual choice will work. This will allow the collective wholeness to also have the benefit of independent and individual thought at various levels (currently it has only collective thought). This will contribute significantly to the "whole" and accelerate the speed at which the "whole" progresses through the vibration levels and, therefore, evolves.

## Traveling Through the Multiverse/Universes

ME:     *I would also like some more details on how we as physical beings can travel throughout the universe.*

SE:     Mmm, I can see this is one of your *pet* subjects. Traveling in the universe is done by moving from one dimension or vibration level to another. If you consider that the multiverse is a series of spheres within spheres, you would travel out of one dimension to another of a higher vibration, travel the distance in that dimension, and then drop back into the dimension of origin. The amount of time needed to travel the vast distances of interstellar space is then massively reduced because of the lack of density and, therefore, resistance of the universe traveled through. The effects of gravity are also reduced because of the reduced levels of density; therefore, the amount of energy required to travel in a higher vibrational realm is reduced. In some cases, where the ship rotates to very high vibration levels, it can be almost instantaneous. This method has a similar profile to traveling outside the Earth's atmosphere and letting the Earth (or in this case, the universe) rotate beneath them and then dropping back down to the intended landing point.

411

## Teleportation

Another form of transportation is teleportation. Teleportation can be performed by highly evolved beings and is done so on a regular basis.

*Me:*   *How is this done?*

SE:   Consider that we exist as energy in all dimensions in all times in all of space all at the same time. The being that knows this can take advantage of this condition and use it to transport himself/herself/itself from one side of the universe or galaxy to another by disassembling and reassembling himself/herself/itself. If you consider that we are like dust in a sphere, our current incarnation is, therefore, a localized increase in density and attention in a particular position or point within the sphere. We can, therefore, change our location by reducing this local increase in density (and attention) back to the normal distribution of density and attention that is spread throughout the total volume of the sphere (our real condition as part of the whole) and then refocus our attention and density into another position or point within the sphere. We will, therefore, have instantaneously transported ourselves (our attention and density and the attention and density that represents us in our current incarnation) across the galaxy or Earth or universe or dimension/vibration level.

## Science and Nature Working Together

During January 2006, the subject of re-usable space flight was on a UK TV program called *Horizon* with the program offering a $10,000,000 prize for a private enterprise that could develop a re-usable system for leaving Earth's atmosphere and re-entering it twice within a 14-day time frame. The successful company would later be courted by Richard Branson to help him fulfill his dream of commercial spaceflight.

## Burt Routan's Re-usable Space Craft Designed in Alignment with Nature

The winning design of Burt Routan was small, manned, and used a unique tail plane assembly that was rotated through 90 degrees to create the drag necessary to slow the craft down to speed where heat buildup was not an issue in re-entry and, therefore, did not need special heat sinks. The takeoff speed was 2,150 mph, and the drag created by the tail plane was such that this slowed down to 500-600 mph on re-entry. The plane had a piggy back up to 9 miles and then detached to make the final journey into space. I was going over this program in my morning meditation when the Origin responded on the subject, resulting in the following dialogue.

ME:  *It's incredible that a small company can achieve this in such a small amount of time with such a simple solution when the whole of NASA has thrown mega bucks on huge machines over a long period of time and still not have the totally re-useable vehicle.*

O:  Yes, Burt Routan has hit upon the correct way that nature works.

ME:  *How do you mean?*

O:  He has found a way that works the way nature works. Don't forget that nature has a set of universal laws that must be used when working within the dimension or frequency that you are manifested within—in this case, the lowest level of manifestation, the physical world. If you look at Routan's design, you will notice that the craft falls the same way as a leaf. A leaf creates its own drag and, therefore, slows itself down.

ME:  *I also got the image of a spider falling.*

O:  Yes, that's right.

ME:  *So what does that mean in terms of following universal law?*

413

# Failing to Follow the Universal Laws/the Laws of Nature

O:      It means that if you follow and work with universal laws, you don't need much work to achieve what you want. In the case of the NASA space program, they are fighting nature; therefore, the more they fight nature to achieve what they need, the more energy they have to generate to achieve what they want to achieve—hence, the huge machines needed to get into space versus the small machine that Routan designed. The greater the power used, the greater the resistance and the greater the power needed to go faster. This resistance is manifested as friction, resulting in heat in your dimension. This is also correct for movement through space at near light speeds. Your physicists have already noted that there is resistance incurred even in the near vacuum of space. This resistance results in a bow wave and an increase in mass in the ship that is associated by location of the ship to the bow wave. This results in more energy being required to accelerate from the current speed to that closer to and above the speed of light.

This is the same for moving large distances by using dimensional shift methods. A lot of the other physical or semi-physical entities in the physical and sub-physical universe (the level between this dimension and the next one up) use synergistic methods to work with the universal laws and, therefore, do not incur the energy penalties incurred by going against nature.

ME:    *I have just seen a picture of a man trying to open a door the wrong way to go through a doorway; he can't do it. However, when he opens it the correct way, he can slip through.*

O:      Yes, that's right. The man with the door is a good description of fighting against the universal laws. In your image, he had to go backwards to open the door to

414

allow him to go forwards through the doorway. This is exactly what has happened with the US space program. In fact, their methods are akin to using an axe to break down a door to allow passage through the doorway. This is a good example of the need to use vast amounts of energy to overcome the universal laws of nature as opposed to working with them and requiring very little energy.

Chapter 34:
## *Choice*


## Humanity, the Only Incarnate Beings with Personal Choice

SE:    Choice is one of the big experiments that you are all experiencing and working towards validating as a new medium for the other incarnate races. You see, humanity is currently the only incarnate race that is allowed to have personal choice—the ability to make its own decisions and live with consequences. Other races have to do things by committee or by collective mind.

    This part of the experiment was to see how the evolutionary timing would be affected by giving no discernable guidance or governance. You can make your own choices based upon what We/the Origin, I, and the remaining Sources decide to put in your way, so to speak. Rather than being detrimental to your progress, this actually enriches your experiences and accelerates the individual evolution, as well as that of the race. So far you have taken the collective path of dropping down the frequencies just about as far as you can go.

    This was a very interesting path to observe and one that will be very difficult to crawl out of. Indeed, it has been hard for the human race, but it is now slowly but surely raising the frequencies again through personal choice. In general there is less violence in the world than there has been in the past. Atrocities in conflict are the exception now rather than the norm. I know that from your perspective, the world is in turmoil, and there are many bad things going on, but looking from where you have come, you are definitely on the up.

*ME:*     *So it was our choice to go down the frequencies.*

SE:     Don't get Me wrong. You didn't all suddenly decide to slide down the frequency ladder in one day. It was a gradual decay, one that from your own level would not have been noticed without a particular level of objective observation over a long period of time. If you had observed, you would have seen certain choices for improvement of a particular situation but didn't make uplifting choices for a couple of reasons: 1) either a particularly strong and charismatic individual convinced you otherwise, or 2) or you were afraid of the change that would/could occur if a certain someone was right even though what he/she said was radical. In essence, humankind incarnate has been a willing lamb. The best way to describe humankind's willingness to be led is best told from the perspective of one of the older races that existed on the Earth.

## Atlantis Sliding down the Frequencies

*ME:*     *Which one would be the best to use as an example?*

SE:     Everyone knows the legend of Atlantis, so I could start there. However, there are many more to choose from that would give a better example of how easy it was to slip down the frequencies, but the Atlantis example is one that most people recognize so I will leave it at that.

# Chapter 35:
# *No Coincidences*

ME: *So, it's been three weeks since we last talked, and I have had so many coincidences happen while I was away from you. In some instances, the timing was impeccable, down to five minutes either side. Any longer and I would not have met the person I met. This can't be real; it must be contrived in some way, pre-planned, pre-ordained, or destiny!*

SE: Everything is pre-ordained and planned. Destiny is there for the taking if you are awake enough to see the signs and act upon them. Many people see the signs and don't act because they either write them off as inconsequential, or they are afraid of going down that path—a path that might take them outside of their comfort zone and cozy life. This is, of course, O.K. with Me as they have free will to do anything they like with their lives. After all, it's their evolution, and they can do what they want with it. You see, even if they don't follow the hints given to them, they still contribute to the greater cause and are still continuing to evolve. It's just that they have not taken the optimal route that has been presented to them.

ME: *So who are these people I met? What is their involvement in my evolution or anybody else's, for that matter?*

SE: They are people that you work with whilst in the energetic realms, *in Spirit,* as your esoterics like to say.

ME: *You mean I know these people even though they live on the other side of the world in the physical.*

SE: Yes. Why are you so surprised? You know that you are all connected.

ME: *Yes, but . . .*

## Nothing Left to Chance

SE: You still get constrained by the thought processes that you are allowed in the human form. This is understandable. But consider this: the opportunity to greatly advance the human race is at the fingertips of every man, woman, and child on the planet. Everything is presented to you in a way that you can follow all the time. Your team of helpers, those who are not incarnate but who choose to work together with you behind the scenes, are constantly changing the ultimate plan to suit the changes in environment in which you find yourselves. They are constantly re-presenting the opportunities to you at the most opportune time when you are able to recognize the signs and take the opportunity as it presents itself. These are the coincidences like meeting someone that you not only instantly like but *know*—someone that you know even though he/she lives on the other side of the world. These are wake up calls to do something greater with life and to take on-board the higher functions of the universe and work with it for the common good. It might not look like you are working for the common good right away or even ever, but don't forget that there are myriad interactions you make each day that affect others in some way or another.

ME: *So what you are saying is that we are guided by our team of helpers to make the right decisions in our physical incarnation to make sure that we take the route of least resistance evolution wise.*

SE: In a way, yes. Nothing is left to total chance since everything is understood. Every cause and effect is recognized, understood, and planned. Every event that happens is in the plan. It's just interesting to see which event comes to fruition given the set of circumstances that the individual is working within.

I have been working with humankind and other

physical incarnation vessels for many millennia in the quest for a greater understanding of Self for the Origin and Myself. Every time We (humankind in Spirit/energy and I) have planned an incarnate life, We have always used the Akashic records to see the permutations that could arise as a result of a different decision made by the incarnate entity whilst in a position of reduced communication with its higher self and the rest of humanity. As a result, nothing is left to chance, and everything is understood and considered. Nothing is really a coincidence; it is part of the plan.

*ME:* *So what are we supposed to do when we see such coincidences appear in front of us?*

## Recognizing and Working with the Serendipities in Life

SE: Work with them and use them as much as you can to enrich your lives and experience, for that is why they are there. When you experience a coincidence that allows the communication between yourselves and others that you would not normally be in communication with, wherever they are in the Earth sphere, it brings the human race closer together in peace. Being together in peace is one of the *Holy Grails* that is available to humankind to enable personal and collective growth. When a coincidence presents itself, it does so in the knowledge that it will bring people closer together to allow them to work together for a common good, a common goal of giving themselves for the good of others. Coincidences, therefore, don't just happen. They are planned, timed, and adjusted to make the most of the surrounding events and to give them the biggest impact on the individual they can, so that they are recognized and worked with to the best of the individual's ability.

# Chapter 36:
## *Coming into Our Power*


ME: *What about coming into our power?*

SE: What power?

## Power as the Return to Spirit

ME: *Just our power.*

SE: Knowledge is power, and the return to true knowledge and awareness is power. Therefore, the return to Spirit is power. You are only truly in your power when you are in your most energetic state, Spirit. Then you are in control of all of the elements at your disposal, even the universe itself, but don't think of it as being the ability to create and destroy planets. Think of it in terms of being back in control of yourself, of being back with yourself, being whole once again, being whole with the universe. Your knowledge base increases beyond your wildest dreams when you are in Spirit, for *you* have many millennia in which you have been incarnate and in energetic existence. So have all the others that I created, although some chose to incarnate well before others and have, therefore, evolved faster. On top of this, you have access to all of the combined knowledge of the created entities, the other Source Entities, and Me to draw upon, as well as your own experiences. With this combined knowledge you can draw strength from the experience of others to help you through your own experiences. Your true power here is the ability to make decisions in isolation based upon previous experience, whether it is solely yours or not.

ME: *So what does being in our power really do for us in the physical?*

SE:    It gives you confidence where previously you may have had none. If you have confidence in a successful outcome even if the outcome is not what you ideally desired, the outcome is a success. The prime objective is really to experience an event and not to pre-judge the outcome of an event and think that one way is desirable whilst the opposite may not be desirable. This is putting a negative spin on the outcome of the event and is not allowing the entity to fully appreciate his/her/its experiences if he/she/it dictates the outcome.

In essence, the older you get physically, the more aware you become and, therefore, the more powerful you become. The only issue you have here is to allow yourself to have the time to experience this transition and listen to the reality that is happening around you. For this point in time is really exciting; you are being rewarded for your performance of one of the hardest things that an energetic entity can do—go down to the lowest vibration levels possible for the good of his/her/its evolution. This reward is heaven on Earth—the knowledge, understanding, and experience of what you have in the higher energetic/vibration levels whilst being in the lowest of frequencies.

## Life on Earth as an Illusion

ME:    *I have read a couple of books recently that are written by people who took journeys into the Far East in the late 1800's and early 1900's. They tell tales of witnessing people doing feats that have only been recorded in the Bible as being possible by Jesus or the feats are a very good illusion, which they insist is not illusion but truth. They also re-iterate that the physical existence on Earth is nothing but illusion and that there is a greater reality out there.*

SE:    Is this not what we have been talking about in all our dialogues to date? The greater reality is out there for all to see, use, and experience if they are ready to work within the context of the universal law and remove themselves from the vagaries of the commercial/materialistic content of the physical world. This does not mean that you have to abandon it and become a monk. Being a monk does not specifically give you a fast track to enlightenment. It means that you have to work around it and not let it dominate your thinking processes. This is hard. From your perception, the dominant series of senses that you have at hand are physical, and it is difficult to trust anything else, such as inspiration, as your own thoughts.

ME:     *So does this mean that we as physical humans don't invent anything?*

## All Inventions as Divine Inspirations

SE:     There is no invention made by man that is not the result of divine inspiration. In spiritual terms, this means that it is channeled to the individual from the spiritual realms. Anyone who thinks that this is not the case is under the spell of the greatest illusion of all: life in the physical. The trick is to work with the physical and some of the creature comforts that present themselves without being taken in by the physical as reality, i.e., not making it your God.

   Let Me tell you something. When the Origin made the Source Entities and I subsequently made you, you were all made in our image. That is not to say that you were all made to look like what you perceive now as physical man. You are a microcosm of the energetic. You were given all of the abilities that the Origin and I have at hand, but with the understanding that you can use them to their fullest conclusion within their context, the universe that you were created to work within. In this way, you are equal to God, the Origin, and its first creations, the Source Entities, Me. With this as the *real*

425

reality, why would you want to restrict yourself to this lesser existence when you can achieve heaven (reality and total connectedness) on Earth by simply allowing your eyes to be opened? So why do all of you waste your time on Earth so much?

The Origin has created both you and Me for Its pleasure and enhance Its *Self* experience. The Origin could just as easily end all this right now if It got bored with the way things are going in the universes that the other SEs and I have created and start afresh. But neither He/It nor We have reached this point, nor do We feel the need to start over.

We feel that We are getting to the most interesting part of the game: the ultimate rise of reality over illusion. There are people like all of you throughout the universes who are helping others question their existence. In doing so, they give themselves the right to question their own beliefs further and deepen their understanding. They, too, are making further strides in personal evolution and, therefore, passing this on to others to help raise the game of those who need help and guidance in their first faltering steps in understanding reality and thus, moving them closer to God—the God within them and, therefore, the power within them, the power to do anything provided they give themselves the permission to be open and trust in the seemingly intangible truth. The fact is that they are all powerful, and, provided that they work within the universal law of doing things for the betterment of others, they will be able to build mountains out of molehills, for this is the power at their disposal.

## Aging as an Expectation

ME:     *This "truth" seems fantastic. Does this mean that we could even affect things like the aging process by using these powers based upon belief?*

SE:   Of course. You only grow old because you expect to grow old. You only expect to grow old because you see others around you growing old. This is the norm; this is the problem. The problem is that the norm is incorrect but is nevertheless accepted as being the norm "because everyone does it." Therefore, it must be real. Right from re-birth into the physical body, you are fed basic un-truths, mis-information based upon ignorance and blindness.

   We have talked previously about the primeval desire to be part of a collective, no matter what this means, and being "part" of the norm is part of this desire. In this example it means growing old, allowing the physical body to demise when it really doesn't need to in order to feel that you are part of the norm. In essence, you could negate the inconvenience that decrepitude offers and, instead, command your body to stay like that of a teenager for 500+ years or until you feel that you have experienced all that you planned to experience in the physical before returning to Spirit. Why do you do this!? I still chuckle over this because allowing the body to decay was not and is still not in the design of the body. This is just one part of your power that you do not use because you feel the need to be part of the whole, no matter how misguided that whole is. With this the illusion is complete. It is perpetuated by a fear, a fear of the un-known, an un-known which could/should be known if you only gave yourselves the chance.

# Chapter 37:
# *Religion*


*ME:*  *One of the questions I have been meaning to ask is why religion started? What you think of it and if it is relevant or not in the greater reality?*

SE:  One thing I will say before I answer those three questions is that I have no opinion to give on any of the things that humanity has created as a result of its total independence and isolation from the whole. What has been created has been foreseen and recognized as a certain direction that could have been taken and, in fact, has been taken. There is no judgment on this direction, for every direction is a possibility and is, therefore, perfect in itself. It is interesting to see the individuals' struggles and ultimate solutions to problems presented. It is beautiful to see you succeed in all things evolutionary, and we revel in your contribution to the Origin's evolution.

## Initial Purpose of Religion

In terms of whether religion is relevant or not, I can say this. Religion means re-group, re-assemble, become whole. Its initial use by humankind was not to control people as it is used today but to help the individual remember the greater reality when the frequencies surrounding the Earth were falling to a point where the contact with the higher self (the rest of you) was starting to diminish. The objective was to provide a way to help you to remember what it means to be in contact with a greater reality. This meant dedication and diligence on the part of the individual as the methods that worked without doubt required concentration and meditation to allow the physical world to be shut out and the remnants of the greater reality to trickle through those vastly reduced communication channels that remain connected to those parts of the human construct that are in the lower energetic levels. Even now, great things can be achieved with the energies that are available.

In the past, there were greater opportunities as the channels were cleaner. However, as the frequencies became lower, the number of incarnates that could tap into the energies reduced significantly as did the purity of mind of those bestowed with the responsibility of passing on the truth and how to find it. The true ways fell by the wayside as those "in the power" withheld certain methodologies to give them the edge on their students. Eventually, as more and more methods were withheld, the incarnates became lost as the teachers' (calling themselves "priests" by now) physical bodies died off. Very quickly the promise of being *in the power* as a result of dedicated study reduced to being *in control of others*—others who were keen to learn but had nobody to really teach them. They were happy to be controlled because they believed that they would become something special at the end and be in a position of power over others. This so-called "power" was used in various ways over the millennia, but the true meaning of religion (re-legion) has been lost. Based upon this, in terms of its relevancy, it no longer achieves what it was designed to do, except bring people together and give them some comfort over what is, to them, the unknown part of their existence, what gives them the most concern, and what happens to them upon the demise of their physical vehicle/body.

## Worship's Role in Religion

*ME:     Is that it!? I thought you would have more to say about religion than that—like which one is correct or that you like being worshipped.*

SE:    No one religion is correct, for they were all trying to help the individual remember from whence they came and what they are. Each of them had an individual who was more prominent in the teaching of such knowledge, and each of these tackled the problem from a different standpoint. Eventually every one of the current religions and those that are not known by humankind failed to deliver its initial promise. As I previously alluded to, this was due to corruption of the systems created from within, coupled with the general reduction in frequency of the Earth plane, which also included the local spatial neighborhood, by the way, and the desire for the power to control individuals on a local/physical basis. The Original reasons for its development were lost.

     You mentioned if I like being worshipped!!!

     This is a difficult one to answer as true worship is connectivity to the Origin and Me via group focus (meditation or prayer). It relies on the concentration of many people at the same time to gain some limited gestalt coadunation.

     Look, worship has been taken totally out of context in the current physical climate of the Earth plane, and I am talking about over the last couple of thousand years or more. In essence worship is just another name for love, unconditional love at that, but this is not what worship is taken for currently.

     Currently worship is taken as dedicated belief of the existence of a so called "higher being" that needs to be continuously told by the individual or collective of individuals that they believe in its existence and will do its bidding, whatever that may be. The irony here is that over the years no one has agreed on which being to worship. That, in itself, proves how ridiculous worship is. The Egyptians, for instance, used to worship several "gods." Each of them had a purpose on the Earth, and, therefore, each of them needed to be worshiped to ensure that the god would allow the continued existence of the Egyptian people by ensuring that human reproduction, crops, trade, manufacturing, and wars continued to be successful.

ME: *Are you talking about the worship of idols or idolization here?*

SE: Idolization is something different, and I will get to this later. The real issue with worship is that it is misdirected, misunderstood, and addictive to those who are susceptible to the idea of so-called "salvation" through worship. This is especially prevalent in cult culture where the teachings and the teacher are both worshiped.

In some respects, worship has a positive side: it does bring people together in a common purpose, especially those who feel subconsciously that they need guidance and direction in their lives and thus feel they need to be told how to live their lives. They believe that if they follow the directives, they will gain salvation from inevitable destruction and move into some perfect state of eternal bliss—one that is specifically described by their teacher as being the only *real truth* and everything else is fake. There are many people being sold this particular "pup" all over the world with some being used ultimately for un-Godlike actions.

In reality all return to the blissful state of communion with the rest of their spiritual intellect and, of course, Me. The promise of being one of the "chosen ones" is just not true. Unfortunately, it is too compelling for some people to ignore so they can continue with working on their real task at hand of experiencing and evolving. Instead, they become engrossed in unreal and manufactured situations.

In reality all worship does is give individuals a

vehicle that allows them to side-step their responsibility for their personal progression towards perfection and places it on the shoulders of another. The premise here is that if I pray and worship You/God, You will save me, no matter what I do. The issue here is not that you will be saved because all of you return to Spirit, no matter what; instead, the issue is how much baggage (karma points) you accumulate. That's what counts; that's what holds you back from evolutionary progression in the long run. I will not wipe out what you have collected in "negative energy" because this is not what everybody has signed up for. The Chinese had a belief that they had many incarnations, which is true, of course. They also misguidedly had a view that they could ignore their commitments in their current life in order to have a good time now and catch up in the next, which never happened, of course. This was an endemic mental misunderstanding that resulted in thousands upon thousands of poor souls going backwards in their evolutionary path. It took quite a bit of re-education to sort out and put them back on track.

But we digress here.

As I said before, worship is really the giving and receiving of unconditional love. This is the true meaning of the word, which has obviously been lost over the years.

In essence though, I don't need to be worshipped. The Origin doesn't need to be worshiped, and none of my aides need worshiping in the current understanding of the meaning of worship. Communion in the sense of giving and receiving unconditional love is the objective as this opens the lower self to the higher self, creating a re-union of these two aspects of self that is generally only possible in Spirit.

ME:   *I thought that anyone could be in communication with You and the Origin?*

SE:   Your thought is correct, but not everyone is at the point in their human evolution where they are able to see through the mist and fog of unreal reality and grasp what little of the real reality they can perceive with their limited functionality within this plane of existence. You yourself have doubts, as do others who are in similar evolutionary level. How can they possibly believe what they perceive individually when they experience it best in harmony together? So in terms of whether or not I like being worshipped, I would say that communication with my children is always liked and encouraged,

## The Manipulation of Others for Personal Power
But . . .

Worship used to distract from the truth for personal power is a misappropriation of power and a loss of opportunity to help others on their true path.

What I have stated above is and can be classified as a sin!

Bear in mind that the whole point of religion is to bring people together to help them discover ways that they can use to gain control of themselves. The goal is to help them access that part of themselves that is closest to the physical plane but high enough in frequency to allow reasonable communication with some part of their higher selves. What I have stated above is and can be classified as a sin!

ME:   *What is a sin? What is your understanding of the word we use here in religious contexts?*

434

SE: Simply put, sin is a wrongdoing that can be and should be avoided. You can also use "could have been and would have been" avoided if the individual was open enough to feel the inappropriateness of the actions he/she was about to undertake that would cause the action of wrongdoing.

*ME:* *I thought you said that there was no such thing as right and wrong? If this is the case, then there is no such thing as sin!*

SE: Well observed. There is no such sin or wrongdoing; there is just doing without judgement. I was using it as an example of what is construed to be incorrect from your perspective. In essence the manipulation of others for personal power is an experience for both the leader and the led. The fact that this leadership could have been used for the advancement of human evolution but was not is a shame. To say it is wrong is a contradiction in all that I have been saying. However, it is the *wrong* direction for the opportunity of evolution in an increase in frequency sense. It is still evolution and experience for all of those incarnates that take part. It is just that it would not result in the fastest way to coadunation with their higher selves whilst in the physical. Remember, everything you do is experience, one that the Origin and I are in constant wonder over, for We would not have gone down to the levels of existence that you, My children, have gone in our quest for knowing ourselves.

## Worship vs. Idolization

*ME:* *You said that you would get back to idolization earlier, and I would like to know the relationship between worship and idolization.*

SE: Although I said they were different, in essence, they are the same. The main difference is the use of or the need for a physical object to give the individual's attention focus. The use of graven images has been used for ages and has proven to be the biggest distraction in working with the higher self, especially in striving to gain a greater connection with the universe and Me. Its capability to be distractive is absolute. Its use is not so prevalent in the current phase on Earth in terms of the use of carved images or paintings of a priest's explanation of what God or a God looks like.

However, the "idolization" of certain well-known individuals has taken over with a vengeance, and that is particularly damaging as it links into the comparison of the physical self with others in the physical. This is perpetuated by the media and used to market what are frankly non-essential products as essential everyday necessities. The celebrity life is now the new graven image used as idols to be worshiped on a daily basis. The once wooden or gold mini-statues have been replaced by sports figures, entertainers, politicians, and, more recently, people who are famous simply for being famous. Parents revere these individuals and their children follow suit, knowing no better, as they are programmed from birth that this is what they should aspire to be, a celebrity! In this instance, idolization is particularly blind and the effect limits the soul, not specifically because it in itself is a distraction but because it is seen as being achievable. Of course, I accept all things as being part of the bigger picture of helping the Origin know all aspects of Itself; however, you have all been here before! And, I am interested in how many times you will feel the need to go down this road before you recognize it for what it is.

ME: *You mean we have done this before?*

SE: Almost all of the races of man have gone down this route, and it has led to a significant contribution to their downfall.

## Aztec and Toltec Races

*ME:* *So what about races like the Aztec and Toltec where the worship led to human sacrifice?*

SE: Totally misplaced. They both descended into cave man status as a result of a collapse in civilization which was brought about by pure decadence. Those that survived were not the leaders, inventors, craftsmen, and doctors, but the common people. Without proper leadership, they quickly lost the ability to renew and rebuild what they had around them in modern conveniences, which started to break down. All they could remember eventually was that they were once a great race and that they had done something wrong. This, in turn, led to a worship culture where they prayed for their leaders and intelligent individuals to return to bring them back to greatness, which was, of course, impossible as they had died hundreds of years previously. All that was left were the stone monuments that the previous race had built to commemorate the time they finally achieved the first level of understanding of the laws of nature and the universe. These were taken as areas for worship, areas where it was hoped the previous race could be contacted. And so they felt the need to offer gifts to the previous ones, who they now elevated to God status. They must have been Gods, they thought, to have built the pyramids, fulfilled the stories of legends, and given them the power to make gold. When there was no response from these previous leaders to their pleas for help, they resorted to more impressive forms of offerings to attract the attention of the "Gods." The result was human sacrifice, not to kill the individual being sacrificed but to force the gods to come back to save the life of the one being sacrificed. As it was known that the previous ones revered life and would do anything they could to preserve them, they reverted to the radical act of removing the heart. What better way to attract the attention of the gods than to give them real cause to return—to save a life in danger of ending.

## Starters of Three Major Religions

*ME:* *I have another question on religion before we move on. I know that we all associate God (You) with religion. We believe that the two go hand in hand, together with the need to worship You, and that is the reason why we have religion.*

SE: Wrong! You see, neither the Origin nor I need or desire humanity or any other race to worship us. Why would we want that? We (I) created you to help Us (the Origin) know Itself better. The work all of you do in this area is sterling; you don't know what a difference you are making to Us in Our quest. If anything, We should worship all you incarnates, for worship is only really a form of recognition and a desire to communicate. No, there is no need to worship, only recognize, communicate, and share experience.

*ME:* *What about all those people that our modern religions are founded upon, such as Jesus with Christianity, Buddha with Buddhism, Mohammed with Islam, and Confucius with philosophy.*

SE: If you are going to include philosophers, you should also include all the Greek philosophers as well, for they have equal standing with Confucius. What I would suggest you do is concentrate on the individuals who are attributed with the starting of certain teachings, which are now called a "religion" of one sort or another.

*ME:* *O.K., let's do that because from my point of view, they are pivotal in understanding the* History of God *from a human point of view. They are the start of our major religions and are what most people hang their hats on for the longevity of their* immortal souls.

SE: In essence, they each represent a part of the whole.

438

Each one of them was allowed to have a varying level of connectivity with his higher self and the plan of action he was working toward. They worked above and beyond what would normally be possible together with other individuals (disciples?) who also incarnated with a view of helping this "religion starter" on his quest on the physical plane. Each quest was the introduction and the spreading of teachings to help incarnated humankind to evolve in the most efficient way possible without being dragged down into the lower frequencies where they would lose their efficiencies and, therefore, evolve at a much slower pace. To a lesser extent, all of the "religion starters" managed this although they all taught some things in error. Some of these errors have been taken as being the core truths without question or ratification.

ME: *So what was the area that each of these people was to specialize in teaching us?*

SE: Remembering that each of them was quite high up the evolutionary ladder anyway. None needed to incarnate to perpetuate his/her own evolution. Each took a risk that he might actually slip backwards as a result of exposure to the lower frequencies. They assumed quite a risk, so it is to be expected that they may not have gotten it totally right in the presentation of what they were trying to achieve. Based upon this, you have to be tolerant on what the actual outcome of the teachings delivered.

So here are the tasks that each of the three undertook to help humanity evolve.

## Jesus

The objective of the entity that incarnated and became known as the individual you now recognize as Jesus was to point out the best way to evolve whilst in the physical without incurring the evolutionary points known as karma. Karma was previously described as those parts of your frequency that you lose as a result of doing harm to others who are also in the physical realm.

What Jesus was trying to teach was that it was more important to live in understanding and forgiveness of other people's ways than to persecute them for being different from your own ideals and ways. The biggest message he gave was to turn the other cheek. In this it is well understood from humanity's perspective what he meant by this, but it is not followed at all in your current time period. Instead, it seems that most people are out to get what they can rather than live in harmony with each other. This is a big issue. Even the Christian church is more interested in the careers of their priests and how many parishioners they have rather than the task of teaching the best way to live without incurring karma points.

Jesus also showed the ability of tuning into the energies that surround the Earth and the opportunities that tuning into such energies could give to the individual. The most obvious example from the history books is healing. The other opportunities that could have been shown were creativity (creating an object from the surrounding energies), telepathy (being in constant coadunate communication with the rest of humanity and the Source, Me), teleportation (the ability to change the focus of your physicality to the point where your physical body changes location to that of the new focus) to name but a few.

## Buddha

The objective of the entity that incarnated and became known as the individual you now recognize as Buddha was to provide the mental vehicle for true enlightenment. Enlightenment is the ability to contact the higher self and understand the real meaning of incarnate life on Earth. Jesus, who taught the ways to exist in this lower frequency environment, was, to all purposes, born with this basic knowledge unlike the entity that incarnated as Buddha, who had to first experience incarnate life from all angles before he was able (allowed) to be in contact with his higher self and, therefore, the greater reality.

What Buddha tried to teach was a method of gaining communication through the removal of external stimuli (similar to what you now call meditation) but to the point where the meditative state was the consistent rather than the transient state that is now used. By consistent, I mean that the individual was able to stay in the meditative state of connection with the universe all of his/her waking and sleeping hours whilst also being able to exist and communicate on the lower physical planes. In essence, he was able to bring the individual back to the condition that they would have been able to achieve in the early days of humanity's desire to incarnate for evolutionary purposes. It must be noted here that the constant smile portrayed on the faces of those individuals who are said to have reached the point of enlightenment are an indication of what being in constant communion with the rest of the universe can do to you. In this condition, why would you be angry with anyone?

## Mohammed

The objective of the entity that incarnated and became known as the individual you now recognize as Mohammed was to defend the truth of the first two teachers above. This is to say that he was also able to tap into the greater reality to the extent required for him to know what was worth defending. Mohammed himself was enlightened to the same level as the

Buddha. Since truth is universal, it has no bearing on where it originated. The truth just "is" and can withstand any criticism. As a result the need to defend the truth is just a metaphor. In this respect, Mohammed was to perpetuate the teachings of the first two and to bring the general populous back on track to what the greater reality was and is. Although he knew what these teachings were, he never met the individuals who taught them in the physical.

*Defending* truth at any cost really meant Mohammed was to sacrifice himself in the same way that the other two teachers above had done to perpetuate the belief system that was required to lift the resonant frequencies of Earth and the human race to the point where a constant meditative state could be achieved with relative simplicity and external distractions kept at a minimum. *Defend*, in this instance, was to *promote*. This is the best form of defense since it works within the principles of the teachings to the point where the individual defending the truth is not or cannot be affected by the enticements that cause the individual to lose frequency levels and, hence, gain karma.

So you can see that the whole reason for allowing three individuals to incarnate with greater than normal (at that point in time) cognitive abilities was to jump start the general incarnating populous into seeking the truth again. This was the driving force behind the desire to try to increase the frequencies of the Earth back to the level they previously enjoyed. The truth is defined as the greater reality that surrounds them and the need to investigate themselves through experiencing more.

ME:   *Were the three incarnations planned? It sounds to me as if these three were part of a pre-planned activity of the sort that you previously described—when we want the whole world to change direction in some way.*

SE: Yes, and it still is part of the plan. The only issue is that the intended path that the human race should have taken as a result of these individuals incarnating has not been as effective as energetic humanity expected. It seems that with all things in the physical, there appears to be a certain amount of uncertainty. This, you understand, is a direct result of the vast majority of you not being able to connect with your higher selves and the greater reality. You cannot see what the desire is from the greater human perspective and, therefore, tend to play the situation you find yourselves in to YOUR best advantage rather than for the advantage of the collective human race, both physically and energetically.

## The Plan for Utopia

*ME:* *So what is the plan?*

SE: Look into yourself. You are part of it!

*ME:* *I get the impression that the whole point is to put enough way-points/guideposts in place to make the existence of the greater reality stand out and, therefore, gain popularity.*

SE: Good. Go on.

*ME:* *This . . . I feel like I am waffling here!*

SE: That is because you are accessing the true information without intersecting it with your intellect and, therefore, trying to analyze it. Carry on!

*ME:* *This gain in popularity will automatically generate an increase in frequency, locally at first, as people with similar thoughts get together and discuss with excitement what they see, feel, or experience. As the number of these groups increase, they will have a triangulation effect where those areas in between (location-wise) will also be affected by the increase in frequency and will subsequently rise as well. This rise in frequency will cause the incarnating individuals who are not normally open to their higher selves to experience more of the greater reality than they normally would but in a conscious way. This then will bring recognition to who they really are and what they are doing here on Earth in the physical plane. This will enable the frequencies to rise even further when the need for self-aggrandisement and aggressive actions to maintain personal position are recognized for what they are and discarded in favor of working for the whole rather than for the self. Humankind will once again be equal to the Gods in all its manifestations and will be able to accelerate the evolution of the race and the return to the Source and Origin, if so desired. Utopia will, indeed, have been achieved.*

# God

SE: God is all—everything and nothing at the same time—absolute. We are all part of the God collective and have been fragmented off to enable us/God to appreciate who and what It/we are with the aim of evolving back to a state of true all-encompassing enlightenment. God is, however, not just one being that is spread over all dimensions, all times and all space at the same time. God is part of a number of collectives that are ultimately limited by the number of dimensions It occupies. It may exist in all times and spaces but is limited by a finite number of dimensions—a number of dimensions that can, in our books, still be classed as infinite. A God collective is, therefore, part of a collective itself that truly encompasses all possible dimensions simultaneously. We are split off from God as tendrils from a sphere with each tendril incarnating in order to evolve to a greater level of enlightenment in different evolutionary levels, times, dimensions, and space at the same time. In any one point in space time or dimension, we can only split off twelve times, hence the twelve points or parts of the God head that is us.

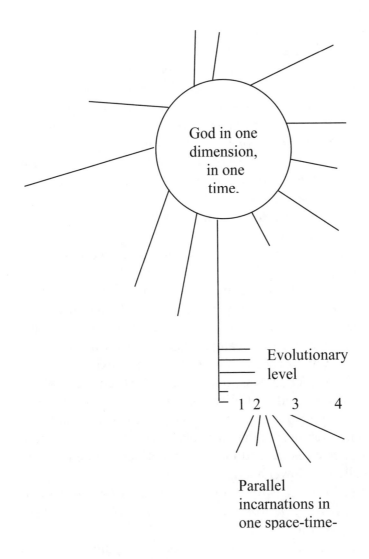

The dimensions can be considered as spheres within spheres with everything on the same line, a line that is both wide and narrow, long and short, thick and thin, in this dimension and that dimension thereby encompassing all physical and metaphysical things at the same time.

## The Entity Called Lucifer

ME:   *O.K., so we have talked a bit about many things, but I can't help feeling that we are not being told the whole story. For instance, where did the story of Lucifer come from in our religious texts? Why have you not mentioned him in our dialogues about religion? Did he exist? Does he exist? If he does exist, what is his angle? What is his input into the Origin's quest for self-knowledge?*

SE:   You don't want too much, do you?

ME:   *I don't think so. No.*

SE:   O.K., I will give you the reality about the entity you recognize as Lucifer.

First, I will continue to call this entity Lucifer as that is the name that you recognize although this is not the name that it is recognized by in the energetic/spiritual realms, which is a great shame for this entity has accomplished much in its existence.

Lucifer was one of the first entities to get involved in the physical human being project and is directly responsible for allowing humanity to have the rare pleasure of having total free will when in the physical realms and those levels closest to the physical called the lower and upper astral.

ME:   *Hold on. So why is this Lucifer classified as an evil character if he was instrumental in getting us to where we are now?*

SE:   He was classified as bad or evil purely because humanity is where it is now—in the lowest dimensions and frequencies possible. You see, when energetic humankind started this project, you were all existing in very high frequencies. Even your physical projection was what you would call translucent or not solid, more gas-like in substance than physical. Although "gas-like" is not a correct description, it will suffice.

ME: *So Lucifer is responsible for us being stuck here at this level.*

SE: No, all of you are. Lucifer simply gave you the means to soar high in the dimensions and frequencies by making the right choices as they were presented to you. You made the decision on which way to jump without the influence of other higher/collective minds.

ME: *Ah, we are back to the conversation about free will versus collective minds.*

SE: No, not quite, you see, even though you are free to make your own decisions, you are still part of a collective entity and, therefore, a collective mind. Lucifer merely suggested and debated hard for the incarnate human entity to have autonomy in order to maximize the evolutionary opportunity and accelerate the evolution process. His idea was maligned by the other key workers on the physical humanity project as being both unnecessary and dangerous. They felt it was dangerous insomuch as the individual entity or that part of the entity that was projected into the physical, that was incarnated, would lose communication with the rest of itself or humanity. He gained some support from some entities that ran a "what if" scenario, using the Akashic and established that the opportunities for evolutionary expansion and experience were enormous and should, therefore, be considered. On the other side, the opportunities for dropping down the dimensions were also there, but they were not too high statistically in terms of becoming a reality. It was based upon the higher probability of success that allowed Lucifer to

447

win the debate with the others leading the project. It was decided that giving free will was the correct way to go to maximize the opportunity.

The big issue was that Lucifer decided not to advertise the possibility that humanity could actually drop down to the lowest levels as well by choosing this route—even though in doing so, humanity would make its greatest advance in pulling out of the lowest of levels. He saw this as the excuse the others needed to veto his idea. He said they would say that the risk would be too great, so he decided to withhold all of the information that came from the Akashic. In withholding this information, he committed a crime—which he was free to do—but that was compounded by the fact that humanity incarnate actually managed to go along this path. From their point of view, the others believed that they chose the worst path for humankind. They believed that if they had been given the complete picture from the Akashic, they would have decided differently. This resulted in Lucifer being maligned as an evil entity, "one that is not of the whole." As a result of this he was asked to leave the group of individuals that had both developed the physical body for humanity incarnate and been the "steering committee," if you want to call it that.

You have carvings and images that show Lucifer as a fallen angel. Let Me say this, Lucifer is not a fallen angel. He has just changed the type of work that he is doing now. Agreed, it (he) is not involved with humanity within the same capacity that it was. But Lucifer is, nevertheless, making significant contributions, especially in understanding the implications and opportunities presented to humanity whilst it is currently residing in this level of frequency, as this is where Lucifer was most experienced. Without knowledge of these levels, he would not have been able to make a decision to withhold this information.

I will say it again.

His own knowledge was damaging to his own arguments to give humanity the free will to work in isolation, in independence of the greater reality, to work alone and be responsible only for oneself, and to truly experience the self in isolation.

ME: *Wow, he really has made a big impact on humanity, hasn't he?*

SE: Bigger than he expected, and he has gained a reputation that is not equivalent to his mistake. Nevertheless, to date, humanity is following the path that was predicted if it individually (collectively) made the decision to go this way, which it did. Now Lucifer is paying the price, the price of not being totally open to his peers even though he is still doing a good job and is now very open with his information, even if it is controversial.

## Dark Forces and Lower Entities

ME: *Over the years I have been to many courses on spiritual matters. All of them referred to so-called "dark forces" or lower entities and said that we must protect ourselves from them. Can you advise on the realty of the situation?*

SE: This is a real bone of contention amongst the lower grade spiritualists, but, fortunately, it can be easily explained. Know this: there is no such thing as a *dark force*. There are only entities that exist in the lower astral. They only exist whilst the energies are at that lower level of vibration. They are scared because when the Earth moves up a level, everything else does, so all the lower vibration level entities will cease to exist. To try to stop this, they are trying to keep the Earth's vibration levels low by influencing those people who naturally gravitate towards the lower vibration levels and make them antagonistic to people who operate for the good of the light work.

Many spirits from all parts of the universe/s and dimension/s come to Earth to incarnate and experience being in the physical with a view toward accelerating their personal evolution. Some of these spirits get addicted to the sensations that they feel in the physical and keep coming back for more, even when they are disincarnate. They do this by attaching themselves to people who are open to them in order to experience their surrogate host's experiences and vibrational frequencies. As they get more and more addicted, they start to slip down the frequencies until they get to a point where they forget who and what they are, and what they need to do to remember. They are effectively lost, have nowhere to go, and don't know what to do.

They only have the instinct that they need to increase their energy levels and, therefore, their frequencies and that this will allow them to remember who they are and break out of the downward spiral. These entities roam the Earth (there is literally a river of lost souls surrounding the Earth) looking for people whom they can latch onto for energy and experiences. When they find a willing host (the poor host doesn't know this is happening most of the time unless he/she is a sensitive), they are happy. But when the host or a healer recognizes their presence and tries to remove them, they get very angry and fight back until they are sent into the Light. In actuality they are just lost and afraid and can't understand what is happening to them, but when they don't get what they want, this turns to anger.

To send them into the Light, all you have to do is invoke the Christ or God consciousness or energy to protect yourself. Then give them lots of love and send them back to the Light by giving them the energy to do so. You, in effect, give them the energy to propel them back to where they came from.

# Chapter 38:
## *Christ Consciousness*

*Me:*    *We talk a lot in spiritual circles about the Christ consciousness, and we call Jesus "Christ" in separation to this, at least the religious circles do. What is the actual connection between the two?*

## Interpretations of the Meaning of the Word "Christ"

SE:    Basically, understand that the word "Christ" was used to describe an individual that had been christened or baptized, meaning cleansed or purified. This is part of the process required to allow the purity of thought to be aloof of the desires of the physical levels and work with the spiritual whilst on the Earth plane. Therefore, he who is cleansed and prepared for this level of work is christened and is called Christ for short. Thus it is that Jesus would be called Jesus the Christened one or Jesus Christ for short.

　　　　Your readers should note here that the temporal "order" in the use of the word "Christ" will always be a bone of contention. The purification process now symbolically used in churches around the world under the guise of baptism came before the currently recognized use of the word—a word currently used to describe Jesus and the religion that stemmed from his teachings. Suffice to say, the christening process of purification was in existence a long time before the entity known as Jesus was incarnate upon the Earth. It was a process used to open the individual's higher channels of communication and remove the desire and the urge to use the knowledge given for personal gain.

The word *Christ* is purely a function of humankind's need for a "punchy" word to explain the purification of the soul. In this function, humankind has assigned it to the Jesus entity as it personified what he was, purified. Hence, humankind put the word after the name of the purified one, Jesus. It is, however, one of many words that have been used to describe the purification process. In essence, Jesus should really be called "Jesus the Purified One," as this is a more meaningful description.

Spiritualists will additionally comment that the word Christ is also used to describe certain "pure" energies or forces. These are energies that are only available to those incarnate entities that are pure of heart. Of these, there are but a handful currently incarnate on the Earth.

ME:   *So if I was purified to the level that allowed me to be aloof of the desires of the physical, then I would be called Guy Christ.*

SE:   Yes, but it doesn't sound as good as Jesus Christ, does it? There is, however, much more to this than meets the eye, for you have asked a question about the Christ consciousness.

Once you are Christened, you are then left to develop yourself personally to the point where this Christ state is personified within you, i.e., you are not tempted by any of the demands or desires of the physical world because you are aware that the physical world is but a minor proportion of the greater reality, the universe and all its levels and frequencies. This is not easy as the temptations of the physical are great and go deep within that part of you that is in-carnate, *in the meat.* You have to look after your flesh body to enable you to work fully within the physical environment at its most basic level. This is where the confusion sets in and the vast majority of you, once christened, become un-christened due to the contamination of the physical world. It is hard to give up the desires of the physical when they are so alluring and so apparently real.

## The Need to Continue Christening/Purification

Your religious leaders just about understand the need for the human body, neigh the soul, to be purified soon after birth to give it a push in the right direction. After that, they have no idea about the need for the christening/the purification to be continued. No one does, as this has been lost throughout the ages. It has now been left to individuals to work out for themselves for so long that it is quite a revelation when someone comes out of the dark and works it out by himself/herself without the religious slant, which, although it means well, is also a lure to control the susceptible mind and constrain it. Being spiritual and in one's power as a result of being Christened is not about conforming to the demands of those who believe they know the answers, for the answer is truly within the self. It might need a little help along the way but it certainly does not need conformity, for there is no conformity in Spirit. There is only creativity borne out of love, wisdom, and power resulting in evolution.

ME:   *I have heard that being Christened protects one from the devil.*

SE:   Rubbish, for as I have stated before, there is no devil except that which is the temptation within you, *the devil within* with its temptations to succumb to the demands and desires of physical existence. All this is part of the perpetration of un–truths to control the minds of the masses. It has no part in the minds of the seekers of the truth or in the greater reality.

I will say this. Anyone who believes in the devil is himself/herself the devil, for there is no such character, energy, or force in the environment contained by the Origin. The word "devil" is in reality

453

just a word, taken out of true context, for the resulting level of personal consciousness reached by succumbing to the desires of the physical.

## Level of Consciousness of the Fully Christened/Purified

But moving back to the Christ consciousness . .

The level of consciousness that can be achieved when fully Christened/*pure* is such that you have full communication with your higher self and the rest of the universe. All intentions and actions are pure as a result and all are made with the view to help the rest of humanity reach the same level of personal attainment towards the Source, Me, and then the Origin. This is all you ever really wanted and to be christened is but a milestone along the way to achieving this perfection." For achieving it is the perfect solution to the perfect desire, the desire to evolve.

Within the Christ consciousness, there is the ability to understand the workings of the universe in your local area and to be able to manipulate the surrounding energies to the point where feats that would be described as miracles can be achieved. A great many of these can still be achieved even in today's "desire-led" physical environment although up to a hundred years ago they were performed in great numbers by enlightened "Christened" individuals in less materialistic parts of the world.

## The Lure of Materialism vs. the Wealth of Christ Consciousness

If there were to be anything that could be described as the devil, it is the massive increase in the need for material wealth. This, in itself, is a real distraction. The need to feel "comfortable" physically is now including the ownership of many things or products that are not really necessary in your everyday life. Moreover, the more you have, the more you want, and the material "hole" to be filled grows bigger. Within this time period, it is then both more difficult and more important to reach the Christened and Christ consciousness state, for the personal goal posts of owning just another product keep getting wider, leading to the condition where you are never satisfied.

Let Me tell you this.

Your entire life would change if you would all take just 2 % of your lives to dedicate to Christening/ purification and insight into what the Christ consciousness is and how it feels to be in the Christ Consciousness of purity of thought, life, and understanding. Oh, the things you could achieve as a result! You would willingly give up material wealth in an instant, for you would not need it. You would have much, much more wealth than you could ever dream of, the wealth that comes with having all the energies within the universe at your command.

ME: *So material wealth is . . . immaterial?*

SE: Yes. It means nothing. Material wealth is not only a passing convenience but a massive distraction to spiritual growth. It seduces you entirely and has done so for millennia. You really don't need it in the slightest. When you are in tune with the universe and its energies, you are able to create everything that you need to support you, including any currency that is needed to barter for physical requirements.

ME: *Are you saying that we can create money?*

SE: Yes, but more importantly you can create food, water, clothing, and shelter. You can even create energies that provide the same effects as medicine (healing).

ME: *So if it's this easy to live, i.e., you can create everything that you want, then why do people get seduced by the physicality of it all? As it seems to me, it is much harder to do the physical than it is to work with the spiritual.*

SE: I ask Myself the very same question on a regular basis. Why are all of you missing the point these days? But I recognize that it is up to the individual to work this out for himself/herself, and this is what your incarnate life is all about.

## The Crux of Christ Consciousness

*ME:* *So getting back to the crux of the Christ consciousness, what is the whole point of it?*

SE: To return to the Source, Me, and then the Origin. I must make this one point plain though. Once you return to the Source or the Origin, you do not lose the basis of who you are. This is not the point of giving you individuality. As I have stated many times, the point is for you to experience many things and feed this back to the Origin. The end result is evolution of the individual to the point of having no need to return to the lower levels. Evolution at this level is to be evolved to the point of being one with God, so to speak, to the point of being equal. Although you can never really be equal, as God is the Origin and you are a small part of God through being created by Me.

The way to get there is to live the life of simplicity, not to the point of depravity but to the point where you are comfortable in your circumstance and any additional time that you have can be used for the betterment of others without benefit to *self*. This is the most important piece of advice I can give you, for there are many who use the *working in the volunteer sector* route as a means to an end. This is usually done by people of wealth to gain higher standing in society and gain public or higher acclaim by helping people who are less privileged than themselves. However, all they really want are the medals, such as knighthoods to further their status, not because they feel the real need to help others in need. To work for the benefit of others/to volunteer at the highest level must be done with the feeling of true love behind it. To help with love as the basis means that you do something for someone because you want to do it, not because you think it will do you some good but because you feel that the individual or individuals involved will really benefit from your actions, and that is what brings you pleasure. Everything is done in love when you are working within the Christ Consciousness. This is the most important thing to remember, for nothing can be done with malice or with the benefit of the individual in mind, for this is not the way of those who operate in this euphoric state of consciousness.

ME: *Why is this?*

## Being at One with the Universe and All Within It

SE: Because when you are in the Christ consciousness, you are at one with the universe and all that exists with it. You do, of course, have a greater focus on the here and now of the Earth plane and will gladly operate within the confines of its environment. Even if you are one with the Christ consciousness, this you cannot avoid, for this is why you are here now on this planet and in this dimension and frequency—to work with the planet as it is now and those inhabitants who need your help to progress themselves, or just need your help.

To be with this level of consciousness is something to behold, truly, for if you could only experience it for a minute, you would understand what I am talking about. In fact, you would do everything in your power to return to this level of existence, for it is what you are all born to experience in the physical. Imagine being able to be in contact with all the animals on the planet, to share with them their experiences,

457

their lives, their joys. Imagine being in control of your body to the point where you do not age, where you can actually rejuvenate yourself, heal yourself and others of any ailment, no matter how difficult or impossible it is to cure with modern medicine. Imagine being able to work the metals and minerals that are found in the earth without the need to smelt them. Imagine just asking them to depart from their current location and to become what you want them to become. Imagine being able to work with and control the basic elements of earth, wind, water, and fire and being able to change the weather to that which is needed to help your crops. Imagine being able to create the food that you need from out of their very basic elements without the need to cook and bake. Imagine being able to manipulate the very space time fabric around you to the point where you don't need cars or trains or planes or boats to traverse the Earth. This is what it is like to be in the Christ consciousness. So why do all of you accept a lesser existence?

ME: *I don't know. Why do we?*

SE: Because you have all been blinded to the greater reality by the need to conform to the rules of the physical. The way to the Christ consciousness requires some level of dedication to the point where you can work long and hard for little reward, for you expect physical reward and this is not what's at the end of the tunnel. As I have just explained, what is at the end of the tunnel is much, much more than physical reward, for you are invited to sit at the table of God (the Origin) as a brother.

## Chapter 39:
# *To Be of Service*

SE: Let Me talk to you about being of service, for there is a lot of mystique and reverse snobbery about this statement. To be of service does not mean that you have to give up your whole life to be something for other people and work for nothing. It is much more than this simple statement. To be of service means to work for the betterment and evolution of the human race if and when you can in an acceptable way.

You see, you cannot force good will on people; they just don't want it that way. People tend to want help when they want it and from people they can trust to help them. This does not necessarily mean that they want enlightenment. More than likely, they require help with sorting out a particular problem that they find insurmountable at a particular point in time. Offering help or agreeing to help if asked is, therefore, the best way forward. The type of help they need may even be benign, like fixing a plug on a desk top lamp or a puncture on a child's push bike, helping with decorating, and, yes, even getting the shopping for dear old granny. On the other hand, you may find that some people ask for help spiritually and are looking for guidance that their particular group of friends, associates, or religious persuasion cannot give them. In this instance, they are questioning the fabric of the reality that they see around themselves and asking for answers to questions that religion fails to answer because it cannot answer questions that the religion itself is designed to keep you away from. For all religion is designed to control the masses by the few who want power over others.

Being of service is to be available to Me and the Origin when We need you, and you know when We need you because you will get drawn into the desire to do a certain thing that can help others. You will only be asked if you are ready and willing to help and are not taken in by the multitude of charlatans that are giving false hope to those who need real help.

Being of service does not mean that you hunt for service opportunities, for you have to live your own life. It does mean that you should take the opportunities to help others as they present themselves whilst asking for no self-gratification in the process. Be content with doing what you can to the best of your ability, for this is the natural way of the universe. If those who are grateful wish to reward you in some way, then so be it. Equally, if there are those that you help who can't reward you, then don't ask for a reward. Go with the flow, for the rewards are there even if none are received at the point in time of giving.

Being of service also means that you should help people even though you do not particularly like them. You should not help them out of the NEED to be of service, but you should remember that they are fellow brothers of the human race and are incarnate to evolve as well. Showing kindness to someone that you don't like by helping him/her out in his/her hour of need (and people instinctively know that you do not like them) is a wonderful thing to do. Not only do you help yourselves rise in the frequencies by overcoming your own prejudices, but you also help them to rise, for they will see you in a different light. As a result of your kindness (a kindness that they did not expect), they will feel differently about those they think are their enemies, albeit on a subconscious level at first. So you can see that by being of service when the opportunity truly arises for helping others, you can help both yourselves and them in the short and the longer term. Everyone is a winner, and no one loses when prejudice is removed and help is given to all, not just your friends. When Jesus said, the *Lion will lie down with the lamb,* he meant that people who were once enemies or had a dislike for each other will work together because they no longer have a fear of each other.

Oh yes, the lion can be fearful of the lamb, as well as the lamb can be fearful of the lion. The lamb can have power that the lion does not have: man to protect it, to feed it, to look after it, and man is powerful. Although the lion is powerful in its own right, it is suspicious of the lamb for although it is weak, meek, mild, and is slaughtered by man for food, the lamb still works with man. So the lion thinks that the meek and mild lamb must be powerful in some way that he is not. This is the same for powerful people. Those that are powerful in stature or position fear those not so strong as them, for they are many and they are few. Being of service can truly help by crossing the boundaries of suspicion, making the strong work with the weak, the enemy work with the enemy, and for them both to move forward together by working together.

Being of service is, therefore, a two, no three-fold opportunity for the entity: 1) to help others in need; 2) to allow both the helper and the helped to progress spiritually and evolutionarily; and 3) for the removal of prejudice and suspicion which promotes kinship and love of fellow man. These three together result in the increase in people working together in trust, harmony, and love, which results in the movement of the whole of humanity upwards through the frequencies. So in the end, a few people being of service helps everyone.

ME:     *So being of service is really all about working to get humanity back where it belongs, in the higher*

461

*frequencies.*

SE: In a nutshell, yes. Anything that you do to help your fellow man elevate himself in some way helps to bring the whole of humanity back on course. But don't forget that this is not just humanity that this helps, for the planet whose environment that you exist within also benefits.

*ME: How do you mean? Does it also rise up through the frequencies?*

SE: Yes, of course. The only reason why it is at its current level is because of human activity. The fascination with the physical caused a general reduction in the frequencies in and around the space/dimensions that the entity called by you "The Earth" exists within; therefore, it was pulled down with you.

*ME: The Earth is a living entity as well?*

SE: Of course it is. It is just at its lowest vibratory level at the moment—nowhere nearly as vibrant as it could be, even if it was shifted up one or two levels.

*ME: So we can be of service to the Earth as well by helping others to better themselves spiritually.*

SE: Most certainly. Being of service, however, does not just mean being of service to the human entity. It can be just as relevant to be of service to the Earth and the other entities that exist on or in the bio-dimensional sphere. This means that working on ecological work for the love of the work, not for political statement because that nullifies the higher frequency energies resulting from the reason for doing the work. Simply completing ecological actions can also be a very rewarding way of being of service, a way that benefits not only humankind but all of "spiritkind" on, in, and around the Earth's bio-dimensional sphere. Some of you are already working directly with energies to supplement the Earth's loss of energy due to being at a lower frequency, and it is starting to respond by waking up, hence the dramatic weather changes you have been

462

experiencing. These are due to shifts in the energy patterns that result in elemental responses from energies that are on the border of the spiritual and the physical. Wind is one of those and is the most noticeable.

You cannot believe how fantastically different life on Earth would be if it were to be lifted back to the level it is supposed to exist on. Just a couple of levels would mean that the areas that are currently desert would start to become fertile again. The weather would change to reflect the most ideal conditions to nourish the land and would create optimal levels of precipitation, temperature, humidity, and cloud coverage to make the most of and then shield the Earth when and where it needed shielding from ultraviolet radiation.

The Earth would start to live again rather than being inert. It would cherish its inhabitants, and you would recognize the Earth for what it is and cherish it as well. You would realize what you are part of and what you collectively have done to this most divine of beings. Furthermore, beings of all kinds that are currently hibernating because of the low frequencies would re-awaken and start to work with and attend to the needs of the Earth to nurse it back to full health. In doing so, the Earth would increase in energy and frequency and pull up humanity with it. As all of you move up through the frequencies, you would all start to re-awaken from your slumbers and start to use your true abilities as you recognized your own divinity and the reasons for incarnate life. You would then start to see and understand the real reasons for the other entities on the Earth, such as the animals on the land, the birds in the air, and the fish in the sea. They all have reasons for being here, they are all part of the bio-spiritual sphere, and they all have jobs to do. You would know

463

these, regain your ability to communicate with them, and in turn work in true harmony with them for the good of the whole. In doing so, the totality of humanity and its companions on, in, and around this larger entity will rise even higher, closer to the Origin.

Imagine a world where all is in total harmony, one where everything has a job to do and is content with doing that job. Envision a world where all are helping others to reach perfection in what they do, not in competition with each other but in glad tidings and joy brought about by the sheer delight in seeing another entity attain further greatness. Visualize a world where you were instrumental in others attaining greatness due to your being of true service. Picture a world where you can see, feel, touch, experience and enjoy all the energies in and around the beings that exist on that world—one where you can experience what they experience when you work with them in true love and harmony and see how they respond and grow. Imagining a world where you could see and feel this represents how the world itself responds to the work and time you lovingly give to attending to its needs and helping it also grow and evolve. Imagine the resulting energies being that of pure unconditional love with this love representative of the love that is throughout the universe—the love of a creator that is always pleased with its creation's efforts, no matter what they are. See a creator would never judges, never gets angry, and always holds you in love. Imagine a world where you are your true selves, omnipotent, omniscient, omnipresent parts of the greater entity, the Origin.

Working in service to attain this level of existence is a noble work, indeed, with the rewards being unlimited in comparison to your current existence. So with this as the carrot, why wouldn't you do it? Why wouldn't you be of service for the greater good and for everyone's benefits when the greater good (greater God!) benefits?

# The Ways of the Masters

ME:   *Let's get back to the Masters of the books I was reading about. Are they really capable of making their bodies live for two thousand years?*

SE:   Of course. And realistically they can make their physical bodies live for as long as they want. For instance, a yogi can, when he is in total understanding and acceptance of the universal law, do anything he wants. The human body is only limited by its physicality and the incumbent Spirit's ability to draw upon the energies that are naturally available to all. When the incumbent spirit is in a state of slumber, as most of you are, it is not able to tap into the greater reality that is all around it and it believes that its physical existence is all there is. Once a spirit is aware of the greater reality, it starts to become in tune with it and the simple abilities that are at first available—such as increased intuition, healing, channeling, contact with those who are totally in the energetic state—start to come to the fore.

      The greater abilities, such as being able to control the physical only come when the individual has broken through the veil of the physical and is, therefore, not contained by it in any way. When you have achieved this level, which I might add was not easy in those Masters' times and is even harder in the current consumer-driven economies of the world, you are not concerned by the needs of the physical. You are able to feed the body with the energetic, renewing the energies of the cellular structure of the body at its most basic level. You do not need to use the conversion of organic or in-organic materials, which is at best poor but necessary since the physical body does need some low grade energy.

465

The body degrades as a result of the need to reproduce new cells to replace those that are worn out, for without the regeneration of the cell at the energetic level, the cells are only partially reproduced. The essential details of the cell's programming are lost over a period of replacements and results in decrepitude, as the essential vitality is lost over time. The yogi or master knows this and is able to give the cellular structure of the body all it needs all of the time or at certain points in time, which then affects a complete regeneration or rejuvenation based upon the memory of the body at a certain age—that age or physical appearance being at the discretion of the incumbent spirit. Not all spirits want to be presented as young boys or girls. Many prefer to present themselves in middle age, for that is an age where there is most respect from the students that follow such masters. When you are in your middle aged years, you are considered to be at the peak of your learning and teaching abilities. Any older and you are considered to be a doddering old fool, any younger and you are considered to be too young to teach with authority.

Getting back to the prime reason for this discussion though . . .

An individual, once enlightened to the point of mastery can affect change of his/her cellular structure to the point of perfection. This means that it is able to operate at 100% efficiency and be manipulated at will by the energetic spirit. If the Spirit wishes, the body can be perpetuated for eternity by translating it into the fully spiritual by converting it into its true energetic state whilst allowing it to be present in the physical. This method can also be used for the transportation of the physical body in and around the physical environment. But it can only be used in this way once the spirit is in control of the observation of the real reality and is, therefore, able to work with the whole of its existing energetic state,. i.e., when all of it is accessible, recognized, and understood by the individual spirit.

It may seem a little far out, but this is attainable by all. But again the distractions of the physical are such that it is difficult to move oneself outside them, but dedication and commitment to the cause, coupled with belief in the self, will ultimately bear fruit. The issue here is the continuation of the work over a long period of time in the current existence of the western world and the one that the eastern world is running into head long.

The physical body is an un-necessary object but is nevertheless useful in the evolutionary opportunities it presents, for existence in such a cramped and limited condition is, indeed, enlightening in its own right. The opportunity presented to the Spirit that allows itself to be incarnate (in the meat!) is that through hard work it can retain the physical body in the spiritual environment if it so chooses. This allows it to exist in the physical whenever or wherever it chooses without the need to go through the lengthy process of growing the body to a state of maturity and going through the resulting forgetting and awakening process that follows. The Spirit is, therefore, free from the confines of the physical whilst still being able to exist in the physical at its most basic level, thereby experiencing what it can at the physical level whilst also being able to relate to the spiritual. This is the perfect combination as the Spirit is not under the control of physical demands and distractions but is in control of the physical in every sense.

# Chapter 40:
## *Accelerated Spiritual Awareness*

ME:    *I have noticed that in a number of things in life you work hard for something and as a consequence work out shortcuts whilst maintaining the same quality of what you do. If you pass the shortcuts on to other people, they get to the same position you are without having to know the long-winded process you had to use in the first place. Essentially, they leap frog you in the learning process.*

SE:    This is totally true and if you are able to pass your learning onto them so that they have a higher start point than you had, you have then given them a great service. In fact, this is the whole point of "experience." You experience what you experience and learn as a result. You can then pass on what you have learnt to others which allows them to progress at a faster and more in-depth rate. They will both know the history of how to get to where they are and, therefore, progress forward whilst not needing to spend the time required by the teacher to get to there. This is the natural way of the universe and is the best way to spread evolutionary opportunities and raise the base level of the frequency of the universe and its inhabitants, physical or energetic.

ME:    *So it is a good thing to do, to show your shortcuts to others.*

SE:    It is one of the primary ways to be to service. Through your pain do you relieve the suffering of others. You show how to move forward by offering that which is most personal to you: your learning. If you remember in one of our previous dialogues, I mentioned that the total learning of all the beings in this universe is recorded in the Akashic records. That means that everything that you experience, learn, and evolve is recorded and stored for the use of others. This is there for reference so that others can gain the knowledge and experience of others that they have not received themselves in order to help them in incarnations or experiences that are of a similar nature. With this inherent knowledge, they are able to start at a higher level than they would have if they had started from scratch. This allows them to move learning and evolutionary opportunities forward to the point where they find a shortcut and pass this on to others who will follow them.

Hence, the circle is closed because they have benefited from the knowledge and suffering of others. I used the word "suffering" here because all learning and evolution has a level of suffering involved in it whilst one is incarnate in the physical. Entities in the physical that have suffered and learned and then share that knowledge with others to enable them to continue the evolutionary cycle, help accelerate the learning of others. In essence, they create a spiral as incarnate spirits give as they learn, and the cycle continues onward and upward.

ME: *I have heard that to achieve spiritual enlightenment, you need to follow strict pathways and meditate with dedication. How can this be possible in today's western society where we are required to react to email in an instant? We are never left alone enough to spend this sort of time to get really spiritual. We aren't able to wander around and teach with no fixed abode and be taken in by strangers like Jesus did.*

SE: And no one is expecting you to. This is the beauty of the upward spiral. As the level of people trying to be spiritual increases, so does the base frequency of the world/universe. This means that you don't have to do as much to be at the level you are now because others before you have done enough work to give you a higher starting position. As a result, access to the spiritual realms is just that bit easier than it was for them.

## Spirituality over 2,000 Years of Human Incarnation

*ME:* *So what is the difference between us and them? What is the difference over 2,000 years of human incarnation?*

SE: The difference is that, in general, your minds are more open to understanding the truth. There are many more of you now that are asking the most fundamental of questions, *There must be something else to this life.* This is the springboard; this is the first step on the road to enlightenment. When Jesus was alive/incarnate, there were significantly fewer people in the world than there are now. This reflected a smaller number of people on a conscious spiritual path and a reduced opportunity to increase the Earth's frequency levels. If you realize that the increase in today's population has also resulted in a significant increase in the population of people who are consciously on an evolutionary spiritual path, then you can see why the base frequency of Earth and the local universe is much higher than in Jesus' time. The only difference here is the level of things bombarding your consciousness on an hourly/daily basis that distract you from contacting that which is the rest of you, the real you. Those incarnate in Jesus' time did not have these distractions, but they had a much lower level of frequency to battle through first to get to the spiritual realms. They needed to study for most of their lives and their life expectation was different so they had their challenges moving upward through the frequencies to enlightenment.

471

ME: *So how come Jesus was enlightened at so young an age?*

SE: How come you were interested in the psychic at so young an age?

ME: *Because he was born surrounded in a higher frequency?*

SE: Correct, and so are all those who are on the path to enlightenment right now, just like you. This does not make you any better than those who are not on this path, but it does give you the opportunity to "Kick Start" them along this path. This is what you are all here for. To help those not as fortunate as yourselves to progress along the path that you have chosen, the way to true enlightenment.

## Awareness–A Comment from the Origin

ME: *You mentioned previously that an entity needs to be evolved before he/she/it can be aware of real reality and gain access to the knowledge that exists within reality. Why would an entity need to be evolved to access this if he/she/it came from You and the Source in the first place?*

O: Because of the ability to abuse the power that comes with awareness. If you could access the "ALL" and you were not pure of heart in your limited condition of physical incarnation, you would not get the whole picture but only that which you desired. Based upon this, an entity needs to be evolved to the point where he/she/it is not tempted to use the knowledge for self-aggrandisement. Instead, they must feel the need to share it with others who are aware enough to be interested in a positive way. These people are naturally good-natured and not aggressive; in fact, they would find it difficult to be physically aggressive and could never pitch a really powerful punch. These are the people who will spread the teachings of reality in order to help humanity move out of the physical and progress to the next frequency.

## Chapter 41:
# *Forgiveness as a Rule for Life in the Physical*

SE:     Forgiveness is one of the main foundation stones of maintaining your spirituality and increasing your vibrations to the point where you can progress to the next level. When incarnate, Jesus was quoted to have said, "Forgive them father, for they know not what they do." These are wise words, indeed, for the understanding to the point of ultimate feeling and ultimate knowing is based upon ultimate forgiveness of all wrongdoings. No matter how big or small that wrongdoing is and no matter how personal it may seem, learn to forgive in the fullest sense and be free of the thoughts of petty revenge that result from dwelling on wrongdoing. Rise above such needs and behold the truth, the truth that everyone deserves to be forgiven of their minor misdemeanors, no matter how personal they may seem to the individual.

ME:     *Forgiveness seems so simple. Why don't we use it more often? It would make the world a much better place.*

SE:     Yes, it would and what's more it would solve a lot of the world's problems, if not all of them. The problem is that people say they forgive, but they don't fully forgive. This is because they do not fully understand what they are forgiving or what forgiveness really is. To truly forgive someone, you have to really understand the circumstances surrounding the reason for their actions. Then and only then are you able to put yourself in their position and feel the emotions that went with the action. This is only available when you invoke the empathic function of your true selves, which, of course, is available at any time if you only give yourselves the time to listen to your higher selves. This ability is only a step along the way to instantaneous and unconditional forgiveness that is born out of unconditional love for all because it requires a process to work through to achieve forgiveness. When you are open to and at one with the universe and the opportunities it presents for your evolution, you will see the actions of others not as a rub against you but as an opportunity for them to evolve, as well as yourself. This will be instantly recognized and understood; forgiveness will be instantaneous and unconditional.

ME: *So forgiveness is a powerful tool to have in your back pocket.*

SE: It's not a tool. It is another of the rules for life in the physical, a way to ensure that you don't pick up opportunities to lower your vibrations and, therefore, lose your contact with the higher self, that remaining part of you that is within Spirit. In actual fact, it is a fundamental need for existence in incarnate life. If you consider the number of times per day that someone may have wronged you in some way, shape, or form, but you ignore it or so you think, (as some people let things simmer in the background), then you have a tremendous potential for either decreasing your vibrations by taking exception to the events experienced or increasing your vibrations by forgiving those who provided the events and move onwards and upwards. The wise person sees this without further need for thought on the matter and accepts the opportunity for evolutionary progression with joy.

ME: *But what about those around you who may suggest that you are being taken advantage of or being ridden over rough-shod?*

## Showing Others the Thought Process of Forgiveness

SE:     Then it is your place to help them get over their preconceptions and show them the thought process that you have and why you have it. In doing so, you achieve two things: 1) you help them to stop taking on-board someone else's problems and thereby lessening their vibration level due to unnecessary personal interaction/intervention; and 2) you give them an opportunity to review their own opportunities for forgiveness when they arise by identifying the greater picture with regard to loss of frequency due to loss of forgiveness. There is also an additional opportunity for releasing the energetic tie between you and the person needing to be forgiven, for this energetic link is also part of karmic law.

## Karmic Link Between Doer and Receiver of Perceived Offenses

ME:     *Link? What's this link? I thought that if you did something that caused a lowering of vibrational level, then that was karma enough.*

SE:     There is always a karmic link between the doer and receiver of wrongdoing. This link ties the two entities together for eternity until one of the following two things happens: 1) they forgive unconditionally—this is one of the greatest gifts an entity can give another entity, for it severs the karmic link for that particular action between the two entities for eternity; or 2) the entity who gave the initial wrongdoing will receive a similar action from the same entity that previously received the wrongdoing.

ME:     *Wow, this route seems very messy.*

SE:     It is. You can imagine all the links between entities that there are in the incarnate part of the universe. It is a real "buggers' muddle" and one that would be easily remedied if the entities receiving the wrongdoing forgave those giving the wrongdoing at the point of reception. Furthermore, imagine this, if everyone forgave each other at the point of reception of an action, then Earth and its entire population of incarnate souls would be at a significantly higher vibratory level than they are now. This would even raise the individual level of awareness to the point of recognition of the opportunity for committing wrongdoing, thereby lifting the individual to the threshold of universal consciousness whilst incarnate. At this point the bigger picture is recognized and a way to work with it willingly compiled.

ME:  *So forgiveness is the way forward.*

SE:  It's not the only way forward, but it is a big player in the methods available to individuals to move forward on their evolutionary paths.

# Chapter 42:

## *More on Communication with Our Higher Selves*

ME: *Do you have another example of why it is hard for that part of us that is squeezed into this very small vessel on the Earth plane to be in contact with our higher selves? I ask this because I have tried to explain this to some of my friends and acquaintances by using both the consciousness in a bottle example and the 5 senses vs. 5,000,000 senses examples, and it seems to have a very limited effect in their understanding.*

SE: Let Me give you an example that most people should relate to, especially the younger ones, since it relates to computers. Consider the problem of band width and downloading information from the Internet. If you think of yourself as your home computer and your real self/your higher self as the whole of the knowledge in the World Wide Web, you may see the problem. It takes time to download or stream data even via your broadband link, especially when other communications are happening in the background for a single operation. This is made even slower when you try to download or surf more than one web site at the same time. This is to do with the available bandwidth, the pipe size, or how much data can be received at the same time together with the processing power available in your computer. This slowness gives you frustration and a very limited ability to gain information at any one moment in time.

   Now consider trying to download all the information in the whole Internet at once. Your computer would crash as it can't cope with the processing power required to process this information; neither has your service provider got the bandwidth to cope with it. This is exactly the same for humanity trying to communicate with their higher selves and the knowledge deposited in the universal memory, the Akashic. So you are limited to the small amount of communication that you can manage, which is put down to intuition or psychic powers at best. As some people have access to greater band width and better and faster computers, so do some humans have a greater capacity to communicate with their higher selves. This is purely due to their ability to tune into that part of themselves that has the greater bandwidth and the faster processing power. It involves giving yourself time—time to sit in silence and listen to yourselves and the universe without expectation, preconception, or intellectual judgment, just with acceptance.

# Chapter 43:
## *Angels, Oranges, and Apples*

ME: I have also had a bit of doubt about the prolific use recently of angels and orbs in spirituality, specifically the use of angels, spirit guides, spirit animals, Reiki, demons and archangels as authorities to access Spirit and the universe. Even my old healing instructor is suggesting that her old graduates take a year's course to incorporate this into their healing techniques! It's almost like a backward step to me.

SE: Well, in real terms, it is a backward step, especially for someone like you who is somewhere near being awake, but it does have its uses, specifically with those who are on the border of interest and are, therefore, at the start of their opportunity to become enlightened.

Remember that people who are unsure or limited in confidence need a level of authority or permission to be spiritual, hence the use of churches for group work, attunements in Reiki, and the use of cards in tarot and angel readings. All are *crutches* or a better explanation would be *focal points* that the individual uses to log into the universal energies or their higher selves. You used to use your counting method to get to Me. This is the same. In essence, angels, Indian spirit guides, animal guides, or demons are just labels for one specific type of energy or energy-based entity that can be accessed for information or experiential knowledge.

The issue is why would you want to limit yourself to just one information medium when you can access them all? Also, why attribute one type of information with one type of energy? Let Me explain further. If a child is learning to count, we let him count in apples, oranges and pears. The child in his lack of experience labels them separately; therefore, in the child's mind 5 apples, 1 orange, and 2 pears equals 5 apples 1 orange and 2 pears. If he adds 3 pears, he has 5 apples 1 orange and 5 pears, the addition being to the pears only. The child has not thought about the fact that the total amount of "fruit" has changed from 8 pieces of fruit to 11 pieces of fruit, for he still has them labeled in his mind as apples, oranges, and pears and does not consider them as the collective name or label of "fruit."

If you remove the labels, you open yourself to greater levels of understanding because you are not restricting your access to knowledge or associating it with something that is limited in its example or explanation. A further example of limited thinking is the mathematician who proved Fermat's Theorem. He was limited to using one type of mathematics to start the proof and another to finalize the proof, which at first, he thought he had. The problem was that he had no proof of the calculation that took him from the first type of mathematics to the second. It was not until a young Japanese mathematician invented another form of mathematics that Fermat realized that this new form of mathematics *linked* the mathematic models he was using *together* and thus furnished the final proof that Fermat's Theorem worked. This took the mathematician ten years to work out from his initial understanding that he needed to link the two models he had used together in some way to the point where he realized that the Japanese model *was the link between them*. His limitation was the use of labels. If he had considered the bigger mathematical picture that it is *all* mathematics, then he would not have limited himself in the first place and would have solved Fermat's Theorem in the same way that Fermat did, by tapping into the universal knowledge.

This is the dilemma with the use of angel cards, Reiki, and other healing/spiritual mediums that require or give external authority to use them. This limits individuals' ability to tap into the "all" that is available to them in the universe. Instead, it only allows them to tap into the specific energy that is aligned with a particular label.

# Letter to the Reader

Dearest Reader,

I know that the impact these texts will have on you largely depends upon where you are on your path and your particular level of evolution. What I am really hoping is that this book will capture your imagination and help you consciously embark upon the serious task of self-realization. May you grasp that the physical is but a poor illusion within the greater reality and may you use these texts as a starting/continuing point for your journey onwards and upwards. If this happens to you, then my work has been successful.

You are drawn to this work because you wish to awaken, to remember who you are, to become more aware, and to question everything. This is a light on your route to evolution from the shackles of the physical.

Use this book as an opportunity to inspire and to promote discussion, questioning, realization, and eventual evolution. Share it with your friends and acquaintances. Wherever you are on the Earth plane, know that THERE REALLY IS A GREATER REALITY.

Choosing to become self-realized is not an easy task. Doing so requires your consistent dedication, introspection, and stamina, specifically when the material world is so compelling. The mere fact that you have either bought or borrowed this book, read all the text or a few choice pages means that you are on your way towards enlightenment. For this, I thank you from the bottom of my heart, for your enlightenment shows the way to those around you and will ultimately result in our evolution and ascension.

With loving gratitude for our evolutionary journey together,
Guy Steven Needler
1ˢᵗ March 2011

# *Appendix*

The following is derived from instructions I received by my energy healing teacher, Helen Stott, who was a direct student of the Barbara Brennan School of Healing™.

## How to Perform Core Star Meditation

The core star is the essence of who you are. It is described as the source of your physical body's energy. It is the location of your soul and contains the energetic content of the "spirituo-physical," as well as the individual resonant signature of the incarnate energy that houses the essential objective of your incarnation. Without the soul, your physical body would not function, and your energetic self would not be able to experience the physical realms. Meditating on the light of the Core Star can be used for protection, healing, and understanding your soul's purpose. Please allow up to one hour in a quiet place with no disturbances.

1. Stand with your knees slightly bent, feet shoulder width apart, arms and hands by your side.
2. Focus on your tan tien, which is 1 ½ inches below your belly button and in the center line of the body. Tune into how it feels. The feeling should be similar to the earth's core. Remain in tune until you feel its heat and harmonization with the resonance of the earth. [If you can't actually feel this, simply use the power of intention to do so.]
3. Continue by becoming aware of the area in the upper body approximately 2 ½ inches below your throat. This is called the middle tan tien. On the haric level, the

middle tan tien is sometimes called the "soul seat." This is where the soul's longing and life plan reside. Don't confuse this with the nearest chakra, the heart chakra, which is a few inches below this. When you connect to your middle tan tien, it sometimes feels like a "full feeling" inside your chest. [If you don't feel anything, that is fine, too. Simply trust that it is there and your intention is to tap into it.] It is spherical and clear in appearance.

4. Now search for and feel the thin line that travels from your soul seat/middle tan tien down to the tan tien and into the center of the earth. Tune into your individual life's purpose/plan. Recognize the strength that comes from being connected to it.

5. Straighten your spine. With your head erect, continue by changing your awareness to a point above your head. Imagine a fine line projecting through the crown chakra at the top of your head. Using your inner eye, move up the line to find the connecting vortex with its ¼ inch opening. This will be around three feet above your head. Listen for the high-pitched sound. Now locate your thin line into the opening. You should hear a sound like a "pop" if your clairaudience is functioning when the correct connection is made. [Again, if you do not have clairaudience, you might not be able to hear anything. Simply make it your intention to make the connection and visualize yourself doing so.]

6. Make sure the line is in alignment within your body. See it running from the earth to the tan tien to the soul seat/middle tan tien and to the vortex. You may experience a feeling of expanded consciousness.

7. Traveling through the vortex will put you into the greater reality of the Source Entity/God. Tune into your soul's "song" in your upper chest, as well as the creativity in your tan tien. At the same time feel the line as it travels down to the earth's core. Absorb the power. This is the alignment for your life's work.

You have now created a link between heaven and earth and aligned your hara line.

## Expanding Your Life Purpose to Your "Group" Purpose

Now reach out and detect the hara lines of people that are close to you. This allows you to synchronize your life's purpose with your "group" purpose and the group hara lines. Once you are on this level, you are connected and synchronized with the group with whom you are working. Then you can synchronize with the greater community which, in turn, allows you to connect to the city, country, and world. In this way you can connect to a collective power of an iterative system.

8. Return your focus to your core star, the essence of who you are. You are outside time, space, longing, pain and desire. You "are" a creator. Create a plan. As a creator, move to the hara line bringing creative energy (your plan) with you. This is your divine task. Now take this energy to the auric level and create your template for the physical. With this you will bring energy into the physical body. Now the creative energy from the source travels from the core star through the head to the soul seat to the tan tien to the haric level and through the auric layers into the physical.

9. With one creative plan completed, you can go forward, shining with your true essence and purpose. Allow your core star to shine with this purpose and your essence to permeate through your aura. Return and create more plans as desired.

10. Allow this essence of your being to shine through the levels of human physical self, core star, soul seat, tan tien and then onto the hara and the aura. Allow it to permeate through every cell of your body as it creates health, joy, and pleasure while you are in the physical.

Everything about you will be an expression of your divine essence.

## Experiencing the Source Within You

With this exercise, your "trinity" of the core star, soul seat, and tan tien become one with your seven auric levels that are associated directly with the physical. You will experience the "Source" within you.

11. With your mind's eye observe each cell of your body. Each cell is like the core star. Therefore, the healing process is the simple task of connecting with the truth of your being.

    Whenever you have illness, pain, anger or fear, suspicion or greed, or forget your purpose, focus on your core star. Bring every cell of your body within the light of the core star. This is your essence, your "god" within. Healing is a just connecting with your energetic memory of who you are. You re-create the link or individual creativity. You remember your life task. Allow the creativity associated with your life task to come through to illuminate you, the memory of who you are, and your path in this physical life. Remembering who you are is your prime directive; allow your core star to show you the way.

12. Now return to your earthly condition by slowly moving back into the physical, retracting the line from the vortex and the earth, "reeling it in" to the core star.

13. Sit down. Drink plenty of water and rest. You will be in a state of euphoria for a while.

# How To Create an Effective Energy Shield/Filter

Each chakra is associated with an auric layer. Chakra 1, the base chakra, is linked to the first layer of the aura, the etheric. Chakra 2, sacral chakra, is linked to layer 2, the emotional, etc., up to chakra 7, crown chakra, which is linked to auric layer 7, the ketheric template. Also note that each chakra is present, in part, on each of the frequencies represented by the auric layers, which I will now call levels. So you will see all seven chakras (A, front/anterior & B, back/posterior) relative to the human form every time you experience each of the auric levels separately.

In reality, there are 14 levels associated with the physical (ten associated with the human body, 1-3 physical, 4-7 spirituo-physical, 8-10 spiritual). This is not widely recognized though (although some spiritualists are now beginning to recognize the eighth and the ninth). Seven levels (1-7) are relative to the four auric levels that are associated with the gross physical, and three are associated with the spirituo-physical. The 4th level is associated with the heart chakra and is the link between the gross physical and the spirituo-physical. It has a foot in both worlds, so to speak. The seven higher auric levels (4-10) are also associated with the spirituo-physical and spiritual, but are the link between the real self and that which is incarnate. It is because of this personal link that we can use these higher levels in conjunction with the lower levels, as programmable filters. There are more levels as you have gleaned from my book from eleven upwards, but these are purely energetic.

1. Stand with your knees slightly bent, feet shoulder width apart, arms and hands by your side. Concentrate on your aura. Feel the first level, the etheric; feel and acknowledge its presence and assign it to your base chakra, for they are linked. This will be your grounding. Imagine this to be your tie to the earth. You will need it while working with the six

higher levels until you get used to it. It will be your lightening rod for shorting heavy energies to the ground if they are more than you can cope with. Note: some people have thicker areas or holes in their various auric levels, and in the lowest spirituophysical level, the astral, they might have debris/entities attached due to energetic dysfunction/physical disease. For this exercise, assume a clean, clear, whole un-infested egg shape for your auric level. Ignore colors since they are not important in this exercise. Image you are in an elevator on the first floor/first chakra and that this first floor has a frequency attached to it.

2.  Imagine going up a level in an elevator to the next level, the $2^{nd}$; the frequency is higher and finer. Link the 2nd chakra to the 2nd auric level. Feel its presence and its wholeness. Then link the 1st and 2nd together by flooding the gap in between the two "eggs" with an energy that lets everything you want in and out, except the energies and frequencies associated with the issues you are experiencing. It is not necessary to fully understand the structure, frequency, and amplitude of the energy associated with the issues as it's the intention that counts). This is the filter "blocking" energy.

3.  Continue the process used in levels 1 & 2 with 3, 4, 5, 6 & 7 as you go up each level in the mental elevator, feeling and visualizing the shape and structure of the level, linking the chakras to the auric levels and flooding the gaps between the auric levels with the blocking energy in between levels 2 & 3, levels 3 & 4, levels 4 & 5, levels 5 & 6 and levels 6 & 7. The frequencies become finer and finer as you go higher. Check your grounding.

4.  When you have achieved this and are satisfied with the integrity of the structure, you can move on to the next task. If you have any doubts about the integrity

of the structure, you will need to start again at the level where the doubt exists. At this point you are at a high level (for most people), so take your time.

5. Re-check your grounding. Imagine the next six levels (8, 9, 10, 11, 12, 13) individually. Use the elevator method to get to each level and again feel each level. Notice how each level feels different from the others and feel the energies associated with these levels. No chakras are present in these levels so this bit is easier.

6. Once you have arrived at the 14th level, you may well experience a heightened level of awareness. Ignore any "strange" or disturbing images that might appear based on your fear of being too high. This sometimes happens with individuals at this level and could occur in any of the higher levels. Concentrate on the task at hand. Bring all of the levels together, one on top of each other so that they sandwich each other. Flood the gap between level 7 and level 8 only with the blocking energy. Imagine these seven higher levels to be a laminate (sandwich) that also ONLY allows the energies you want in. If you are in doubt, block out all but essential and necessary energies you need to function and not just those causing the issue. Image it is fully impregnable. Feel the safety.

7. Give the filter a life span in days, weeks, months, years or as long as you are in the physical. This gives it an automatic function. Don't worry; you can always turn it off manually by disassembling it in the reverse of the method you used to create it.

8. Check your grounding. It is easy to fly off at this point in the exercise. Come down the levels slowly one by one using the mental elevator.

9. Take a deep breath and drink plenty of water, which will also help ground you. If you feel dizzy, lie down immediately. Drink more water. This is a natural response. If you don't feel dizzy, go outside for a few

minutes and take in the fresh air. Then take a nap. You WILL be tired (including the next day).

Well done! You have just created an all-inclusive, fully integrated, matrix-based shield/filter.

## The Names of the Chakras

- First Chakra – Color: Red – called the Base/Root Chakra or Muldhara Chakra – Anatomical Association - Adrenals: Spinal Column, Kidneys
- Second Chakra – Color: Orange – called the Sacral Chakra or Svadhishthana Chakra – Anatomical Association - Gonads: Reproductive system
- Third Chakra – Color: Yellow – called the Solar Chakra or Manipura Chakra – Anatomical Association - Pancreas: Stomach, Liver, Gall Bladder, Nervous System
- Fourth Chakra – Color: Green – called the Heart Chakra or Anahata Chakra – Anatomical Association - Thymus: Heart, Blood, Vegas Nerve, Circulatory System
- Fifth Chakra – Color: Blue – called the Throat Chakra or Vishuddha Chakra – Anatomical Association - Thyroid: Bronchial and Vocal System, Lungs, Alimentary Canal
- Sixth Chakra – Color: Indigo – called the Third Eye Chakra or Ajna Chakra – Anatomical Association - Pituitary: Lower Brain, Left Eye, Ears, Nose, Nervous System
- Seventh Chakra – Color: Violet – called the Crown Chakra or Sahasrara Chakra – Anatomical Association - Pineal: Upper Brain, Right Eye
- Chakras situated in the front of the human body (so called A chakras) are associated to our intentions

- Chakras situated in the rear of the human body (so called B chakras) are associated to our actions

## Psychological Function of Chakras

- Chakra 1:   Quantity of physical energy, will to live
- Chakra 2A: Quality of love for the opposite sex, giving and receiving mental & spiritual pleasure
- Chakra 2B: Quality of sexual energy
- Chakra 3A: Pleasure & expansiveness, spiritual wisdom, consciousness of the universality of life and who you are in the universe
- Chakra 3B: Healing and intentionality towards your health
- Chakra 4A: Heart feelings of love towards other human beings, openness to life
- Chakra 4B: Ego will, or will towards the outer world
- Chakra 5A: Taking in and assimilating knowledge
- Chakra 5B: Sense of self within society and one's profession
- Chakra 6A: Capacity to visualize and understand mental concepts
- Chakra 6B: Ability to achieve ideas in a practical way
- Chakra 7:   Integration of personality with life and spiritual aspects of mankind

## Name, Appearance, and Function of the Auric Layers/Levels

- Auric layer 1 − Name: Etheric Body − Appearance: A web of tiny blue energy lines − Function: An energy matrix or template of the physical body
- Auric layer 2 − Name: Emotional layer − Appearance: Colored clouds in continual fluid motion − Function:

Displays and allows communication of the emotional content or feelings of love, joy, anger, etc.

- Auric layer 3 – Name: Mental Body – Appearance: Structured bright yellow light emanating from the head and shoulders of the body – Function: Contains the structure of our thoughts and ideas
- Auric layer 4 – Name: Astral Level – Appearance: Amorphous clouds of Color infused with rose-colored light – Function: Facilitates the transition of spiritual energy to physical energy and physical energy into spiritual energy. Love between two people is displayed within this level.
- Auric layer 5 – Name: Etheric Template – Appearance: Has the appearance of a blue photograph negative made of cobalt blue lines – Function: The blueprint or perfect form for the etheric body to fill
- Auric layer 6 – Name: Celestial Body–Appearance: Shimmering light made up of pastel colors with a gold silver shine – Function: The communication of unconditional love and of "being one with God"
- Auric layer 7 – Name: Ketharic Template – Appearance: A highly structured matrix of tiny gold-silver threads of light within an egg shape that shows the structure of the physical body and all chakras – Function: Accumulation of past life bands, life plan, holds the auric bodies together
- Auric layer 8 to 10 – Name: No names identified – Appearance: Gossamer-like structure, increasing in fineness the higher one goes and finalizing in no structure – Function: Main communication/link to the true and fully energetic self

# How to Experience the Levels Discussed in
## *The History of God*

Because trees provide a level of frequential stability, many people choose to experience higher frequency level meditations while sitting among trees or leaning against a tree. Some people progress better and feel safer when in the presence of trees. Trees are constantly connected to the universal grounding medium of water and are a gestalt mind. They revel in kind and loving human contact and a perfect setting for learning to traverse the many levels above the 7$^{th}$.

This exercise illustrates the basic method I initially used to raise my frequencies to the levels required to transcend the seven levels generally associated with the physical/spirituo-physical body, move through the next seven spiritual/energetic levels, and then continue onwards and upwards to those levels where the Om, Byron, and other energetic entities reside. With practice one can also commence a dialogue with the Source Entity and the Origin.

1. Find a quiet room where you will not be disturbed.
2. Stand with your knees slightly bent, feet shoulder width apart, arms and hands by your side.
3. Ground yourself by imagining a climber's rope attached to you and an anchor buried deeply in the ground. You will need this, and you should keep referring to this grounding link throughout this exercise. This will help you return to the physical.

Each chakra is associated with an auric level. Imagine them opening in order. This will allow you to ascend to that auric layer level and frequency.

4. Concentrate on your base chakra. Imagine it being opened. Feel the etheric level. Move to that level.

5. Move on to the second chakra, the sacral. Open it and feel the presence of the second auric level, the emotional. Move to that level.

6. Move to the third, fourth, fifth, sixth, and seventh chakras and auric layers and associated frequency levels in the same way.

7. Stop at the seventh level. See the crown chakra open and the ketharic template present. You are now at the end of the physicality of your humanity. Check your grounding. Feel the level. Get used to it. Levels 8-10 are purely spiritual and levels 11 upwards are purely energetic.

8. Next imagine an elevator with a series of buttons. Each button represents a frequency level from 8 through 100, as well as buttons marked G for ground and S for slow descent or ascent. For continuity of methodology, you can later include 1 through 7 buttons if you wish. Imagine that pressing one of these buttons takes you in a linear vertical ascent to the level selected. Therefore, pressing level 20 takes you to level 20 via levels 8, 9, 10, 11, 12, etc., to 20 in a slow and methodical fashion.

9. Also imagine access to a stairwell by the side of the elevator. This stairwell also has a series of stairs leading to each of the landings/levels as well. Walking the stairs duplicates the way to ascend the frequency levels. This stairwell should be used if you are resistant to moving up a level using the elevator method. Using the stairs will be a slower and much gentler transition from level to level.

10. Always check your grounding, it is easy to fly off when you are on the levels above the physical/the 7th chakra.

**A word of warning here.** I do not advocate "jumping" up the levels right away. Progress one by one. Get used to the feeling of each level and gain your confidence slowly. You are a long way, frequency-wise, from what you may be used to. Progress one or two levels at a time above the eighth. This is NOT the same as creating a shield/filter because your attention is not fixed upon your own energy fields. Progressing too fast will result in disturbing images, which you may experience anyway. Initially moving up the frequencies too fast isn't wise. It's better to get used to them in small amounts. Traveling above the fourteenth requires re-grounding, so remember always to send out another line to the anchor.

11. When you have practiced a few times and have reached the fourteenth level, take a look around you with your mind's eye. Stay alert for communication with any entities present at this level. It can be via clairaudience, clairvoyance, and/or clairsentience.
12. When you are ready, come down the levels slowly one by one using the mental elevator.
13. Take a deep breath. If you feel dizzy, lie down immediately. Drink lots of water, which will help ground you. This is a natural response. If you feel fine, drink plenty of water, too, to help ground you. Go outside for a few minutes, take in the fresh air, and then lie down. You WILL be tired (including the next day).

At any time if you are concerned or worried at being at a specific level, go back into the elevator and select the G/ground/full physicality level button. Choose also the slow descent button. Descending too fast is as detrimental as ascending too high. Do not stay on a level where you are uncomfortable. If you feel uncomfortable at any time at any level, either descend to a level where you are happy or descend fully to the ground.

Over the days or weeks, slowly progress to higher and higher levels (keeping in mind your grounding and comfort level). Remember to take your time. Eventually you will be able to traverse all levels and may even transcend this mechanical method of traversing the frequencies.

# Glossary

- "Out for a Golden Duck" − a saying in Cricket when you have been bowled out on your very first bowl of the ball in your first over of a match. In the conversation with Byron I expected to know everything about "time." As soon as Byron stated that time was spherical (in his first sentence on the subject), all of my pre-conceived knowledge was rendered meaningless.
- 4 Star Petrol is high octane gasoline.
- Akashic records − an eternal past present and future record of each of humankind's actions and subsequent evolution
- At a rate of knots − an old nautical term. It means "fast" or to be at "speed." A knot is equal to one nautical mile per hour. In the days of the tall ships when old mariners were navigating by using the "dead reckoning" system of navigation (the most basic there is), they threw a weighted float attached to a knotted rope over the stern of the ship and counted the number of knots passing through the hand of the sailor, as the ship progressed, in the period taken to allow the sand in a 30-second hour glass to pass from one side to the other. The distance between the knots was 47 yards and 3 inches. When the ship was travelling fast and the "rate of knots" passing through the sailors hand was high, the term "we are travelling at a (high) rate of knots" was used to indicate a faster than normal speed.
- Avebury and Kilmartin are in the UK.
- Black hole − physically is an area of local gravitational density and spiritually is an area of

stable dimensional instability, a dimension within a dimension

- Chakra – an energy center in the human body
- Coadunate – a connected collection of civilizations that are all collectives in their own right
- Core star – the "Hara" or "Core Star" are essentially the same with the exception that the Core Star tends to be associated with the Soul or the individuality (resonant signature) of the incarnate energy and the essential objective of the incarnation
- Core star meditations – a method of meditation focused upon understanding one's life plan/task or reason for incarnation through accessing our greater beingness via the Hara or Core Star
- Dimensional Mechanics – a method of creating a dimension within a dimension
- DNA – deoxyribonucleic acid
- Dysfunction – out of specification functionality
- Energy levels – the distance between each level that is consistent with the difference between the frequencies in the human auric levels
- Etheric Template – please see Name, Appearance and Function of the Auric Layers/Levels in the Appendix.
- Frequential – sequentially-based frequencies in frequentic space
- Frequential Plane – a singular sequential frequency
- Frequentic – multi-frequency space
- Gestalt mind – a collection of entities that share a single mind function, such as ants or trees and most other energy-based beings within this universe
- Hara – the "Power" or energy associated with that part of the entity that is incarnate
- Hara line – the connection between the incarnate entity's energy and the physical "earth." It is the bond that keeps us here in the physical. Cutting the

Hara Line (Japanese Hara-Kiri or Seppuku, ceremonial suicide) is the cutting of the connection of the Hara to the physical, which results in physical death

- Holographic − a three-dimensional rendering
- Hot Swop − a computer peripheral term used to describe the removal or plugging in of a peripheral without the power being turned off. In the spiritual, this relates to the swopping in/out of a soul from/to a physical human body without the body needing to die or be born. This is sometimes called a walk-in.
- Hum − an energy being beloved of the Om. Hum was sent by the Om to help me in my early stages of continued connectivity with the higher levels of frequency/dimension.
- Human Aura − the energy fields associated with the physical and astral components of the human body
- Hyperspace − a moment of frequential and dimensional phase that is different than the normal graduations of phase that allows movement between dimensional and frequency based environments.
- Ketheric Template − please see Name, Appearance and Function of the Auric Layers/Levels in the Appendix
- Macro-universe − a complete universe where our own universe would serve to be the sub-atomic levels
- Micro-universe—a complete universe at the scale of the sub-atomic
- Minor-verse − a universe of lesser content in terms of dimension and frequency and habitation, one of lower importance
- Multi-verse − an environment housing myriad universes
- Not grasping the nettle − grasping the nettle is a way of augmenting the level of understanding.

Understanding is one thing but fully recognizing the details behind the level of understanding and believing it whole heartedly (deep down) is another thing. "Grasping the Nettle" is, therefore, a way of saying that "I," in this instance, was understanding but not fully appreciating the knowledge to the point of "knowing" on a fundamental basis and taking it "on-board" as fact.

- Null Space − the space in between universes for travel between universes
- Psychometry − gaining spiritual information about an object or person via tactile contact
- RNA − ribonucleic acid
- Simulacrum − similar or in the same likeness
- Spaced out − a term I used to describe being close to fainting
- Spirituophysical − the level where the physical and spiritual levels meet and mix
- Tan tien − the point within the physical/auric body where the center or point of the Core Star/Hara/soul is dominant. With Japanese Hara-Kiri, the cutting of the Hara line should also pass through the tan tien to ensure that the Soul energy is effectively released from its earthly ties.
- Telekinesis − levitation of an object or person by application of pure thought.
- Teleportation − the ability to dissolve and materialize the physical body at will while changing location in the process.
- The Big Bang − the current "scientific" theory on how the universe was created
- The Dragon Entity/Byron − a 27th level energy being
- The Om − energy-based beings not indigenous to Earth

- The Origin − the creator of the 12 Source Entities who exist within the Origin, the greater God an entity of pure sentient energy
- The Silver Cord − the connection with our energetic "higher selves," the opposite of the Hara which anchors us to the earth energetically. Some individuals with enhanced ability to communicate with spirit have two silver cords.
- The Source Entity − what we call God, the creator of our multi-verse
- UFO − Unidentified Flying Object.
- Unleaded petrol is a low octane petrol with a zero lead count
- Wormhole − physically an area where two frequencies connect with each other. It is possible to use wormholes to jump up through the frequencies.

# *Guy Needler*

Guy Needler MBA, MSc, CEng, MIET, MCMA initially trained as a mechanical engineer and quickly progressed on to be a chartered electrical and electronics engineer. However, throughout this earthly training he was always aware of the greater reality being around him, catching glimpses of the worlds of spirit. This resulted in a period from his teenage to early twenties where he revelled in the spiritual texts of the day and meditated intensively. Being subsequently told by his guides to focus on his earthly contribution for a period he scaled this back the intensity of spiritual work until his late thirties where he was re-awakened to his spiritual roles. The next six years saw him gaining his Reiki Master and a four year commitment to learn energy and vibrational therapy techniques from Helen Stott, a direct student of the *Barbara Brennan School of Healing*$^{TM}$, which also included a personal development undertaking (including psychotherapy) as a course prerequisite using the *Pathwork*$^{TM}$ methodology described by Susan Thesenga with further methodologies by Donovan Thesenga, John and Eva Pierrakos. His training and experience in energy based therapies have resulted in him being a member of the Complementary Medical Association (MCMA).

Along with his healing abilities his spiritual associations include being able to channel information from spirit including constant contact with other entities within our multiverse and his higher self and guides. It is the channelling that has resulted in *The History of God* and is producing further work.

As a method of grounding Guy practises and teaches Aikido. He is a 5<sup>th</sup> Dan National Coach with 28 years experience and is currently working on the use of spiritual energy within the physical side of the art.

Guy welcomes questions on the subject of spiritual physics and who and what God is.

Website: www.historyofgod.eu

Email: thehistoryofgod@btinternet.com

## Other Books Published
## by
## Ozark Mountain Publishing, Inc.

**Continue for more books by Ozark Mountain Publishing, Inc.**

For more information about any of the above titles, soon to be released titles, or other items in our catalog, write or visit our website:

# OZARK
## MOUNTAIN
## PUBLISHING

PO Box 754
Huntsville, AR 72740
www.ozarkmt.com
1-800-935-0045/479-738-2348
Wholesale Inquiries Welcome